TIME
IN
FEMINIST
PHENOMENOLOGY

TIME
IN
FEMINIST
PHENOMENOLOGY

Edited by

Christina Schües,
Dorothea E. Olkowski,
and Helen A. Fielding

INDIANA UNIVERSITY PRESS
Bloomington and Indianapolis

Support was received from
The University of Western Ontario,
J. B. Smallman Fund.

This book is a publication of

Indiana University Press
601 North Morton Street
Bloomington, Indiana 47404-3797 USA

www.iupress.indiana.edu

Telephone orders	800-842-6796
Fax orders	812-855-7931
Orders by e-mail	iuporder@indiana.edu

♾ *The paper used in this publication meets the minimum requirements of the American National
Standard for Information Sciences—Permanence of Paper for Printed Library Materials, ANSI
Z39.48-1992.*

MANUFACTURED IN THE UNITED STATES OF AMERICA

Library of Congress Cataloging-in-Publication Data

Time in feminist phenomenology / edited by Christina Schües, Dorothea E. Olkowski,
and Helen A. Fielding.
    p. cm.
    Includes bibliographical references and index.
    ISBN 978-0-253-35630-7 (cloth : alk. paper) — ISBN 978-0-253-22314-2 (pbk. : alk. paper)
1. Time. 2. Feminist theory. 3. Phenomenology. I. Schües, Christina. II. Olkowski, Dorothea.
III. Fielding, Helen, [date]
    BD638.T564 2011
    115—dc22

                                                                        2010049852

1 2 3 4 5   16 15 14 13 12 11

CONTENTS

TIME
IN
FEMINIST
PHENOMENOLOGY

1.

INTRODUCTION: TOWARD A FEMINIST PHENOMENOLOGY OF TIME

Christina Schües

The book *Time in Feminist Phenomenology* brings together several approaches to a subject that is always present in life but that has been largely disregarded by feminist phenomenology: namely, time. This lack is perhaps surprising since feminist phenomenology is now well established and arises out of the reevaluation and extension of the work of classical phenomenologists for whom time was central, including Edmund Husserl, Martin Heidegger, Hannah Arendt, Maurice Merleau-Ponty, Emmanuel Levinas, and Paul Ricoeur.[1] In addition, Simone de Beauvoir, Luce Irigaray, and Julia Kristeva are among the influential feminist thinkers who combine phenomenology with feminist *theoretical reflections on time*.[2]

Given the diversity of philosophies in the phenomenological tradition, it will come as no surprise that each of the essays in this volume approaches the question of time in a different manner. Yet, as different as their approaches are, all texts share one thing: each one engages with feminist phenomenology or feminist theory. If we are to call these essays feminist philosophy, we would not articulate this as a feminist love of wisdom; rather, it would imply a theory in the sense of "theoria," a distant observation from a critical feminist point of view. For this reason the feminist phenomenologists contributing to this volume share an interest in a variety of themes that seem to have been forgotten or disregarded in the history of philosophy. Thus, they focus not simply on the negation or destruction of specific concepts in the history of ideas, but on the productive appropriation and critical rethinking of classical texts and theories, themes and questions. Focusing on these neglected themes means not only enlarging the realm of topics, but also shifting the methodology and meaning of phenomenological discourse. Of course, feminist phenomenologists' special interest is to relate phenomenology to the issue of gender; but central to this relation have been the ontological questions of the nature of space, time, and the body. So there have been numerous feminist discourses on space, the body, sexual differences, and gender, as well as male-female relations with their intrinsic power structures, and the theme of alterity. However, the issue of time has been neglected. Given that feminist phenomenology has, since the 1990s, engaged in rereading the classics in a most fruitful and productive way, it is even more remarkable that feminist phenomenology has never really considered, or reconsidered, questions of time and temporality, even though, and especially because, they have been central not only to phenomenology, but throughout the history of philosophy starting with the Greeks.

The founding father of phenomenology, Edmund Husserl, whose primary interest *lay* in the structures of consciousness and its relations to the world, saw clearly that not only our experience, but our existence in general, is temporal. This insight, initiated by Augustine, is central to all phenomenological considerations of time. Well known is the experience Augustine describes in the *Confessions*, where he says that he understands precisely *what* time is when he does not think about it. But as soon as he directs his attention to it and to saying *what* time really is, then he does not know it. These famous sentences typify our basic and common philosophical *difficulties* (*philosophische Verlegenheit*) regarding time. We are concealed in our thoughtlessness about time, even as we take time for granted (*Selbstverständlichkeit*). No wonder there is a resistance to thinking about time that philosophy in general and phenomenology in particular are up against. Our inability to think about time is due precisely to the fact that we take it for granted. To think our taken-for-granted relations with the world is the basic task of phenomenology, and, of course, time is preeminently taken for granted. Time withdraws and therefore remains in the background; as such, it is continuously unsettling (*beunruhigend*). This sort of withdrawal of what should be obvious, as well as the thoughtlessness concerning what we take for granted, is typical of philosophical problems. Some phenomena withdraw from our access and our concepts and, nevertheless, keep haunting us even as they withdraw. To be drawn into and by "something" that withdraws and is hidden is one of the basic philosophical problems; but it is a fascinating problem, *for it involves questioning the very concepts out of which the questions are themselves posed.* One could even say that the real philosophical problem is a question, such as the question of time, that one does not know how to "pose." Perhaps this is why it appears that thinking *is most at a loss* when it tries to say what time is.

One reason for which it is at a loss, which is reflected in the essays in this volume, has its roots in the Greek tradition with which our contemporary thinking still struggles. For the Greeks, time was understood on the basis of movement and change, meaning, as the now moment of the present (*Gegenwärtige*). However, we no longer accept the idea that time is only the now of the present moment (*Jetzt der Gegenwärtigkeit*). It seems clear to us that time is not present simply in the now of the present because, whatever is now, will immediately become a past. The dimensionality of time, its status as past, present, and future, is not included in the notion of the now moment as present, as it was for Greek thinking.

Augustine's big achievement arose from his investigation of the relation between personal experiences and time, which led to the realization that time is multidimensional. Augustine was the first philosopher to propose a concept of internal time in order to explain movement in relation to experience.[3] For him, time is not in the world or a property of the world, but rather the *extension of the soul*. The soul measures the time of movements in the form of a continuous presence: "The present considering the past is memory, the present considering the present is immediate awareness, the present considering the future is expectation."[4] Past, present, and future are psychic or mental functions, which do not have their corresponding temporal order in the world. The soul measures impressions that are found in the soul, in consciousness, and hence, only the soul has time. In other words, time has a subjective structure.[5] With Augustine, time has its real location (*topos*) in the soul, and, thus, time means temporality, and redemption from temporality is accomplished only by the grace of God. The tension of the soul, unifying itself out of the dispersed manifold, is the result of the *curiositas,* an aspect of truth; Augustine posits this as the way to overcome the limitations of Greek thinking about time. However, the problem remains: Does time have reality? Is time real? Does time exist? Or is time only an a priori form of the idea of subjectivity?[6]

Aristotle addresses this question when he argues that the determination of time is the counted succession of "nows," in which movements enfold themselves. This does not imply that space or location (*topos*) is more real than time or that time exists only in the human understanding (because counting takes place in the human understanding). But Aristotle knows that human beings are beings who have a sense for time (*aisthesis chronou*) because they have expectations. However, in this context, expectation means having foresight concerning something not present, whereas having a sense of time seems to imply having foresight regarding something futural. By defining time as merely the distinction between the present and the non-present, Aristotle loses a true concept of time. Although he construes human beings as having goals and purposes, this only means being able to distance oneself from the present in order to look at that which could next be present. As such, we can see that this anthropological thesis does not explain anything about temporality, that is, how it is that we have a sense of time.

In the twentieth century, phenomenology sets out to investigate time with respect to subjective, lived time—the time of experience. Husserl understood this problem, and he showed that as soon as we reflect upon the nature of time and upon subjective time consciousness, the lived experience of time, its familiarity vanishes, leaving us "involved in the most extraordinary difficulties, contradictions, and entanglements."[7] Nonetheless, Husserl focused on internal time consciousness in contrast to objective, physical time. In this regard, the threefold experience of time—past, present, and future—was considered by many phenomenologists to be the fundamental approach to time. However, differences emerged over the concept of presence and the origin of time as presence. Husserl, in his transcendental phenomenology, constructed the structure of time out of a passing presence as a fundamental moment of genetic time constitution. Husserl's phenomenology of time lays the foundation for the analysis of how time is constituted, how experiences are temporally structured, and how different modes of consciousness can be distinguished in reference to their time structure. Thus, the founding father of phenomenology is a rich source for the successors who all have set off in very different directions. Henri Bergson, whose work belongs to the realm of life philosophy but who has been in close relation to phenomenological and existential research, especially concerning his study of memory, puts more emphasis on the past and, hence, the concept of memory as constitutive of the creation of the present.[8] Martin Heidegger's guiding principle in *Being and Time* is the idea that being-there projects itself into the future and, therefore, "the primary phenomenon of primordial and authentic temporality is the future," and thus, is being toward the future.[9] The ontological concept of being-there is put in relation to the existential fact that all humans are "being driven toward death."[10] The individual being finds his or her authenticity and liberty only in acknowledging the existential fact of his or her mortality. Jacques Derrida criticized Husserl's conception as metaphysics of presence by referring to different levels of speech and meaning: "Signs represent the present in its absence."[11] With this basic insight he opens the ground for hermeneutics and deconstructive approaches of different kinds.

These differences in the phenomenological tradition evoked further phenomenological reflections on time such as Paul Ricoeur's reflections on narrative identity as discussed in this volume by Annemie Halsema, discussions of differences between the time of the world, the time of life, and personal time (Alfred Schutz, Wilhelm Dilthey) invoked in particular by Gail Weiss, as well as Maurice Merleau-Ponty's emphasis on bodily anchorage in the world and in time (in Stoller and Fisher).[12] Modern and contemporary philosophy has developed a number of varied and sometimes incompatible time concepts. However, explorations of the relation between time and gender, or feminist issues and time concepts, have been completely neglected by many phenomenologists. That is, even though various rapprochements between feminism and phenomenology have examined different aspects of lived experiences from the aspect of gender, comparatively little attention had been paid to the exploration of time and temporality in relation to gender. This is particularly extraordinary since time is a fundamental category for modern and contemporary philosophy and its reflection on ontological, epistemological, political, aesthetic, and ethic dimensions, dimensions that are issues for feminist phenomenology and gender theory. Moreover, it is particularly surprising since even the classical phenomenologists and hermeneuticists have developed concepts and linkages, such as time and lived experience (Husserl), the lived, anonymous, habitual body (Merleau-Ponty), or narrative identity (Arendt, Ricoeur), that are fundamental and useful for the thematization of gender and feminist theory in relation to issues of time. The field, which had been set out by classical phenomenologists, can be *shifted* into, even *transformed* by, gender theory and feminist phenomenology. Moreover, this transformation from classical philosophy of time into time concerning gender theory and feminist phenomenology can be traced back to our ideas about the origins of time itself. That is, at least for a moment we shall look at the beginning of questioning time, meaning the historical transformation from mythos to logos, from myth to reason. Ancient philosophers, such as Plato in the *Timaios,* struggled with the question of how to think about the simultaneous emergence of the cosmos with time. This question was of great importance for the astronomical and physical explanation of movement and change, and has important implications for the feminist phenomenological view of time. Thus, the starting point for this collection, the essay by Dorothea Olkowski, is appropriately concerned with the beginning of time, that is, the mythological prehistory of occidental philosophy. Since the question of myth and of the beginning of time concerns history *before* the logos, her essay is systematically located and literarily named *Prologue.* That is, it is a prologue in its double sense: as the beginning of history and as the situation before the history of logos.

Greek mythology tells the story of the god Hades, who comes from the underworld. Made imperceptible by the gift of the Cyclops, the helmet that conceals him, he comes to earth to abduct Kore, daughter of Demeter. For the Greeks, this abduction is a defining act that creates the seasons and so becomes the original determination of time for human beings. Olkowski argues that this conception of time is the determining act of the god of the underworld and a function of death and disjunction. Thus, for the Greek poets and philosophers, every so-called act of creation is ultimately an act of destruction and death. Olkowski finds this notion developed further in Western philosophy by Plato, for whom Nature is the "God of All Things," who creates nothing, but who unravels all the elements, a "setting in due order." But what this means, she claims, is that with respect to time, the invisible world of Darkness and of the dark god Hades asserts its "rights" over the *visible world*, the world of the goddesses Demeter-Kore.

Thus, Olkowski posits that the visible world might be reinterpreted as the world of the Pelasgian goddess Eurynome. Eurynome was called the wide-wandering goddess, the visible moon and diffuse light. She was the universal goddess who set the cosmos in motion by dancing with the wind. But from her union with the wind, the goddess also brings forth the snake Ophion, who exasperates her by proclaiming himself the author of the self-created universe, until she, incredulous, "bruised his head with her heel, kicked out his teeth, and banished him to the dark caves below the earth." Olkowski suggests that according to the myth of Eurynome, Hades and the Western philosophers are the descendants of the serpent Ophion. This is why their *episteme* begins its surveying, measuring, and calculating on the basis of *shadows* projected upon surfaces, screens, and supports in the caves beneath the earth, while they liken the visible realm of the goddess to a prison dwelling. Olkowski then proposes that the goddess, along with the myth of Demeter-Kore, be taken as concepts that constitute a first philosophy, a description of the nature of reality and of the origin of time as creative and transformational, rather than as the deathly thought of an invisible and powerful destroyer.

This narrative and myth-based account, by expanding the horizons of our concept of time, allows us to move into the center of the reevaluation of the phenomenological tradition, which is based on the Greek tradition and a philosophy of logos, in terms of a philosophy that turns the privilege of death and mortality, solitude and contemplation, into a recognition of beginning and natality, human relation and action, and that is therefore able to thematize gender theory in relation to a philosophy of time.[13]

In order to account for two basic levels of discussion, this volume of *Time in Feminist Phenomenology* is construed in two principal sections: first, a phenomenology of time read from a feminist perspective and focusing on concepts and methods arising out of gender theory; second, a phenomenology of time taken in its ethical and political aspects. The former perspective focuses especially on methodological questions of phenomenological conceptions of time, such as change and becoming, different modes of experiences, and the relevancy of time for feminist phenomenology. A feminist approach always concerns the reevaluations of power relations within society, as, for example, the question of the relevance of time when discussing power relations or asymmetrical hierarchies between men and women. Thus, in a certain respect, feminist phenomenology is always also at least implicitly political and social. In the second section these implicit traits are made explicit. It focuses on temporal structures of the political and the social that affect gender issues, particular female experiences, questions of gender identity, and questions surrounding our concepts of the body. Thus, the two sections are kept together by specific concerns, which are, however, discussed in relation to varying perspectives and themes.

Overall, several assumptions weave through the collection. These assumptions can be followed up as the central themes of *time in feminist phenomenology*. First, phenomenology concerns *methodological considerations*. Hence, the task becomes, as Sara Heinämaa argues, to explicate the temporal constitution of the experience of sexual difference as well as its pre-predicative foundations. If we want to develop a philosophical account of sexual difference, we need to engage in genetic phenomenological inquiries. We must also raise questions about the differences between the temporal structure of experiences, the self-constitution of time, and the temporal structure of reflective thinking. To this end, Christina Schües shows that they are grounded in very different time structures and that an understanding of these structures is relevant for further research in the political and social sphere, particularly in the realm of power relations, which are held in place by way of domination over time. The implications of this analysis are the subject of the second section of this book. Throughout these essays there is a shared view that we need a clarification and elaboration of the concepts of temporality and sedimentation, and a discussion of the differences between empirical and phenomenological inquiries, and from there a clear account of sexual differences.

Second, central to more or less all authors is the belief in the *intertwining between the temporality of experience and gender*. Experiences are gendered insofar as they are bound to the body and to the world. Experiences, as phenomenologists have clearly shown, are always temporal, and, as feminist theorists have argued, experiences are also gendered; thus, the interrelation between time and gender must be examined. The difficulty of thematizing this relation lies in the fact that neither time nor gender is "something" that can simply be thematized *as* something. Both are involved in the most extraordinary difficulties, contradictions, and entanglements. Because of these difficulties, contradictions, and entanglements, it may be that philosophical methods and questions utilized to explore time may also be applicable to gender. Martin Heidegger, for example, asked the insightful question "how does time show itself?"[14] As soon as we try to understand time as objective time or clock time, we actually lose it, because we then measure only the movement from now to now and then homogenize the now points. *The same might hold for gender;* as soon as we try to objectify gender and find a list of attributes, the issue disappears or we find ourselves in some ungrounded naturalism. The alternative approach put forward by phenomenologists, and most explicitly by Heidegger, maintains that "time is temporal"; *Dasein*, or existence, is not objective time but is temporality. Alternatively, one could say that "gendered is gendering."

The gender, *the* woman, and *the* man are concepts that are as senseless as saying *the* time. Thus, for both we might pose the same kind of question: How does time show itself? How does gender show itself? And: how does gender show itself in relation to time? And how does time show itself in relation to gender? Thus, temporality is gendered, gendering is temporal. Time as an issue in the framework of feminist philosophy requires addressing gender in relation to temporality. Theorizing the relation between temporality and gender in the framework of feminist phenomenology means making use of the phenomenological tradition.

Time and gender, or better *temporalizing* and *gendering,* both force upon the philosopher the task of the thematization of their concrete realization as well as what is known as the *constitutive transcendental realm.* That is, in order to consider the question of "how time or gender shows itself," we have to look at how experiences are constituted with respect to temporality and gendering. We have to focus on their concrete realization in different realms of experiences.

Time and gender seem to be particularly experienced in their negation or exaggeration. When we lack time or when time seems to flow away, when we do not have time for something, or when we are too late, then—so it seems—time shows itself with all its realistic force. But is this the time that we experience? Certainly our language seems to suggest that time is always passing by and not creating itself, but is this true? What is it that we face when we are too late? The feeling of boredom, or the sense of having free time and nothing to do, seems to suggest a different experience from what is normal, and a sense of time. "Normally" our gender recedes into the background; we are not always conscious of our gender; we experience, speak, or act as somebody gendered, but the gender becomes present to consciousness only when it is a problem, is emphasized, or the like. Hence, the notion of gender is strongly associated with a notion of anonymity and a focus on the body. Here the work by Merleau-Ponty is central to this discussion, since it is in his work that the idea of anonymity has been so clearly formulated. Explicitly taken up is this theme of anonymity by Silvia Stoller. However, her main interest in this paper consists of introducing an aspect of temporality that seems to be widely unrecognized, not only in feminist philosophy and phenomenology, but also in theories of time in general: the anonymous aspect of temporality. She proposes that there is an anonymous temporality that is not yet named or determined, but that lies at the basis of all temporal experiences, women's as well as men's. It is an indeterminate sphere from which experiences such as "female" or "male" temporality arise, and it is what makes them possible. Thus, recognizing such a general sphere of lived temporality allows us to think gendered temporality in nonbiological terms while at the same time considering the dynamic dimension of gendered temporality. Intersecting habits and gender, as well as time and anonymity, allows any biological essentialism to be avoided (Stoller) and the masculine or the feminine to be regarded as different variations of human existence (Heinämaa). The dimension of anonymity must be complemented by further dimensions that are relevant for the constitution of time, namely the body.

Thus, the *third central theme* of this volume is the thematization of concepts of the body. When considering time and the body, the body is interpreted in different senses; it may be taken as lived, anonymous, or habitual. Starting with Merleau-Ponty's *Phenomenology of Perception,* Linda Fisher discusses how habit, enacted through motility and bodily meaning, mediates between bodily space and spatiality. She then examines how habit, taken as an understanding body, is formed and forms a temporal character, and consequently, gender is read as habitude within a well-developed phenomenology of embodiment. Taking up the argument that embodiment includes both subjectivity and belonging to a genre, Fisher maintains that bodily identity, or more specifically, sexuate identity, is a construction that implies, as Judith Butler argues, an appeal to develop ourselves within the context and restrictions of society. Thus, the embodied self articulates itself within a social context for which it cannot account. This articulation can be narrated, but not entirely. For feminist purposes it is especially the limits of what is narratable that are worth considering, for these limits mark out the futural possibilities for us and for generations to come.

So we find Annemie Halsema explaining, in her essay "The Time of the Self: A Feminist Reflection on Ricoeur's Notion of Narrative Identity," how Ricoeur's notion of narrative identity moves in between *idem* and *ipse,* between self-sameness and constancy on the one hand and the flux of time on the other. The narrative itself contains a notion both of time as passing and of time as enduring. For Halsema, Judith Butler exemplifies the position that it is not only in narrating our life story that we refer to time and use time, but that also the process of constructing an identity includes time, or rather *is* time. Moving along these lines of thought, Halsema then turns, with Luce Irigaray, to a bodily account of the narrative self. Not only the aging self—with its body that grows older and the perception and interpretation of the self that change in correspondence or in dissonance with it—but also the concept of the self itself includes time. These three basic assumptions—the concern about methodological considerations, the intertwining of the temporality of experiences and gender, and different concepts of the body—cannot be thought of independently from society and culture.

Precisely put, the experience of time depends upon the habits and the social norms of our society. The political (Fielding, Vasterling) and the social (Weiss) are inherently temporal, and not to be grasped without reference to the experiences, the body, identity, or certain habits. And this assumption about the temporality of the political and the social is the fourth underlying theme of this volume. So, for instance, psychologists discovered that time, next to money, is one of the major issues in quarrels between couples. Walking too slowly, taking too much time in the bathroom, moving about hectically in the kitchen, or arriving too late or too early for an appointment are all familiar issues that can provide grounds for irritation in our relations with others. This observation about the importance of time holds true as well for intercultural relations. Each culture has its own structure of time, its own speed of time, and its own norms of time. And again, the different time concepts are also gendered in different ways. For instance, in the United States hard work and long working hours tend to be associated with norms of manhood, while family time is associated with women and children. In Japan, hard and fast working is considered to be one of the highest virtues, and it is associated with patriotism and being part of the collective.[15]

Particularly in Western countries, most people say that they need more time and that they lack time: many employees complain about the tempo at work; women especially feel that given their different roles as mothers, employees, partners, housekeepers, and caretakers, they lack time for themselves. The fight for balance among the different female roles is a temporal problem. However, paradoxically, one could also argue that people have more time. Officially we are working fewer hours than in the past. We have helping machines, and we live longer than the generations before us. Nevertheless, we can observe that time has sped up. But the faster pace of time might not be the root problem; rather, the question is how time is structured qualitatively, and how it is lived by women and men. Thus, the essays in this volume discuss differences in these time structures. Sociologically speaking, we can observe that we live in a multi-optional society in which so-called multitasking seems required. In this manner, the experience of time has been multiplied. We find several tracks of simultaneous (linear) time: 24-7 open hours, day and night business; every time and everywhere all options are open; everyone must be present at all times via mobile phone, e-mail, Internet blogs, and online groups. Following up on all these demands and communicative options results in stress. Withdrawing from the multi-optional society of simultaneity requires constant decision making, the ability to choose one particular option out of many possibilities. The multiplication of times results, therefore, in a lack of time, which brings stress and contributes to the lessening of the capacity to concentrate.

However, the question of our need for more time is also the question of our point of view: the question is not how much work does one have to do, the question is also what is considered to be work, and how is this distinguished from time filled with activities that I like, as well as time for myself. For example, some women see time spent with their children as playful leisure time, and their work in the office as duty, and perhaps as stressful. Others might feel the opposite: time spent with their children is a mad rush, whereas life in the office is quiet, peaceful, and communicative, and hence, a relief. Although the images I draw upon might seem rather simple, I think the point is clear. No specific activity can be regarded as the source of time's quick passage, or as the source for stress. The root problem is not a particular activity or a lack of time, but the *rhythm of time*. By the rhythm of time I mean the temporal structure of society and of the way activities are to be carried out. In many Western societies, life is organized according to economic guidelines that can be followed without temporal stress only for individuals without children, without social dependencies, that is, people who can be anywhere whatever at any time. But as implied above, it might be that even if more flexible work hours were introduced, it would not necessarily mean that employees would use the flexibility in order to spend more time, for example, with their families.

The rhythm of time concerns the appropriateness of the time structure of our activities. Who is in control of the rhythm of time, and why? The more somebody else determines *when* and, most of all, *how* something must be done, the more we feel these determinations are not appropriate. We feel more stress, and our need for more time evolves. Hence, understanding the forces and the different structures of time lays the ground for understanding the relations between human beings, between men and women, between different groups and styles of living. To understand the sense in which time can be a powerful instrument to rule others and their activities means to take the first step toward active participation in the constitution of human relations and social norms. Thus, in order to understand these general concerns, the second section of this volume focuses explicitly on political and ethical aspects of time. Here it is important to notice that the political and the social are inherently temporal; it is action that is, in effect, interaction, the speaking and acting before others that gives potency to the act of saying rather than to what is actually said.

These concerns take us, once again, to the understanding of time held by the ancient Greeks, for whom the possibilities of the *polis* are revealed as embodied intermittent relations or spacings. But the *polis* is not just a space as such; it is not a physical location at all, but rather, as Hannah Arendt emphasizes, it is an "organization of the people as it arises out of acting and speaking together."[16] Understanding this relation of speaking and acting together must privilege the "relational and contextual" aspects of language over the "normative, rational and universal" ones.[17] Consequently, the political is temporal in that the potency or power that is generated through interaction is effective only when it is actualized and lasts only as long at there is an active relation.

Helen A. Fielding supports her thesis of the temporality of the political by referring to Yael Bartana's video artworks, in particular *Wild Seeds* (2005). One theme of these videos is the specificity of embodied voices to reveal the fissures in national identity. She shows how videos necessarily involve temporality and, hence, are useful for the investigation of identity. Temporality is woven into its structure not only in terms of sequences, the length of the work, or the user's reception. Even more interestingly, the temporal aspects of video allow for the opening up of time-spaces. The thesis that time-spaces are made up of relational structures is strongly supported by the interpretational context of Maurice Merleau-Ponty, Adriana Cavarero, and Hannah Arendt, who push the idea of the primacy of the interrelation among all people, people in their families, communities, or neighborhoods. However, these relations, which are based on an opening of the temporal and special dimension, may also take place when an artwork sets to work in its engagement with viewers, that is, when the video is playing in a public space.

Fielding argues that the intersubjective engagement with the film is based on the intercorporeal relation with the world, and thus, with the experience of haptic sound and vision; hence, she can show how subjectivity is always already relational and an engagement with the world. This subjective intertwinement shapes what is seen and heard in terms of its given temporal structure. With Arendt we know that politics depends on the relational structure of people and their engagement, that is, acting and speaking, in the world and toward the world. Also, for Arendt political action is a space-opening undertaking, that is, a spacing (*ein-räumen*), as Martin Heidegger would also say. Thus, also politics as well as the aesthetics of these videos privilege the temporal structure in the enactment between people. Both politics and video art feature the in-between, whereby a space is rather a spacing, a taking place between people, where they appear to one another. Of course, since spacing depends upon interacting and speaking for Arendt, or aesthetic interaction for Fielding, the place, the in-between people, is always contingent.

Any philosophy that takes time seriously will have to deal with contingency. Even though modern and contemporary philosophy have left the *sub specie aeternitate* stance behind, there are scant reflections on the impact and consequences of contingency. The work of Hannah Arendt is one of the few exceptions. Contingency plays a prominent role in her work. Important concepts in her work such as natality, action, willing, history, and understanding are explicitly elaborated in the light of contingency. Arendt uses these concepts to shift and transform the history of thought to a different perspective. Not the death and the desire for immortality, but the birth and the consequent natality, which opens the grounding space for beginnings and relations, motivates human action and even feminist politics. Human beings are born to begin and not born to die; this phrase characterizes an attitude that is extremely attractive for feminist thinking. Furthermore, what is so interesting about Arendt's reflections on contingency is the emphasis on "newness," both in the historical and the political sense of the possibility of a change for the better or the worse, and in the anthropological and the psychological sense of the shock of the unexpectedly new.

"Contingency, Newness, and Freedom: Arendt's Recovery of the Temporal Condition of Politics" is the title of Veronica Vasterling's explorations of the meaning and consequences of contingency in the sense of "newness" in Arendt's work. She relates this exploration to what she calls Arendt's political hermeneutics, that is, to a political philosophy for which the ability to understand and the ability to judge are central. From this we may hypothesize that Arendt's political philosophy resembles a political hermeneutics exactly because of the prominent role of contingency in the sense of newness. The discussion on newness and political beginning is made possible by Vasterling's emphasis on Arendt's deconstructive move from the binary opposition of necessity versus contingency, and its corresponding concepts of timelessness and change. Subversively Vasterling works out along the line of Arendt's work that the opposition of necessity is not contingency but freedom: freedom that is essential to political interaction and foundational plurality. Thus, human *life* is determined by the linear time conception with its possible interruptions, whereas human *nature,* to the contrary, can be described by the circular, repetitive time structure. However, this distinction is not ontologically, but methodologically, important when one focuses on the relation between time and the political realm.

The political realm, so one might argue, coheres with the experience of a common time for its members. The notion of "common time" was introduced by Husserl in the *Cartesian Meditations* and powerfully used by Schutz in order to describe the idea that even though people might not have precisely the same experience, they still may have some common experience and a common past. Schutz understands common time in a Bergsonian sense: the other's temporal duration and my own are to be found in one united act that embraces both courses of time. Because of the coexistence of both durations they have a similar structure, and hence age together. This basic and common temporal ground is seen as grounding the community in the future, allowing members of the community to act in concert. But is this actually real?

Gail Weiss takes on this pressing political and social issue by arguing against such a harmonious understanding of "common time." In her essay "Sharing Time across Unshared Horizons" she draws a different picture of the question of finding one's identity in time. Weiss argues forcefully that real social, temporal, and spatial "barriers" exist between individuals and groups of different races, bodily capacities, and genders. In particular, disabled persons are frequently excluded from the "common world" and the standard world of working, and their identities are stigmatized accordingly. Often society regards marginalized individuals, as Weiss points out with Rosemarie Garland Thomson, as "misfits" because they are born into the "wrong" race, gender, or body. With this diagnosis in mind, Weiss offers a critical analysis of different theoretical approaches for understanding identity. She discovers that, depending on the philosophical position, different features of identity are emphasized, and accordingly different consequences for the individual ensue. For instance, identity can be seen as unified, multiple, or hybrid; it can be understood as chosen by oneself, imposed by others, referred by a social class, and so on. Weiss claims that we must attend more carefully to the "invisible identities" that help to constitute an individual's self-understanding as well as other people's views of that individual because they are actually "just as salient for a given individual and her community" as her more visible attributes such as her race and gender. Moreover, by deemphasizing "the distinction between the visible and invisible attributes of an individual, we could shift the focus to acknowledging the temporal and "interpretive horizons" in which identities are dynamically enacted and transform over time. This focus on the interpretive horizons that situate one's identity, as Linda Martín Alcoff and Annemie Halsema also suggest, must necessarily take into account temporal experiences, their differences and implications in regard to the possibility or impossibility of interrelating with one another and of having a "common time." Thus, any study of human interrelation and understanding, of political spacing and ethical acting, is required to account for the inherent structure and concepts of temporality. And to account for the inherent structures and concepts of temporality requires methodological considerations, the awareness of the intertwining of experiences and temporality, close studies of different body concepts, and the insight that life is inherently temporal.

*   *   *

Finally, the editors of this volume, *Time in Feminist Phenomenology*, would like to extend their gratitude to Dee Mortensen from Indiana University Press for her enthusiastic response when confronted with this proposal of interrelating time and gender theory and time and feminist phenomenology, and for her competent guidance through the process of publication. Also we thank the editorial board of Indiana University Press for accepting this book in their program. Marianne Averbeck (University of Vechta) deserves our gratitude and admiration for her assistance in formatting the manuscript, and also we thank Lisa Clark for her assistance with the index. Last but not least, all members of the Feminist Phenomenology Group are thanked for their discussions . . . in the past and for the future.

Notes

1. Stoller and Vetter, *Phänomenologie und Geschlechterdifferenz;* Fisher and Embree, *Feminist Phenomenology;* Dorothea Olkowski, "Phenomenology and Feminism," in *Edinburgh Encyclopedia of Continental Philosophy* (Edinburgh: Edinburgh University Press, 1999), 323–30; Heinämaa, "Feminism"; Stoller, Vasterling, and Fisher, *Feministische Phänomenologie und Hermeneutik.*

2. Beauvoir, *The Second Sex;* Irigaray, *Key Writings* and *Speculum of the Other Woman;* Kristeva, "Women's Time" and *Revolution in Poetic Language;* Chanter, "Female Temporality and the Future of Feminism."

3. Augustinus, *Confessions,* 221–45.

4. Ibid., 235.

5. Thus, for Augustinus, the one who has a spiritual life and who is close to God lives most in the present.

6. Kant, *Critique of Pure Reason.*

7. Husserl, *The Phenomenology of Internal Time-Consciousness,* 22.

8. Bergson, *Matter and Memory.*

9. Heidegger, *Being and Time,* 378.

10. Ibid., 426.

11. Derrida, *Speech and Phenomena,* 138.

12. Ricoeur, *Time and Narrative;* Schutz, *The Phenomenology of the Social World* and *The Problem of Social Reality;* Merleau-Ponty, *The Phenomenology of Perception.*

13. In almost all philosophical and political works Hannah Arendt explicitly posits natality as the existential human condition for action and for politics. For a further study on the theme of birth and natality see Schües, *Philosophie des Geborenseins.*

14. Heidegger, *Begriff der Zeit.*

15. See Levine, *A Geography of Time,* ch. 8.

16. Arendt, *The Human Condition,* 198.

17. Ibid., 180; Cavarero, *For More than One Voice,* 192.

Bibliography

Arendt, Hannah. *The Human Condition.* Chicago: University of Chicago Press, 1958.
Augustinus. *Confessions.* Trans. H. Chadwick. Oxford: Oxford University Press, 1998.
Beauvoir, Simone de. *Le deuxième sexe I–II.* [1949] Paris: Gallimard, 1991, 1993. Trans. and ed. Howard M. Parshley: *The Second Sex.* Harmondsworth: Penguin, 1987.
Bergson, Henri. *Matter and Memory.* Trans. Nancy M. Paul and W. Scott Palmer. New York: Zone, 1991.

Butler, Judith. *Gender Trouble: Feminism and the Subversion of Identity.* London: Routledge, 1990.

Cavarero, Adriana. *For More Than One Voice: Toward a Philosophy of Vocal Expression.* Trans. Paul A. Kottman. Stanford, Calif.: Stanford University Press, 2005.

Chanter, Tina. "Female Temporality and the Future of Feminism." In *Abjection, Melancholia and Love: The Work of Julia Kristeva,* ed. John Fletcher and Andrew Benjamin, 63–79. London: Routledge, 1990.

Derrida, Jacques. *Speech and Phenomena: And Other Essays on Husserl's Theory of Signs.* Evanston, Ill.: Northwestern University Press, 1973.

Fisher, Linda, and Lester Embree, eds. *Feminist Phenomenology.* Dordrecht: Kluwer, 2000.

Heidegger, Martin. *Begriff der Zeit.* Tübingen: Max Niemeyer, 1995. Trans. John Macquarrie and Edward Robinson: *Being and Time.* Oxford: Blackwell Publishing, 2006.

Heinämaa, Sara. "Feminism." In *A Companion to Phenomenology and Existentialism,* ed. Hubert l. Dreyfus and Mark A. Wrathall, 500–513. Malden, Mass.: Blackwell, 2006.

———. *Toward a Phenomenology of Sexual Difference: Husserl, Merleau-Ponty, Beauvoir.* Lanham, Md.: Rowman and Littlefield, 2003.

Husserl, Edmund. *Cartesianische Meditationen und Pariser Vorträge.* Husserliana, Band I. Ed. Stephan Strasser. The Hague: Martinus Nijhoff, 1950. Trans. Dorion Cairns: *Cartesian Meditations.* Dordrecht: Martinus Nijhoff, 1960.

———. *The Crisis of European Sciences and the Transcendental Phenomenology.* Trans. David Carr. Evanston, Ill.: Northwestern University Press, 1970.

———. *Phänomenologische Psychologie, Vorlesungen Sommersemester 1925.* Husserliana, Band IX. Ed. Walter Biemel. The Hague: Martinus Nijhoff, 1968.

———. *The Phenomenology of Internal Time-Consciousness.* Trans. and ed. James S. Churchill. Bloomington: Indiana University Press, 1964.

Irigaray, Luce. *Key Writings.* London: Continuum, 2004.

———. *Speculum of the Other Woman.* Trans. Gillian C. Gill. Ithaca, N.Y.: Cornell University Press, 1985.

Kristeva, Julia. *Revolution in Poetic Language.* Trans. Margaret Waller with an introduction by Leon S. Roudiez. New York: Columbia University Press, 1984.

———. "Women's Time." In *The Kristeva Reader.* Ed. Toril Moi, 187–213. Oxford: Blackwell, 1986.

Kant, Immanuel. *Critique of Pure Reason.* Trans. Paul Guyer and Allen W. Wood. Cambridge: Cambridge University Press, 1998.

Kortooms, Toine. *Phenomenology of Time: Edmund Husserl's Analysis of Time-Consciousness.* Dordrecht: Kluwer Academic Publishers, 2002.

Levine, Robert. *A Geography of Time.* New York: Basic Books, 1997.

Martín Alcoff, Linda. *Visible Identities: Race, Gender, and the Self.* Oxford: Oxford University Press, 2006.

Merleau-Ponty, Maurice. *Phénoménologie de la perception.* [1945] Paris: Gallimard, 1993.

———. *Phenomenology of Perception.* Trans. Colin Smith. London: Routledge, 1995.

Ricoeur, Paul. *Time and Narrative.* Vols. 1–3. Trans. Kathleen Blamey and David Pellauer. Chicago: University of Chicago Press, 1984–88.

Schües, Christina. *Philosophie des Geborenseins.* Freiburg/München: Alber, 2008.

Schutz, Alfred. *The Phenomenology of the Social World.* Trans. George Walsh and Frederick Lehnert. Evanston, Ill.: Northwestern University Press, 1967.

——. *The Problem of Social Reality: Collected Papers I.* Ed. Maurice Natanson. The Hague: Martinus Nijhoff Publishers, 1982.

Stoller, Silvia, Veronica Vasterling, and Linda Fisher, eds. *Feministische Phänomenologie und Hermeneutik.* Würzburg: Königshausen & Neumann, 2005.

Stoller, Silvia, and Helmuth Vetter, eds. *Phänomenologie und Geschlechterdifferenz.* Vienna: WUV-Universitätsverlag, 1997.

2.

PROLOGUE:
THE ORIGIN OF TIME,
THE ORIGIN OF PHILOSOPHY

Dorothea Olkowski

Many of the essays in this volume put forth the hypothesis that there is a significant relationship between feminist phenomenological concepts of time and that of lived experience, in other words, that lived experience is inextricably intertwined with the temporal conditions of human life. To this end, the philosophy of Hannah Arendt provides many feminist philosophers with an account of temporality that proceeds by uncovering forgotten lived experiences and articulating the narratives describing those experiences, insofar as the latter give meaning to human reality. By setting forth her philosophy in this manner, Arendt alerts us to the fundamental role of time and temporality in philosophical structures. Starting with an account of the dominant philosophical models of time and temporality, she addresses the possibility of introducing her own phenomenological models. However, as Sara Heinämaa argues, in the lead essay in this volume, in order to address these questions it will be necessary to pay attention to different aspects of concrete human existence in its lived temporality.

The essay by Veronica Vasterling also takes up this project, focusing on Arendt's argument that Plato introduced the greatest metaphysical blunder with respect to the notion of time when he simply eliminated the striving for immortality through noble words and deeds in favor of the philosopher's "unspeakable" (*arrhēton*) experience of the eternal.[1] What distinguishes the experience of the eternal, "the standing now," is that, for Plato, it can be accessed only through silent contemplation. Temporally outside the realm of human affairs, the time of eternity is experienced as a kind of death because it is the absence of any activity, including the activities of thinking and speaking with words. The implications of this view of time are hard to ignore for feminist thinking. First of all, as Christina

Schües points out, we must become aware of the difference between the temporal structure of experiences, the self-constitution of time, and the temporal structure of reflective thinking. As such, although a feminist account of the temporal structure of experience might eschew the notion of deathly eternity in order to focus on an experience such as Arendt's conception of temporality as natality or birth, this does not mean that feminists do not withdraw from the world in order to contemplate, only that they wish to do so from within the framework of the lived experience of natality. This is all the more important for, as Schües convincingly argues, time is an instrument that reinforces power relations. This will become evident later in this essay when we describe the abduction of the goddess Kore, who is taken into the underworld just at the moment in time when she begins to reflect on her own experience.

From the Platonic vantage point, Arendt's appreciation for the other Greek model, that of striving for immortality or attempting to prove oneself to be of a divine nature by means of noble words and deeds, was judged to be vanity and vainglory.[2] In spite of the Greek gods' proximity to humankind, their immortality was understood by most Greeks to be an aspect of nature's cyclical repetitions, its immortal order. By contrast, given the mortality of human existence, human beings had to produce works, deeds, and words that deserved to be preserved and remembered through time.[3] In this manner, it is precisely the ability of human beings to produce enduring things that connects them to Arendt's reconfiguration of time. Arendt formulates a conception of time linked to the specifically human capacity to produce works, deeds, and words. Thus, unlike Plato, Arendt links time to the birth of speech and action rather than death and wordless contemplation.

This conception of time contrasts strongly with the Platonic conception of time as eternity, an eternity that can be experienced only by analogy with death; and, as we will see, it contrasts, as well, with the time of the Greek gods understood to be cyclical and natural, because they represent natural events. Perhaps it will not be too far off the mark to suggest that Arendt's conception of time is both phenomenological and feminist: phenomenological as a description of lived experience, and feminist as modeled on the experience of birth or natality rather than deathlike contemplation. As Vasterling suggests, the temporal, existential condition of natality refers both to physical birth and also to the birth of political speech and action. Moreover, both types of birth give rise to effects that are completely unpredictable, thus free. In the case of human, physical birth, the newly born human being can in no sense be the effect of the contemplation of Platonic eternal ideas. Likewise, the effects of noble words and deeds are free, not only in the sense of unable to be determined in advance, but also because they give rise to new words and deeds, equally free, equally unknowable in advance. As Arendt argues, action grows and multiplies so that action has no end, making it difficult for human beings to bear the burden of unpredictability.[4]

Given this analysis, it will be our purpose in this essay to formulate a feminist phenomenological conception of time. In addition to Arendt, this task also finds inspiration in the philosophy of Luce Irigaray. In her short essay, "Korē: Young Virgin, Pupil of the Eye," Irigaray offers a feminist critique of the meaning of Plato's conception of the origin of time by means of a phenomenological analysis of vision. Citing Plato's creation myth, the *Timaeus,* Irigaray focuses her attention on Plato's warnings against looking directly at the sun "for fear of burning up the membrane at the back of the eye, screen for production and projection of forms in the eye's camera obscura."[5] For Plato, "the consuming contact of light will also be avoided by paying attention to the forms alone."[6] The forms represent Plato's conception of time as eternal. Eternal time is thus something that can be seen, but it can be seen only when light has been reflected, stopped, or trapped, when the light merely outlines what quite possibly always, already existed. "What is that which always is, and does not have generation, and what is that which is always becoming, and never is."[7] In other words, the eternal time of the cosmos can be seen only by means of reflected light. And just as in the cave of Plato's dialogue *Republic,* "the *epistēmē* begins its surveying, measuring, and calculating on the basis of shadows projected by/upon surfaces, screens and supports."[8] The eternal presence of forms, which is the form of eternity, can be discerned only by the light that outlines the forms. For this task, we must be assisted by a system of mirrors that chill the light and shield us from its touch and sight.[9] For in fact, the chief value of vision, as we will see, would have been to view the image of the eternal and unchanging intelligence of the heavens, the image that we call time, but that will never truly mirror the invisible shadowy realm of eternity.

The Field of Flowers

"It was a place where dogs would lose their quarry's trail, so violent was the scent of the flowers. A stream cut deep through the grass of a meadow that rose at the edge to fall sheer in a rocky ravine into the very navel of Sicily. And here, near Henna, Kore was carried off."[10] It was a place that would attract a young girl, virgin daughter of two gods, beloved child of Demeter, born of a violent coupling with brother-father Zeus, whose nostalgia for the radiant light out of which all life emerged found perverse expression and whose acts, although they were the acts of a god, could never approach the everything of she/he who had been the "first-born" of the world, the first appearance emanating from light.[11] Some claim the girl picked poppies, identifying her with their soporific qualities, their red color promising resurrection after death. Others, perhaps more attuned to the continuous usurpations of the male gods who, of necessity, fixed upon Kore's eye, these others who may also have been more attentive to the sensibility, the mind, of a young girl, daughter of the goddess of three worlds—the heavens, the earth, and the caves beneath—these others assert that the girl, Kore, was looking at a narcissus, or perhaps it was a lotus, a lily, or a rose. For them, "the psyche as flower, as lotus, lily, and rose, the virgin as flower in Eleusis, symbolizes the highest psychic and spiritual developments . . . the birth of the self in the Golden Flower."[12] In any case, the accounts of the Greek poet say it was a narcissus, so overwhelming, so seductive, "a thing of awe . . . from its root grew a hundred blooms and it smelled most sweetly, so that all wide heaven above and the whole earth and the sea's salt swell laughed for joy."[13] Obviously, a flower begging to be picked.

If "Kore was looking at a narcissus. She was *looking at the act of looking.*"[14] She is said to be looking at the flower of the youth, Narcissus, who, it was prophesied, would live to a ripe old age only if he never came to know himself. But this did not happen. Spurning all others, Narcissus was condemned to fall in love but denied the possibility of consummation. Seeing his own image in a spring "clear as silver," undisturbed by animal or plant, the already heartless, self-absorbed boy saw himself and came to know himself. Unlike the double-sexed goddess-god, Phanes-Eros—whom men say is the offspring, the luminous male principle, the divine son of Persephone-Kore—unlike Phanes-Eros, Narcissus is unable to copulate with himself. Moreover, in seeing and knowing himself, Narcissus does not gain understanding. Self-love merely enhances his pride. Overly proud, overwhelmed by self-love, overcome by grief, he plunges a dagger into his own breast. Little wonder that narcissus came to be used in the ancient wreaths of Demeter and Persephone, also called Kore.[15] For if to look at and to pick narcissus is to look at and to pick the act of looking, it is to see it and through seeing, to understand. So Demeter-Kore may well be the expression of seeing and seeing as understanding. But for Persephone-Kore, for this girl, understanding was, at the beginning, denied. Wandering alone on a sunny morning amid clusters of blossoms, Kore stops to look. Precisely at the moment when she reaches out to pluck the flower, precisely at the edge of her own look at the act of looking, at the edge of understanding through seeing, the earth opens and she is taken away by an unseen power to a dark, invisible place. Is this not the fate of many young girls? In the full light of the sun, at the very instant when they begin to look at the act of looking, on the verge of seeing and of coming to understand through sight, are they not also swept away by some unseeable power, a power that sees itself in them but that they cannot see? And unlike Persephone-Kore, most do not return.

Why does Hades come from the underworld with his golden chariot and four black horses? He sees and understands nothing of the world above but is made imperceptible by the gift of the Cyclops, the helmet that conceals him.[16] Is Hades the descendant of the serpent Ophion, created with the wind by the "Goddess of All Things," the naked Eurynome? Eurynome, wide-wandering goddess, the visible moon, diffuse light. Eurynome, the exalted dove, the first and only, the universal goddess who arose from yawning Chaos, danced with the wind, and gave rise to all things. Eurynome, the dove, tumbles above the waves and is fertilized by the wind. Out of the union of dancer and wind is hatched the Universal Egg, from which all things emerge, a cosmos set in motion by the goddess that is forever transforming itself, its seven planetary powers now ruled over by the Titanesses whose interests the Titans serve and safeguard. But Ophion soon exasperates the goddess, claiming to be himself the author of the self-created universe, until she, incredulous, "bruised his head with her heel, kicked out his teeth, and banished him to the dark caves below the earth."[17]

And now it is Hades who claims supremacy in the dark caves below the earth; the other world, an invisible world defined as isolated, separated, and silent.[18] In the myths reported by men, this new Ophion returns to the earth, but not to see and not to understand through sight. On earth, once again, a snake wraps itself around a goddess. Hades returns to the self-created and visible world, where formerly only deities ruled the seven days of the sacred planetary week: the Sun to illuminate; the Moon for enchantment; Mars giving growth; Mercury giving wisdom; Jupiter giving law; Venus granting love; Saturn granting peace.[19] There are no dark powers, no isolated, separated, silent, deathly powers among the *conceptions* of the goddess Eurynome. The snake wanders in the caves beneath the earth; it is nothing more than wind whistling through cracks and crevices. Banished, defanged, not a god, for gods give, they do not take anything away. But men, Hesiod, Ovid, ensure the return of the once powerless, defanged creature in a much more despotic and dangerous form. They make him a sightless god who seeks a vision of himself. Perhaps then, we should note that for them, Eurynome, Goddess of All Things, has vanished from the cosmos she brought forth; she is the first goddess to disappear, but will not be the last.[20] For these men, poets and philosophers, Darkness is first, and from Darkness springs even yawning Chaos. And from Chaos springs not illumination, enchantment, growth, wisdom, law, and love, but Doom, Old Age, Death, Murder, Sleep, Discord, Misery, Vexation, Nemesis, and later, Terror, Anger, Strife, Vengeance, Intemperance, Altercation, Oblivion, Fear, Pride, and Battle. What little can Sleep or Joy, Friendship or Pity, do to ameliorate the force of the dark planetary powers now unleashed?[21] And for them, for the philosophers, Nature is now the "God of All Things," *he* who does not bring forth but who *separates,* who *separates* earth from heaven, water from earth, the upper realms from the lower, unraveling all elements. And this unraveling is called "setting in due order," but it is an endless task in a cosmos set in motion by the Goddess of All Things, a cosmos ceaselessly transforming itself through the powers of illumination, enchantment, growth, wisdom, law, love, and peace.[22]

Perhaps then, given the arrival among men of the idea of setting the cosmos in due order, we should anticipate and acknowledge the importance that comes to be placed on the eternal model of the cosmos, that which always is and has no becoming, from which the world order is created in a *symphony of proportion* according to which what fire is to air, air is to water, and what air is to water, water is to earth. It is a structure that arises from a symphony of self-love ("he who framed the universe . . . wanted everything to become as much like himself as possible"), and it produces a symphony of proportions consisting of Originals and their imitations. As such, Different is to Same as men are to gods, and female to male (female being the inferior nature, the poor imitation, the formerly male soul that fails to live a good life).[23] Given all this, it is not surprising that Hades emerges from his separated and silent realm, from the realm of the invisible, into the field of flowers, into the visible, to abduct the daughter of Demeter, daughter of the "triple goddess of the cornfield," whose priestesses initiate the young and newly wed into "the secrets of the couch," but who takes no husband herself, who remains independent of all dark powers.[24] Perhaps we should not be surprised that the separated and silent world, the invisible world, asserts itself, asserts what have been called its "rights" over the visible world, meaning over the visible body of a young girl about to reach out and pluck the act of looking, about to take this open flower, this opening to understanding for herself. Where do these rights of the invisible over the visible arise? What justifies such rights? Are they also the effect of the symphony of proportion?

We have been told, "I'm sure you've noticed that when a man looks into an eye his face appears in it, like in a mirror. We call this the 'pupil' (*kore*), for it's a sort of miniature of the man who's looking."[25] If an eye is to see itself, it must look into a mirror or an eye. Moreover, the best part of the eye is said to be the part with which it sees, and this is likened to the best part of the soul, said to be the part that knows. The best part of the eye and the best part of the soul are said to resemble the divinity, perhaps because the pupil is thought to be that part of the eye that gives vision and the intellectual soul is that part of the soul that gives understanding. In spite of a general injunction against the senses, which disturb the proportions to near breaking point, sight is acknowledged to be a great benefit to humankind. "None of our present statements about the universe could ever have been made if we had never seen any stars, sun or heaven."[26] Our capacity to see

Nature is the gift of vision. And from the human ability to observe day and night, months and years, equinoxes and solstices, has come the invention of number, the idea of time, as well as numerous inquiries into the nature of the universe. And from these pursuits has arisen philosophy! Thus from vision—understanding, and not the reverse. But the philosopher is rather blind to this relation. He reasons that vision is the effect of particles shot out of the eyes, the *pure fire* that flows through the middle part of the eye, that part which is close-textured, smooth, dense, so that pure fire and only pure fire passes through. From the contemporary perspective, "it is difficult to imagine now why Plato did not try to settle the matter with a few simple experiments."[27] But his conception of vision was inextricably linked to the mixing of fires, like coalescing with like, the pure fire from the eyes coalescing with daylight, mixing and forming a *homogeneous* body, a medium that is able to transmit the motions of whatever comes into contact with it. The homogeneous body transmits motions from objects that contact it or that it comes into contact with; it transmits these motions through the eye straight into the soul! Fire meets fire, and *kore*, the young girl about to pick a flower, must be blinded, lest vision lead to understanding. She must be abducted so as to become the pure, virgin opening onto knowledge of an Other self. Eyefire and dayfire mix, homogenize, and convey directly whatever they come into contact with to the invisible soul, the only thing said to properly possess understanding, by which is meant, self-knowledge.[28]

And the soul? The soul is conceived of as a dark box, part of a *camera obscura* consisting of a pinhole opening through which passes one single ray of light; a single ray cuts through the *kore*, the tiny pupil, and is projected onto a screen for *direct* viewing. To see clearly, the soul must be completely dark, dark as the unlit and invisible place from which the god Hades emerges; it is the dark place into which the pinhole opening of the eye projects inverted images of the objects outside.[29] This is what the philosopher calls understanding, but it is little more than a view of the self, a view of the tiny image of oneself in the eye of the other, the very image of what is called self-knowledge. Precautions are put in place to ensure that nothing will enter the soul that should not enter—no diffuse or scattered light, scattered like flowers in a field. The *camera obscura* operates in accordance with the principles of the dark soul, the soul that knows what the eye perceives, but what the eye perceives is oneself. Contemporary perception theory agrees with the ancients that the mind does not record an exact image of the world but in fact creates its own picture.[30] Nevertheless, it can be argued that perceptions are neither arbitrary nor illusory; that they are unaffected by knowledge of ourselves or knowledge of the world. Our so-called direct perception of the world must be mediated by the senses, but as they are veridical; our perceptions do correspond to things in the world when those things are considered objectively, meaning, independently of viewing conditions, meaning, something obtainable through some form of measurement.[31] But *is* vision direct perception, as has been claimed? Geometrical optics tells us that light does travel in straight lines, but the "law of refraction" operates due to the requirement that the speed of light can be constant only in a perfect vacuum. Strictly speaking, if a ray of light passes from something like a glass of water (a dense medium) into air (a less dense medium), the ray of light will refract or bend. Light does travel more slowly in a denser medium and mediums do vary; they are not, as the philosopher hypothesized, homogeneous. Bending, refraction is inevitable and is the basis of image formation by all lenses including those of the eye.[32]

Shadows and Light

The goddess, Eurynome, dancing in the wind across the sky, sets in place the sun to illuminate the daytime sky and the moon to illuminate the nighttime sky. Eurynome is both the *Goddess of All Things* from whom all things emerge and the transformative, dynamic element, the creative element, setting the cosmos in motion and impelling it toward change.[33] In the cosmos set in motion by the goddess, it is the luminous moon and moonlight that form the background against which the sun and the cosmos stand out, light being the fruit or flower of the night. Ancient cultures calculated time from light of the stars and the planets, and especially of the moon. From this point of view, the light-bearing goddess of the night was identified with the moon and the moon was identified with life.[34] Such was the basis of the great mysteries of Eleusis, a celebration of the phases of the luminous moon, the joyful birth of the new moon, following the dark-moon, when the light of the heavens, the flourishing girl, Kore, is abducted by the death-sun.[35] Darkness corresponds, then, to the disappearance of the moon, with its luminous, reflective rays, and death, the darkening of the moon, *comes from the sun*. The winter solstice celebrates not only the return of Kore to Demeter from the caves of Hades, but also rebirth, Kore giving birth to the moon, the full moon, and the transformation of the girl Kore, herself becoming a moon goddess.[36]

A daring proposition? Dare we propose that time is the true transformation, the return of Kore to Demeter and to the moonlit earth, her transformation from girl to goddess, from sunlight to moonlight, an "immortal and divine principle, the beautific light . . . [so that with] Demeter, she becomes the goddess of the three worlds": the heavens, the earth, and the caves beneath?[37] This conceptualization of time, speculative, and at its inception untestable, is grounded in the idea of transformation. There is a transformation of material or natural elements, a quantitative and qualitative transformation in which something new is achieved, something that, like the moon, illuminates the heavens with its reflective light and that by means of this reflective illumination, transforms all, not once, but again and again. Its limits are found, perhaps, in the ancient idea of the cosmos as finite and bounded, having actual edges beyond which . . . nothing, nothing to sustain an object's structure. In such a cosmos transformations are limited, possibly little more than repetitions or maximally a finite number of variations. Still, is there any reason to believe that the universe created by the goddess is not at least *unbounded,* a sphere that is finite in area but delimited by no boundaries?[38] Nevertheless, what matters for the moment is the transformational aspect of this conception of time, for which it may prove to be of the greatest importance that, whether it is called *cosmos* or world-order, there is no severance of the connection between the concept and the reflective moon, the luminous aspect of the night.[39]

The philosophers too began with a concept. What the goddess has consigned to the dark caves below the earth diffusely lit by the reflective rays of the moon, they raised up to the highest heights. What had been lowest will be highest; what had been little more than the sound of the wind whipping through the caves below; what had no being and so no gift giving, planetary power; the invisible realm of Ophion and Hades, the dark realm of the death-sun, this will be the model for a cosmos made in the image of being. No longer a cosmos undergoing transformation as time of its natural elements, but *mimesis,* a world made, guarded, and limited by a nameless *demiourgos,* now little more than a maker, a craftsman.[40] The philosophers therefore, begin with the eternal *a priori,* with *sheer being,* "that which always is* and has no becoming."[41] No transformation, no *genesis,* meaning no dawn, no dawning, no engendering, no generation, inception, opening, no origin. If it is only visible and perceptible, the cosmos lacks sheer being. If it has come to be as it now is, it is grasped not by understanding but only by opinion. But the cosmos has a cause. It is not simply set in motion out of its own material and natural elements. It has a maker, a father who makes it from fire and earth bonded together by water and air according to rules of proportion applied to these materials. Such rules belong to the a priori realm of what is stable, fixed, and transparent to understanding, in the hope that what is ruled over will have the same fixed and stable character. Nonetheless, there is something disturbing, something wide-wandering in these heavens (*ouranos*), for we are told that the god "took over all that was visible—not at rest but in discordant and disorderly motion—and brought it from a state of disorder to one of order. . . . He made it a single visible living thing, which contains within itself all the living things . . . *one* universe."[42] For the goddess, who is Goddess of All, the "All" is first, the sun arising from the night sky that is the totality of all things. For the philosophers, the discordant particulars precede the whole, and although the universe resembles a Living Thing, of which all other living things are parts, disorderly elements and unrest somehow crept into the maker's world, from where it is not clear. What is clear is that the maker orders them.[43]

This brings about a paradox. The begotten universe lacks eternity; it is a shrine for the gods, a copy of an everlasting Living Thing, but not eternal. The maker must nevertheless master the media. He makes a *moving image of eternity,* moving according to number, but as unified, eternal. He makes "time," using the planetary powers, but not to bestow the gifts of illumination, enchantment, growth, wisdom, law, love, and peace. When the philosopher's god kindles a light in one of the heavenly bodies that moves in a circular motion, it shines over the cosmos for the purpose of setting limits and standing guard over the numbers of time. The Sun serves as the measure of the slowness and quickness of all the other bodies; its circle providing the measure of a day and night; its cycle the measure of a year. And beneath the stars the maker made men to whom were shown the laws of this cosmos and to whom were given sense perception, as well as love mixed with pleasure and pain, fear and spiritedness. Those who fail to master these emotions are reborn as women or wild animals.[44] And the wandering Goddess of All Things, stripped of her lunar reflection, is the wet nurse, made invisible, dragged down to the dark and invisible realm of the death-sun, the intelligible realm where she can, at best, provide a necessary, a priori fixed space with no characteristics of its own, *chora.* An indeterminate space for whatever comes to be, for those things that resemble and imitate self-knowledge, that which remains forever unmoved by persuasion, that which keeps its own form unchangingly.[45]

And strange to say, for "men" (made from leftover fire, earth, water, and air, impure but not discarded)—whose purpose in this eternity remains a mystery, since the maker wanted everything to be as much like himself as possible—for men, some adjustments are needed. There is the necessity of visibility, the eye being a condition of the possibility of inquiries into the nature of the universe. The eye that sees by the light of the sun remains subject, in this account, to something else, something other than vision and the principles that govern sight. "The god invented sight and gave it to us so that we might observe the orbits of intelligence in the universe and apply them to the revolutions of our own understanding."[46] Crafted by "Intellect," the eye allows us to stabilize our own understanding through the symphony of proportions, through *mimesis.* Thus the human being may imitate the unstraying revolutions of the god—but only by seeing them first. And yet, self-knowledge seems to require something else. Not a view of Nature, but a view of the self, perhaps a view of the soul? For this it is helpful to look into the *kore,* the pupil of the eye, to capture the young girl, in order to come to know oneself. The question remains, for self-knowledge, why look into the *kore* of the eye; why not simply gaze into a mirror, which after all would give one a much clearer image of oneself rather than a tiny doll-like image, an image reminiscent of a young girl? Perhaps the fascination with gazing into the eye of another is due to the suggestion that to know itself a soul must look into another soul. Looking at the pupil allows another eye to see itself. Kore is both "girl" and "pupil," that part of the eye in which one must look in order to see oneself; to see oneself in the eye of the girl who does not yet see and understand makes it possible to know oneself. To look into the *kore* is to look into that Kore who reaches out to pluck the flower. She exists "on the brink of meeting a gaze in which she would have seen herself. She was stretching out her hand to pluck that gaze."[47] Hades asks brother Zeus for a living woman. Zeus, the god who does not set the cosmos in motion, who can only reproduce what he has devoured—the skies, sea, and earth along with the Titanesses and Titans—this god devours the cosmos, then spits it out, an act of mimicry, not of creation. Henceforth "the world from end to end is organized as *mimesis*; resemblance is the law."[48] This same god whose own power is nothing but *mimesis* is eager to acknowledge the reality of a second world, a separate and silent world of resemblance. He is ready to embrace the dark realm of an invisible mind, to let the power of shadows and darkness invade and overtake the world of the enchanting moon goddess, the Goddess of All who danced with the wind.

The Visible and the Invisible

The earth splits open and Kore is plucked so to be taken away by Hades. Did Kore's eye meet Hades's? Did her eye meet the eye of Ophion, risen up from the world that until that moment had been invisible to her, who remains invisible under the vaunted helmet? Or, does the invisible Ophion, the god Hades, not see himself in the eye of Kore? Is this not his only reality? Far from recognizing herself in that invisible eye, is it not Hades who needs and seeks recognition, who can find himself only in the pupil, in the *kore* of Kore, daughter of the triple-goddess? "But Hades wanted Kore as his bride, wanted to have a living person sitting on the throne beside him. . . . In the kingdom of shades, there is at least one body, and the body of a flourishing young girl at that."[49] The necessity of this move may prove to be multiple. If Hades sees himself in Kore's eye and Kore sees nothing but his shadow, then indeed, vision is the prey. The beautiful visible world, the world granted by the powers of illumination, enchantment, growth, wisdom, law, love, and peace, is invaded by the invisible world. Someone and something are taken from the visible to the invisible. The "girl," young and flourishing, is abducted from the beautiful, visible world transforming itself through its material and natural elements, and she is dragged down to the shadow world. "The eye pounced from the shadows to capture a girl and shut her away in the underworld palace of the mind."[50] Is the invisible realm, the realm of shadows, the realm of Hades, of death, one with the unchanging mind? How can this be? Are not the sun and sunlight thought to be the very image of the Ideas or forms and the intelligible world? And if death and the unchanging mind are one, then what of the so-called divine Ideas? What of philosophy itself? Is it possible that the love of "Sophia," the goddess "Wisdom," has been transformed into a love of death? Sophia is also the flower. And what if it is the flower, Sophia, that Kore reaches out to pluck? What then? "Vessel of transformation, blossom, the unity of Demeter reunited with Kore, Isis, Ceres, the moon goddesses, whose luminous aspect overcomes . . . nocturnal darkness, are all expressions of this Sophia, the highest feminine wisdom."[51]

It has been asserted that "the Olympians developed a new fascination for Death."[52] Is not the reality that men, the philosophers and poets who told the stories about the Olympians, these men developed a new fascination for Death, a fascination not present in the earliest stories of the creation, the stories of the Goddess of All Things? Perhaps the fascination with death is related to the philosophers' and poets' fascination with the world of shadows. "The everlasting correctness of things seen, perceived rightly, has banished not only the darkness of night but also the fires of noon. The *episteme* begins it surveying, measuring, and calculating on the basis of *shadows* projected by/upon surfaces, screens, and supports."[53] The living, flourishing girl, ready to embrace vision and understanding, to affirm visibility and the beautiful world transformed in and through its material and natural elements and tended by the goddess Demeter, this girl is swept away by a shadow to the world of shadows, a world where nothing happens, where nothing changes. What would Kore have seen of Hades made invisible by his helmet? Only his shadow. So it has been noted that the divine Ideas or forms, absolutely invisible themselves, are able to be detected only by the light that they stop, that outlines them, the light they block or cut off.[54] Certainly it is true that the strange prisoners in the cave when forced up the rough, steep path into the sunlight would be pained and irritated, able at first to see shadows and nothing more. Only at night would a former prisoner be able to see and so to study the stars and the moon, and only after a long time would "his" eyes adjust to the light so as to be able to see and to study the sun.

But perhaps we misunderstand this tale when we forget the warning of the philosopher that "the visible realm should be likened to the *prison dwelling*, and the light of the fire inside it to the power of the sun. . . . The upward journey and the study of things above [are] as the upward journey of the soul to the intelligible realm."[55] The visible realm—all visibility—is on this account a prison. The invisible realm in which one's eyes are blinded is the intelligible realm. If a person were to turn from the study of what is divine to the human realm, their sight would indeed be *dim*. The visible, human world, the beautiful, self-created cosmos of the goddess, would be difficult for them to see insofar as they would be unaccustomed to using their eyes at all! Vicious, clever people are said to have keen vision. Their sight is not inferior at all insofar as they are able to sharply distinguish all that they survey. How much more keen must be the vision of these individuals who live in the realm of that which is *coming to be*, what is *becoming*, as opposed to those who see nothing because they look only at *true things*, which is to say, they do not look with their eyes at all, but only with the intellect. For such an individual, the return to the cave is the only possibility of seeing at all; their eyes function at all only in the deepest shadow. Indeed, there in the cave, they see vastly better than the people who dwell there.

Poor vision as well as insufficient, strained views wreak havoc throughout the cosmos.[56] When Zeus drives his winged chariot looking after and putting in due order the heavens, the gods follow him to a place beyond the visible heavens, a high ridge whose circular motion carries them round and round. It is a strange place, without color, shape, or solidity, where Justice, Self-Control, Knowledge are each invisible to the eye yet are visible to intelligence.[57] Souls that cannot move themselves fast enough and with enough self-control fail to "glimpse" these truths. Not only that but they trample and strike one another, their wings breaking, their plumage shredding in a heavenly image of carnage and destruction. So they fall, fall, fall to earth where they are burdened by earthly bodies, hence mortality, finally losing the wings of angels to foulness and ugliness. They are the victims of a weak memory and of senses "so murky that only a few people are able to make out, with difficulty, the original [Idea] of the likeness they encounter here."[58] Initially it seems that only "if it does not see *anything* true" does a soul fall to earth "burdened by forgetfulness and wrongdoing," and yet, "a soul that has seen the most will be planted in the seed of a man who will become a lover of wisdom."[59] Thus in spite of having seen some truth, glimpsing some Reality, some additional souls are still condemned to earthly existence. How then does this account of souls—both those crippled and opinionated and those close to things divine—how does this accord with the claim that *every* soul is immortal, for what is *psyche* if not something self-moved that never ceases to move and so is immortal? As a source of motion for itself and other moving things, immortal soul must not be able to be destroyed, otherwise it would never start up again. Absent immortality, the cosmos itself would collapse, never to be reborn.[60] Absent immortality, no souls would ever glimpse "Reality." Perhaps this is why some souls are looked after by philosophers who are not, strictly speaking, mortal but who are in some sense divine and immortal and grow wings. Those philosophers stand outside human concerns and draw close to the divine. They are said to practice philosophy without guile, they look after the boys—philosophically—perhaps it is only these souls, the philosophers and the boys they look after who will ever return to the realms where Justice, Self-Control, and Knowledge reign. The rest, it appears, are condemned, punished in places beneath the earth.[61]

So it has been argued that strictly speaking, non-philosophers, those who are truly mortals, do not, indeed cannot, *look* upon the invisible Good since such "beings" have their ideal inscription only in the *psyche*. A young girl, daughter of the triple-goddess, who wanders through fields of flowers is thought to be too close to the light, which is too close to the senses. Her *guileless virginity,* her *flourishing body,* are not left undisturbed; she is not to be allowed to come to understanding through vision in the flourishing cosmos of the goddess. Little wonder that Hades looks into the pupil of Kore to see the soul, for he would make her the soul, the psyche, the receptacle of his self-knowledge. Little wonder too that the image of the sun, useful in pointing to the power of Truth, nevertheless "must fall once more below the horizon. [Its] rays of light, *flashing,* burning, glaring, must cease to harry the Truth—*aletheia*—unchanging in the guileless virginity of the *logos.*"[62] But is this so? The philosophers make claims. They say the maker looked at an appropriate form for each thing made, that these things once made exist in time, that time is a moving image of eternity. They articulate a hierarchy of imitations, reflections that *chill the light,* shielding us from the capacities of light to diffract and to vary our perceptions. May we not question their claims? May we not, like Kore, return from the dark, invisible realm to the daylight of sight and diffused reflections, from vision to understanding (*Sophia*)? Or are we to be confined to the direct passage from the visible to the invisible, from the so-called prison of vision to the self-knowing realm of the intelligible, a passage that may be nothing less than the passage from life to death?

Unable even to risk looking into a mirror, Ophion-Hades, the snake, gazes directly into the eye of Kore seeking to see and to know himself. Her retinas focus the light, keeping it from dispersing. Looking directly into the darkest part of her virgin eye, he sees and he seeks . . . and what he seeks there is the reflection of his own soul. Looking into the virgin pupil, seeing himself, "the lover takes pleasure in seeing [gazing at] his beloved" which would be, himself.[63] Still, the philosophers claim that "people with bad eyesight often see things before those whose eyesight is keener."[64] The eyes of any philosopher who turns from the study of divine forms in the invisible, intelligible realm to human life, "his" eyes are filled with darkness, his eyesight dimmed.[65] Moreover, the craftsman and his followers operate, always, within the "*matrix of appropriation.*"[66] The god "makes" the being, the form of each thing: heaven, earth, Hades. But even the work of the god is an imitation, every "being," Sun, Moon, and Stars, a moving *image* of eternity. The apprentice philosopher, less skilled in *mimesis,* uses a mirror to imitate each thing that the god makes. But better not to look at what is made, better to have bad eyesight or no eyesight at all. Better to seek and to see one's soul only, in the virgin eye of the Kore.

Unlike the wide-wandering goddess, Eurynome, whose constant motion and diffuse light illuminate all things, the philosopher's god is "the result of systems of mirrors that ensure a steady illumination, admittedly, but one without heat or brilliance. . . . And the presence, the essence of forms (usually translated under the name of Ideas) will be determined only by the light they have stopped, trapped, and that outlines them. The force of ideas, and their hold on memory, will be a function of the intensity of light that they are able to block or cut off."[67]

What Is Philosophy?

Let us see and understand then, two images of philosophy.

There is the powerful and dark image that lurks nearby, one whose shadow is cast over the cosmos to this very day. It is the image of the snake made god. It is the image of the continuum, the perfection of the undifferentiated, the one, the image of he who wanted everything to be as much like himself as possible.[68] Thus, it has been argued that for the apprentice philosopher, for the "man" in the cave, only death will lead to something more, to something beyond the realm of shadows, of blocked light and direct vision. Is the philosopher the messenger of death since "were it not for the words of the philosophy teacher who talks to you about immortality, who would be preoccupied with such an issue?"[69] Conception, rather than the transformation into energy of the light that enters the eye that is then transmitted to the brain, instead finds its proper meaning as the rebirth into truth, a truth situated in an eternity beyond appearances, in the *One,* that is always, as a wise philosopher among us has noted, mirrored at least twice, once by the god himself and once more by the philosopher or "his" apprentice.[70] Let us dare to question this image of philosophy; let us use the reflected light of the moon and let us conceive of a second image of philosophy, not an imitation but a transformation of the material and natural elements, an image more difficult to obtain. So much has been lost, so much appropriated.

The pre-Hellenic Pelasgian account of creation survives only in the most frag-mented manner, but the standard interpretation of even these fragments overlooks the wide-wandering goddess Eurynome and seeks to establish the patrimony of Ophion. His banishment by the goddess does not prevent the resurrection of his myth. Let us recall again that the hierarchy of mirroring chills the reflected light of the moon and shields us from its capacity to vary our perception of forms. No wonder, in the tales of men, Kore is abducted. How else to fill life with shadows? "What happened in Eleusis was the separation and reunion of the dual goddess Demeter-Kore (*Deó*), she who sometimes appears as two barely differentiated figures."[71] Kore, the reflected light of Demeter, Demeter who is the life-giving light, the photon whose energy is transmitted in diffracted light rays. Demeter-Kore is the story of the reflected, refracted, and diffracted energy of that light, wandering in the world, transmitting its energy. In this cosmos, Kore returns from darkness to her origins; light and energy are conserved. Thus, even for the gods, Kore is a thing of wonder. She is divine evidence of the conservation of energy. The dark gods claim that the girl, after eating nothing for the entire period of her abduction, suddenly, forgetfully, outwitted or worse, full of secret desire, eats the seeds of the pomegranate. They claim that the fecundating light within her is the divine child, Phanes-Eros, who will force himself upon her. Let us resist the reduction of radiant light to psyche, that is, to a dark soul that sees nothing but itself in the emptiness of the eye of the Other. Let us be skeptical of the reports of the derisive "gardener" of Hades who jubilantly proclaims the downfall of the young girl, who hoots that she has eaten the seeds of the pomegranate. What, after all, is a gardener doing in the dark caves of the snake where no flowers bloom and no moonlight gives life? Let us also then be skeptical of the scholarly claims of the new gardeners of the dark, those who argue that Demeter-Kore is the psychological manifestation of the feminine psychology. And let us be equally skeptical of the philosopher, for whom Demeter-Kore is the origin of the philosophical receptacle of all becoming, the wet nurse of the cosmos. Let us instead propose, imagine, theorize that the goddess, that Demeter-Kore are themselves concepts, concepts that constitute a first philosophy, a description of the nature of reality and of its creative and transformational structure. Let us not forget that energy is not lost, only transformed, constantly transformed. And let us then propose this new image of philosophy.

Notes

This paper is reprinted by permission of Edinburgh and Columbia University Presses. It first appeared in Dorothea Olkowski, *The Universal (In the Realm of the Sensible)* (Edinburgh and Columbia University Presses, 2007), 229–46.

1. Hannah Arendt, *The Human Condition* (Chicago: University of Chicago Press, 1958), 20.

2. Ibid., 21.

3. Ibid., 19.

4. Ibid., 233.

5. Irigaray, "Korē," 147.

6. Ibid., 148. Emphasis added.

7. Plato, *Timaeus*, t 27d–28a, in Henry Teloh, *The Development of Plato's Metaphysics* (University Park: Pennsylvania State University Press, 1981), 212.

8. Irigaray, "Korē," 148.

9. Ibid., 149.

10. Calasso, *The Marriage of Cadmus and Harmony*, 209.

11. Ibid., 203.

12. Neumann, *The Great Mother*, 319, 262.

13. The claim that the flower is a narcissus is made in the Homeric "Hymn to Demeter," in *Hesiod, the Homeric Hymns and Homerica*, 289. Cited in Neumann, *The Great Mother*, 308.

14. Robert Graves reports that Ovid claims Kore was picking poppies, based on several goddess images found in Crete and Mycenae. Graves, *The Greek Myths: 1*, 24.15.

15. Ibid., 287–88.

16. Ibid., 31e. Graves relates Kore's abduction to the male usurpation of female agricultural mysteries (24.3).

17. Ibid., 1.a,b,c,d; 1.1 In this archaic religion, paternity was nonexistent, fatherhood being attributed to various accidents, and snakes were associated with the underworld.

18. Calasso, *The Marriage of Cadmus and Harmony*, 208. Calasso does not make this connection between Ophion and Hades. But see Graves, *The Greek Myths: 1*, 2b, and Homer, *Iliad*, xvi, 261. Hades's claim on Zeus is that "Zeus senses the time had come for a new ring to be added to the knot of snakes" (Calasso, 208).

19. Graves, *The Greek Myths: 1*, 1.d, 1.3. The planetary powers of the goddess Eurynome appear to correspond to the deities of Babylonian and Palestinian astrology.

20. "The Orphics say that black-winged Night, a goddess of whom even Zeus stands in awe . . . the triple-goddess ruled the universe until her scepter passed to Uranus . . . with the advent of patriarchialism." Graves, *The Greek Myths: 1*, 2.a, 2.2.

21. Hesiod, *Theogony*, 211–32.

22. Graves, *The Greek Myths: 1*, 4.a,4.b,4.c; 4.1, 4.2. Graves cites Hesiod, *Theogony*, 211–32, and Ovid, *Metamorphosis*, i–ii.

23. Plato, *Timaeus*, trans. Zeyl, 29d-e. Also, 32b,c; 37a; 42a,b,c. Plato requires two middle terms for solid objects (e.g., a cube that is represented mathematically as 2 to the power of 3), so air and water together are the middle terms for fire and earth.

24. Graves, *The Greek Myths: 1*, 24. Demeter was the general name of a tripartite goddess: Core, Persephone, Hecate (green corn, ripe corn, harvested corn) (24.1).

25. Plato, *Alcibiades*, 133a.

26. Plato, *Timaeus*, 47a. Philosophy is the supreme good that eyesight offers.

27. Gregory, *Eye and Brain*, 23.

28. Plato, *Timaeus*, 45b,c,d,e; 46d,e. Vision and all sensations are auxiliary causes of all things because they do not possess reason or understanding.

29. Irvin Rock, "The Intelligence of Perception," in *Perception*, 15–16. The eye, however, is not analogous to a *camera obscura*.

30. Rock, *Perception*, 16, 3.

31. Ibid., 4. Rock also notes how different our perceptions are from what appears on the retina, thus the extent to which there is no direct perception.

32. Gregory, *Eye and Brain,* 25–26. Newton, Hugens, and Foucault (the physicist) all contributed to these realizations.

33. Neumann, *The Great Mother,* 56–57, 25–33. See my *Gilles Deleuze and the Ruin of Representation,* especially ch. 7, "The Ruin of Representation."

34. Neumann, *The Great Mother,* 56–57, 314–15.

35. Ibid., 315.

36. Ibid., 319, 320. Often called a divine son, the moon nonetheless is a "mere variant" of the goddess's own self.

37. Ibid., 319.

38. For a clear explanation of the difference between finite and infinite, bounded and unbounded, see Rucker, *The Fourth Dimension,* 91–93.

39. I am moving away from the limitations of the psychological analysis of an archetype. See Neumann, *The Great Mother,* 55–58.

40. Ibid., 58. Neumann cites Bachoffen as the source of the thesis that what comes last will be looked upon as first and original, a hypothesis found in Aristotle. Bachoffen, *Das Mutterrecht,* 412, and Aristotle, *Parts of Animals,* 2.1.

41. Plato, *Timaeus,* 27d–28. The Greek word for "coming-to-be" used in the text is *genesis.* See Neumann, *The Great Mother,* 55.

42. Plato, *Timaeus,* 30a,b,c,d, 31a. Neumann claims that with this, the moon principle was devalued and made into the soul, the highest material development that contrasts with the pure spirituality of the male. Neumann, *The Great Mother,* 57.

43. Plato, *Timaeus,* 30a–32b.

44. Ibid., 42a,b c.

45. Ibid., *Timaeus,* 51e, 52a,b,c.

46. Ibid., *Timaeus,* 47b–c. There is "kinship" between the undisturbed orbits of the planets and our own disturbed orbits of understanding. Not quite *mimesis.*

47. Calasso, *The Marriage of Cadmus and Harmony,* 209.

48. Irigaray, "Korē," 150.

49. Calasso, *The Marriage of Cadmus and Harmony,* 211.

50. Ibid., 210. The richness of Calasso's text allows the reader to draw contradictory conclusions.

51. Neumann, *The Great Mother,* 325–26. Sophia has been completely lost to us.

52. Calasso, *The Marriage of Cadmus and Harmony,* 214. Calasso seems to forget that "revisions" of myths are the creation of poets and philosophers, not of the gods themselves.

53. Irigaray, "Korē," 148.

54. Ibid., 148.

55. Plato, *Republic,* 516a, 517b.

56. Ibid., 519a, 520b.

57. Plato, *Phaedrus,* 246e.

58. Ibid., 250.

59. Ibid., 248d. If this is not a discrepancy or mistranslation, then we have to take it seriously. Emphasis added.

60. Snell, *The Discovery of the Mind*, 8–10. Plato, *Phaedrus*, 245e, 248b,c,d.

61. Plato, *Phaedrus*, 248e–249a. Women, it appears, are entirely absent from the list of souls who may eventually glimpse truth.

62. Irigaray, "Korē," 148.

63. Aristotle, *Nicomachean Ethics*, 8.1157a3–14. Cited in David Halperin, "Why is Diotima a Woman?" 113–51.

64. Plato, *Republic*, 595c–596a.

65. Ibid., 516e–517e. Such beings are unwilling to involve themselves in human affairs.

66. Irigaray, "Korē," 151. See Plato, *Republic*, 596c–597b.

67. Irigaray, "Korē," 148. Irigaray continues, "light is too corruptible, too shifting and inconstant to form the basis of the relationship to the self and to the All."

68. Calasso, *The Marriage of Cadmus and Harmony*, 207; Plato, *Timaeus*, 29e.

69. Irigaray, "Plato's *Hystera*," 354.

70. Ibid., 355.

71. Calasso, *The Marriage of Cadmus and Harmony*, 210. The previous sentence is a restatement of Irigaray, "Korē," 149.

Bibliography

Arendt, Hannah. *The Human Condition*. Chicago: University of Chicago Press, 1958.

Aristotle. *Nicomachean Ethics*. Trans. Arthur L. Peck. London: Loeb Classical Library, 1937.

———. *Parts of Animals*. Trans. Arthur L. Peck. London: Loeb Classical Library, 1937.

Bachoffen, Jakob. *Das Mutterrecht, Gesammelte Werke*. Vol. 1. Basel: Schwabe, 1948.

Calasso, Roberto. *The Marriage of Cadmus and Harmony*. Trans. Tim Parks. New York: Alfred A. Knopf, 1993.

Graves, Robert. *The Greek Myths*. Vol. 1. New York: Penguin Books, 1980.

Gregory, Richard L. *Eye and Brain: The Psychology of Seeing*. Princeton, N.J.: Princeton University Press, 1990.

Halperin, David. "Why Is Diotima a Woman?" In *One Hundred Years of Homosexuality: And Other Essays on Greek Love*, 113–51. New York: Routledge, 1990.

Hesiod. *Theogony*. Trans. M. L. West. Oxford: Oxford University Press, 2009.

Homer. "Hymn to Demeter." In *Hesiod, the Homeric Hymns and Homerica*. Trans. Hugh G. Evelyn-White. London: Loeb Classical Library, 1920.

———. *Iliad*. Trans. Peter Jones, D. C. H. Rieu, and E. V. Rieu. New York: Penguin Classics, 2003.

Irigaray, Luce. "Korē: Young Virgin, Pupil of the Eye," 147–51; "Plato's *Hystera*," 243–364. In *Speculum of the Other Woman*. Trans. Gillian C. Gill. Ithaca, N.Y.: Cornell University Press, 1985. Originally published in French as *Speculum de l'autre femme*. Paris: Les Editions de Minuit, 1974.

Neumann, Erich. *The Great Mother, Analysis of an Archetype.* Trans. Ralph Manheim. Princeton, N.J.: Princeton University Press, 1974.

Olkowski, Dorothea. *Gilles Deleuze and the Ruin of Representation.* Berkeley: University of California Press, 1999.

———. *The Universal (In the Realm of the Sensible).* Edinburgh and New York: Edinburgh and Columbia University Presses, 2007.

Ovid. *Metamorphosis.* Trans. Charles Martin. W. W. Norton, 2005.

Plato. *Alcibiades.* Trans. Anthony Kenny. In *Plato, Complete Works,* 586–608. Ed. John M. Cooper. Indianapolis: Hackett Publishing, 1997.

———. *Phaedrus.* Trans. Alexander Nehamas and Paul Woodruff. In *Plato, Complete Works,* 506–56. Ed. John M. Cooper. Indianapolis: Hackett Publishing, 1997.

———. *Republic.* Trans. George M. A. Grube, rev. C. D. C. Reeve. In *Plato, Complete Works,* 971–1223. Ed. John M. Cooper. Indianapolis: Hackett Publishing, 1997.

———. *Timaeus.* Trans. Donald J. Zeyl. In *Plato, Complete Works,* 1224–91. Ed. John M. Cooper. Indianapolis: Hackett Publishing, 1997.

Rock, Irvin. *Perception.* New York: Scientific American Library, 1984.

Rucker, Rudy. *The Fourth Dimension: A Guided Tour of the Higher Universes.* Boston: Houghton Mifflin, 1984.

Snell, Bruno. *The Discovery of the Mind: The Greek Origins of European Thought.* Trans. Thomas G. Rosenmeyer. New York: Harper and Row, 1960.

Teloh, Henry. *The Development of Plato's Metaphysics.* University Park: Pennsylvania State University Press, 1981.

Part 1

METHODOLOGICAL CONSIDERATIONS AND THE BODY

3.

PERSONALITY, ANONYMITY, AND SEXUAL DIFFERENCE: THE TEMPORAL FORMATION OF THE TRANSCENDENTAL EGO

Sara Heinämaa

In the manuscripts from the 1920s, Edmund Husserl introduces the concept of *the transcendental person,* and distinguishes it from the concept of the empirical person. Whereas the empirical person is a constituted spatial-temporal reality, a worldly object, the transcendental person is a form of activity, and as such, a constituting ground.

The main thesis of this chapter is that Husserl defines the transcendental person as a temporal structure and that his genetic concept of personality allows us to develop a transcendental philosophical account of sexual difference. Thus understood, sexual identity and difference would not just be research topics for empirical human sciences and empirical life sciences, such as anthropology, psychology, biology and physiology. More fundamentally, they would allow and require a phenomenological analysis, and would belong not to the margins of phenomenology—to phenomenological psychology or eidetic anthropology—but to the very center of this philosophical enterprise, that is, to the transcendental eidetic studies of experience.[1]

To argue for this claim I will first present Husserl's concept of the transcendental person and study its relation to the other senses of selfhood that Husserl distinguishes. My main point here is that Husserl's concept of person is one of the central concepts of his genetic phenomenology, which aims at disclosing the habituation and sedimentation of intentional experiences and ontic meanings in inner time. This means that when sexual difference is understood in accordance with the concept of transcendental personhood, it becomes an issue of genetic transcendental phenomenology and belongs to the heart of the philosophical inquiry.[2]

In the second part of the chapter, I will answer to one obvious counterclaim that has been raised against this conceptualization of sexual difference. The critical argument is that the Husserlian approach leads to a voluntaristic or intellectualistic theory of subjectivity and makes impossible any adequate understanding of sexual difference while overemphasizing conscious activities and neglecting the contributions of desires, drives, and instincts. I will focus on the most important form of this critique, which consists of the argument that Merleau-Ponty rejects Husserl's account of personal subjectivity as egocentric and intellectualistic and offers an alternative based on the anonymity of sense perception, sensation, and motility.

This leads to an investigation of the concept of anonymity as it was explained and used by Merleau-Ponty in *Phenomenology of Perception*. I will respond to the anti-Husserlian critique by arguing that Merleau-Ponty does not develop his concept of *anonymity* in opposition to Husserl's theory of personal subjectivity but offers it as an extension of Husserl's genetic theory of sedimentation. I do not claim that Merleau-Ponty would just repeat what Husserl had already pointed out; there are obvious differences in their arguments. While Husserl explains that the transcendental person is formed by the habituation of egoic acts, Merleau-Ponty claims that our perceptual operations are sedimented results from earlier forms of conscious life, very different from our cognitive and volitional activities. For him, we are formed by our own activities as well as by sediments that come from the activities of our predecessors—both human and animal. Merleau-Ponty calls "personal" the layer of subjectivity that is based on decisions, volitions, and judgments, and "anonymous" the layer that is formed in perceptions, motions, and feelings. My main argument is that both levels are *included* in the *Gestaltung* that Husserl calls the "transcendental person." Accordingly, both levels—the level of explicitly egological decisions and volitional acts, and the level of anonymous operations—contribute to the establishment of sexual difference.

The Living Body of a Person

My phenomenological understanding and framing of "the problem of the sexes" starts from Husserl's account of the ontic meanings that living bodies have in experience. As is well known, Husserl argues that the primary way in which living bodies are given to us is personalistic and expressive.[3] We do not perceive our own bodies or the bodies of others (animals and humans) primarily as bio-mechanisms or as cultural artifacts, but as expressions of sensations and feelings, motivated and directed by intentions and purposes, and responsive to the appeals and rejections of the environment. More fundamentally, my own body is given to me as a field of sensations and as a zero point of orientation and movement. It stands out from all the other things in being the only "thing" that I can move immediately and spontaneously. It differentiates also by appearing in sensation in two different ways at the same time, both as touching and as touched.[4] The bodies of other human beings and animals are similar to my own body in that they too belong to sensing, moving subjects, but this similarity does not cancel our fundamental separation: the sensations, feelings, desires, and volitions of others are irrevocably beyond my reach. As such, our living bodies are not perceivable things, but, as Simone de Beauvoir puts it, "our grasp upon the world and the outline of our projects."[5]

The expressivity of the body has two aspects. First, a living body appears as an *expression* of a person, his or her conscious life and stream of experiences. Second, this expressive relation binds the different parts, movements, and sections of the body into an indivisible unity. Accordingly, sexual identities and sexual differences are given to us not primarily as properties or subsystems of biological organisms (sex) or as cultural artifacts (gender); they belong to the expressive living bodies of *persons*.[6] As such, they are defined by our motivational and intentional relations to the world, and not by any causal or functional relations that obtain in the world. So the phenomenological understanding of sexual difference offers an alternative to naturalistic and historistic theories of sex and gender, from biological reductionism to social, historical, and discursive constructionism.

The personalistic account of the body is obviously dependent on the concept of person. But in developing it, Husserl does not fall back on an empirical notion of personhood. Already in the second book of *Ideas* he starts to outline a *genetic* investigation of experience, its transcendental origins and history. The concept of the transcendental person is introduced for these purposes, to enrich and specify the analysis of the different levels and meanings of selfhood. In a manuscript from 1921, Husserl writes:

> The concrete Self is an identical [one] which extends itself through immanent time, one through its "spiritually" determining content, one that changes through its acts and situations, and carries always in itself the absolutely identical Ego-pole. . . . [Addition in margins:] But this whole examination gives no concretion, as I eventually see it. The "Self" is always constituted (constituted in a completely unique way) as a personal Self, as the Self of its habitualities, its capacities, its character.[7]

In another manuscript, he states:

> I, the human being in the world, living naturally only as this human being and finding myself in the personal attitude as this human person, am accordingly *not another ego as that* which I find in the transcendental attitude. . . . The transcendental ego as pole and substrate of the totality of potentialities is, as it were, the *transcendental person* which comes to be primarily instituted through the phenomenological

reduction. This ego now enters the universality of the concrete transcendental and takes on for itself the all-embracing life which brings into play all potentialities and which can now actualize all possible modes of self-sustainment.[8]

The critical feminist question that I want to pose to the tradition on the basis of these text fragments is the following: What happens when we write, instead of the abstract "human being," the concrete "man," or alternatively "woman," and think through Husserl's proposal. So what happens when we write and think as follows:

I, the man in the world, living naturally only as this man and finding myself in the personal attitude as this man, am accordingly *not another ego as that* which I find in the transcendental attitude?

And more interestingly, what happens when we write and think:

I, the woman in the world, living naturally only as this woman and finding myself in the personal attitude as this woman, am accordingly *not another ego as that* which I find in the transcendental attitude?

To begin to answer to this question, we need to study more closely Husserl's concept of the transcendental self. This is the task of the second section of the chapter.

The *Gestaltung* of the Person

Already in the 1920s, Husserl clarifies his concept of the self or the ego, the I, by distinguishing between three different senses of selfhood: first, the ego as an act-pole or ego-pole, as he also calls it [*Ich Pol, Ego Pol*]; second, the personal ego [*personales Ich, Person*]; and finally the ego in its full concreteness as a monad.

This tripartite conceptual framework of selfhood is transcendental for Husserl. The terms "act-pole," "person," and "monad" refer to different structures of transcendental consciousness as it is given *after* the phenomenological-transcendental reduction; and thus the descriptions and explications are supposed to be purified of all existential theses. So what is at issue is not any worldly beings or parts, levels, or properties of such beings, but the nature of the consciousness in its constitutive work on being. For the purposes of my main argument, I will focus on Husserl's distinction between the subject understood as the transcendental person and the subject understood as the ego-pole.[9]

In Husserl's explication, the ego as an *act-pole* or *ego-pole* is the subject of intentional acts, that is, the ego studied merely as the performer of transient acts. Husserl argues that every act discernible from the stream of experience radiates or emanates from one identical center; every act is given to us as such a ray. So to begin with, the ego is the unifying pole of all the acts (factual and possible) that stand out from the streaming continuum of consciousness.

However, having made this basic point, Husserl argues that the transcendental ego is not merely an act-pole. It is also a temporal formation, and as such it refers to its own past. This idea of temporal formation is presented in *Cartesian Meditations* as follows: "This centering Ego is not an empty pole of identity (any more than any object is such). Rather, according to a law of 'transcendental genesis,' with every act emanating from him and having a new objective sense, he acquires a *new abiding characteristic*."[10]

Husserl uses the terminology of "habits" [*Habitus, Habitualität*] to describe the temporal constitution of the ego as distinct from the ego in its function of performing acts. He warns that we should not take this terminology in its everyday sense of routines and social customs. The reference is to certain processes in internal time in which acts are established and new acts are sedimented on earlier ones, thus forming a kind of act-form or act-*Gestalt*. This *Gestalt* is unique to the individual, and we can thus say that the ego has a specific mode or style of acting. The unique styles of individuals can be classified as belonging to general types, but they cannot be classified as belonging to any naturally determined class.[11]

Husserl calls the "transcendental person" or "personality" of the transcendental ego [*Person, Persönlichkeit*] the *Gestalt* that is formed in the establishment and habituation of acts in internal time. For him, the ego is not a momentary actor that wills, enjoys, and posits being, but is "historical" and has already willed, enjoyed, and posited being.[12] The ego is not merely the totality of simultaneous acts but is formed in time. In other words, the ego has a *genesis,* an internal past and an origin. And more: the ego is its own past.

Husserl illuminates this process of habituation of acts by studying the case of judgment formation. He explains that always when we make a judgment, the judgment becomes our own in a specific way: it becomes part of our transcendental habitus. The judgment remains our own in this way until we refute it by another act, and after this it still remains ours as a judgment once held and acted on, and then refuted. This does not mean that we repeat the judgment every moment until we refute it, but that we are, from the very moment of making the judgment, the ones who thus judge and believe.

The same process of *Gestaltung* covers also non-thetic, non-judgmental acts, that is, axiological and practical acts. Thus the transcendental person is not just a pile of habituated judgments but includes also habitualities of valuations and goal-directed acts. Moreover, Husserl argues that all this is founded on the passive synthesis of sensation (and not on the body as an objective reality).[13]

So as a summary, we can say that with the concept of person, Husserl starts a new discussion about the temporality of the transcendental ego: the ego-pole or the act-pole is an identical center of acts, but the concrete ego is a person constituted as the whole of experiences streaming in time, transient as acts but permanent as accomplishments, and also sedimented one upon another. The act-pole and the person are not two separate parts, levels, or phases of the ego but are essentially bound together, and distinguishable only by analysis.

As the transcendental person is essentially a temporal formation, investigations of its nature belong to *genetic phenomenology*. In the fourth *Cartesian Meditation,* Husserl explains: "With the doctrine of the Ego as pole of his acts and substrate of habitualities, we have already touched on the problem of phenomenological genesis and done so at a significant point. Thus we have touched the level of *genetic phenomenology*."[14]

Genetic phenomenology explicates the temporal order of meaning constitution. It does not confine itself to the investigation of individual histories but, by the methods of eidetic variation, aims at illuminating the essential steps and phases in all temporal institution or establishment of meaning and sense. The mature Husserl argues that static analyses are a necessary part of phenomenology, but not sufficient in themselves because phenomenology aims at accounting for the structures of meaning as well as for their eidetic genesis and origins.[15] Thus Husserl's concept of the transcendental person enriches and concretizes his account of subjectivity by disclosing the essence of the temporal unfolding of the self.

We can draw several important conclusions from this explication. First, we see that the self as a pole is merely an abstraction from the concrete whole of the ego, constituted as a process of change and development in inner time. Accordingly, the ego-pole is not a-temporal but trans-temporal.[16] Second, the transcendental self should not be understood as a universal principle in which all humans or all rational beings take part. Rather it is an individual with individual characteristics and with an individual style of changing and developing. To be sure, this individual exhibits certain essential structures such as the structures of inner temporality and development, but these structures do not have any separate being or existence as distinguished from the stream of lived experience. On the contrary, the essential structures of experience show or disclose themselves only within such a stream.

From these results we can draw further conclusions that concern sexual difference. My crucial idea is that Husserl's personalistic concepts of style and type offer the possibility of formulating the question of sexual identity and sexual difference in a radical philosophical way. We do not need to restrict ourselves to explaining such identities and differences by empirical realities: hormones, genes, stimulus response-systems, social roles, or historical facts. More fundamentally, we can understand sexual difference by using intentional and temporal concepts as a difference between two types of personality.[17] As characteristics or attributes of persons, masculinity and femininity, "manhood" and "womanhood" (if we want to use these terms), are not anchored on any particular activities or objects, but are given as two different modes of relating to objects, acting on them, and being affected by them. Moreover, as sensation, motility, and sense perception exhibit specific forms of intentionality, we can include an account of the sexed body in this framework and ask in what sense sensuous experience is fundamental to sexual identity and sexual difference. Thus understood, sexual identities are not constituted on top of physical bodies, or in addition to them, but are formed together with our sensing living bodies. And insofar as the sensing, moving body takes part in the constitution of spatiality and spatial objectivity, sexual differences may also have constitutive significance for the sense of the world.[18]

When sexual identity is understood as a stylistic identity, it runs through the person's whole life as a way or manner in which lived experiences and acts follow each other, continue, and change. And when this manner of changing itself changes—for example, in childhood, adolescence, sickness, or old age—then "it does so in a characteristic way, such that a unitary style manifests itself once more."[19]

The Anonymous Subject of Drives and Instincts

As pointed out, there is an apparent problem with this way of conceptualizing sexual difference and sexual identity: it seems highly intellectualistic and voluntaristic while emphasizing the role of conscious activity in constitution at the cost of unconscious drives and instincts. The concept of the transcendental person, as Husserl develops it, is dependent on the concept of act, and its paradigmatic cases are volitional and judgmental acts. Thus, the critical argument runs, any account of sexual difference that takes this concept as its starting point would give us an idealistic and abstract understanding of sexual difference. This suspicion is worded most clearly by Judith Butler while questioning the Cartesian presumptions operative in the existential-phenomenological tradition. Butler writes: "If we agree to understand this becoming of gender as a kind of agency or volition, then . . . a problem emerges: what sense does becoming gender have in a world where gender relations appear to be firmly established and deeply entrenched? What kind of freedom is this?"[20] In *Bodies That Matter,* Butler reformulates her antivoluntaristic view as follows: "The 'activity' of . . . gendering cannot, strictly speaking, be a human act or expression, a willful appropriation . . . ; it is the matrix through which all willing first becomes possible. . . . In this sense, the matrix of gender relations is prior to the emergence of the 'human.'"[21]

But, as Butler and many others have pointed out, phenomenology is not confined to Husserl's "Cartesian approach"; the tradition includes several other alternatives. It has been argued in particular that Merleau-Ponty offers a fundamentally different account of sexuality by developing his concept of anonymity. In this understanding, sexual difference does not belong to the self-conscious active and egological levels of experience but stems from the more fundamental layers of life or existence that are anonymous, non-egological, or non-personal.

Certain sections in *Phenomenology of Perception* seem to justify the notion that Merleau-Ponty saw sexuality as part of an anonymous generality opposed to personal life. In the chapter on sexuality, he writes, for example: "Thus sight, hearing, sexuality, the body are not only the routes, instruments or manifestations of personal existence: the latter [personal existence] takes up and absorbs into itself their existence as it is anonymously given."[22]

And in the previous chapter, titled "The Body as Object and Mechanistic Physiology," he explains: "There appears round our personal existence a margin of *almost* impersonal existence, which can be practically taken for granted, and which I rely on to keep me alive . . . it can be said that my organism, as a prepersonal cleaving to the general form of the world, as an anonymous and general existence, plays, beneath my personal life, the part of an *inborn complex*."[23]

Several commentators have argued that with the concept of anonymity Merleau-Ponty breaks away from Husserlian phenomenology, which is methodologically based on the first-person perspective. The descriptions that we find in *Phenomenology of Perception* concerning the anonymous life of the body, as distinct from the personal life of the ego, are claimed to abandon the egocentric approach and imply or posit a level of experience in which the self and the other are fused.

Rosalyn Diprose, for example, claims that Merleau-Ponty rejects the idea of transcendental subjectivity as the foundation of meaning constitution. For her, Merleau-Ponty's analyses show that we exist not as singular selves that constitute a world by our objectifying acts, but as aspects or parts of a general existence. I am not a singular self or a singular body, Diprose argues, because "I am for-myself merely by virtue of being first of all with and for other lived bodies." This implies, moreover, that I "cannot easily tell the difference between what I live and what the other lives."[24]

In the rest of the chapter, I will question this view. By studying crucial sections from *Phenomenology of Perception,* I show that by *anonymous perception* Merleau-Ponty means neither self-less experience, nor any experience with a general or collective subject. Rather than theorizing some egoless form of experience, he struggles to disclose and find expression for certain hidden ingredients of concrete sense perception, ingredients that are implied by the necessarily bodily character of the perceiving self and by the perspectival disclosure of the perceived thing. These ingredients include sedimented accomplishments of earlier activities, some of which are not our own activities but activities of others unknown to us and preceding us in time. Thus understood, the perceiving subject is "prepersonal," not in the sense of being an undifferentiated fusion or a collective of several simultaneous subjects, but in the sense of having a history, and a "prehistory."[25]

This means that Merleau-Ponty does not conceive the personal as a super-structure that is laid on top of some anonymous generality, nor does he conceive the anonymous as a separate realm of permanence in which the directions and parameters of sexual difference would be fixed. Rather than being two different types or levels of subjectivity, the personal and the anonymous are "two moments of a unique structure which is the concrete subject," as he himself characterizes them at the end of his *Phenomenology.*[26]

The implications for our understanding of sexual difference are crucial. Sexual difference is not constituted by decisions or volitions, but neither does it reside in or emerge from some separate level of mere instincts and drives. Rather, it is constituted in the constant intertwining between affective sedimented perceptions on the one hand and the acts of the will and the intellect on the other hand. Thus, we can understand what Merleau-Ponty means when he characterizes sexuality as an emblem of our manner of being related toward the world.[27]

So let us start by studying Merleau-Ponty's *Phenomenology of Perception.* In the chapter "Other Selves and the Human World," he writes: "Through phenomenological reflection I discover vision not as a 'thinking about seeing,' to use Descartes' expression, but as a gaze at grips with the *visible* world. . . . When I turn towards my perception, and pass from direct perception to thinking about that perception, I re-enact it and find at work in my organs of perception a thinking older than myself of which those organs are merely the trace."[28]

This paragraph and other similar sections suggest that Merleau-Ponty's phenomenological inquiries into perception disclose several subjects: in addition to the personal self, there is "someone" involved in my perception. It is crucial to notice, however, that the anonymous subject that Merleau-Ponty's reflections disclose, together with the self, is not plural but singular. He states quite explicitly, and repeatedly, that it is *someone* who sees in me or along with me.[29] The most well known of these sections is in the chapter "Sense Experience," where he states: "If I wanted to render precisely the perceptual experience, I ought to say that *one perceives in me,* and not that I perceive."[30]

Thus, there is no multiplicity or generality of subjects but rather a couple or pair: me and an unspecified, nameless, or unnamed singular, someone else in me. Moreover, these two subjects, the personal and the anonymous, do not take part in perception on equal footing so that we could express the experience by saying that "They perceive" or "We perceive." Rather, the one perceives *in me,* or I perceive *due* to the one or *according* to the one. There is a fundamental interdependence between these two subjects: my personal acts unite and integrate the anonymous operations of the "one," and on the other hand, the sense of the anonymous subject, its very subjectivity, is founded on the sense of my self.[31]

Who or what then is this one in me who perceives with me or who helps me to perceive? Even though Merleau-Ponty wavers somewhat on this issue and formulates his view in different ways in different contexts, he is perfectly explicit and clear in certain sections. The someone who perceives in me or with me is *my own* living, sensing body. We find this clearly explicated in several sections of the *Phenomenology,* for example, in the following paragraph:

> My personal existence must be the resumption of a prepersonal tradition. There is, therefore, another subject beneath me, for whom a world exists before I am here, and who marks out my place in it. This captive or natural spirit is my body, not that momentary body which is the instrument of my personal choices and which fastens upon this or that world, but the system of anonymous "function" which draws every particular focus into a general project.[32]

So Merleau-Ponty argues that the one who perceives in me or with me is not any other soul or body separated from me in space, but my own living, sensing, and moving body. Or to put it in Merleau-Ponty's own words, it is me, myself, insofar as I have a body. But this is not all. We find other sections that are even more revealing, and help to understand what he means by "anonymity." He argues, for example, as follows: "By sensation I grasp, on the fringe of my own personal life and my own acts, a life of a given consciousness from which these latter emerge, *the life of my eyes, my hands, my ears, which are so many natural selves.* Each time I experience a sensation, I feel that it does not concern my own being, but another self which has already sided with the world."[33]

As this paragraph indicates, it is my body not just as a sensing and moving subject but also as a system of *individual organs* that operates in my perception. When *I perceive,* several interdependent "agents" function in my living body: my eyes, my ears, my head, my hands, and my skin. These "agents" are not any separate others but are dependent parts of my own body. The perception, my perception, integrates these functions, and integrates them into the whole of my personal life.[34]

The functions of my perceptual organs remain non-thematic in ordinary experience, but they can be disclosed by reflection, and they "demand" or "require" our attention in abnormal circumstances, such as sickness and fatigue. My perception is directed at the external thing, but at the same time it involves my non-thematic self-awareness. What phenomenological reflection and analysis is able to show, according to Merleau-Ponty, is that this self-awareness is not any simple formal structure but a complex whole including several factors: I am given to myself as a sensing body, and my sensing body incorporates an integrated system of sense organs and sensory functions.[35]

Moreover, Merleau-Ponty argues that my sensations—these "most rudimentary perceptions," as he calls them[36]—are given to me in a special way: they do not appear to me as my original accomplishments or as my creative inventions, but on the contrary, are given as *variations* of a general mode or style of sensing required by the sensible and perceivable thing. He states, for example: "Between my sensation and myself there is always the thickness of some *original acquisition* which prevents my experience from being clear to itself. I experience the sensation as a modality of a general existence, one already devoted to a physical world and which runs or streams [*fuse*] through me without my being its originator [*l'auteur*]."[37]

So I sense, not according to my habits or my will, but *according* to the thing. It is as if the qualities of the thing would demand these movements from my body and its organs or would invite them to move in certain ways.[38] What Merleau-Ponty then compresses with his concept of anonymity is the idea that our own movements are given to us as particular variations or modifications of a general sensibility and motility implicated in the sensible thing.

Thus understood, perception is passive, and the perceived thing active, in a specific sense. It is not only that my body and my sensory organs react or respond to the stimulation of objects; they also receive their own functions—or at least the general style of functioning—from things. How is this to be understood? Merleau-Ponty answers by describing the perceived thing as *a track*. We must focus on this idea in order to understand what he means by anonymous operations or functions.

Merleau-Ponty argues that the perceptual thing is a sediment of earlier activities. Reflection discloses it not as an independent objectivity existing in-itself but as a track or as a relic of sensations and perceptions that have been performed *prior* to our own activities. This idea came up in the quote above, but let me cite the relevant sentences again: "While I perceive . . . I am aware of integrating absentminded and dispersed 'consciousnesses': *sight, hearing and touch, which their fields,* which are anterior, and remain alien to my personal life. The natural object is the track of this generalized existence."[39]

So the perceived object is a sediment or a trace of earlier perceptive acts. This holds for cultural things, instruments, utensils, and artworks, as well as for natural things, mountains, plants, and animal bodies. *As perceptual objects,* all these are accomplishments or acquisitions of earlier motor intentionality, prior to our own perceptual acts. In addition, also my own sense organs are given to me as such relics or sediments. Merleau-Ponty states this explicitly in the paragraph quoted above: "When I turn towards my perception . . . I re-enact it and find at work in my organs of perception a thinking older than myself of which those organs are merely the trace."[40]

The idea of the perceived thing as a trace is twofold. First, it suggests that what is given to me in my perceptual life is not any subject-independent objectivity but an accomplishment of somebody else prior in time. My own body indicates other sensory-motor agents or living bodies, and a whole history and prehistory of them, sensuous subjects who have acted on their environments and constituted what I now find in my perceptual field: the perspectival thing and my own moving, sensing body. Second, this picture proposes that our own perception is not an originative or creative activity, but a reestablishment. At best, we produce modifications or new variations of earlier perceptions and add new layers of objectivity to the foundation of the perceived world as it is handed down to us by our predecessors—human and animal.[41] In the chapter on sense experience, Merleau-Ponty explains:

> Taken exactly as I see it [the spectacle perceived], it is a moment in my individual history, and since sensation is a reconstitution, it presupposes in me sediments left behind by some previous constitution, so that I am as a sentient subject, a repository stocked with natural powers at which I am the first to be filled with wonder. I am not, therefore, in Hegel's phrase, "a hole in being," but a hollow, a fold, which has been made and which can be unmade.[42]

And, as the spatiality chapter adds: "My first perception and my first hold upon the world must appear to me as action in accordance with an earlier agreement reached between x and the world in general, my history must be continuation of a prehistory and must utilize the latter's acquired results."[43]

This obviously brings in the problems of time and temporality. We must ask how it is possible that our subjective time includes references to other lives, prior to and after our personal existence; in what sense can we speak about "priority" and "succession"?

At the end of the chapter "Other Selves," Merleau-Ponty introduces Husserl's concept of de-presentation (*Ent-Gegenwärtigung*) to account for such relations. He argues that the task is to understand and clarify "how the presence of myself [*Urpräsenz*] which establishes my own limits and conditions every alien presence is at the same time de-presentation [*Entgegenwärtigung*] and throws me outside of myself."[44]

By this formulation Merleau-Ponty refers us back to the third part of Husserl's *The Crisis of European Sciences and the Transcendental Phenomenology* (1936, 1954). There Husserl distinguishes between two different types of self-distancing or self-deferment, one temporal and the other spatial. The two principal forms of de-presentation belong, respectively, to memory and to empathy. In the case of memory or recollective de-presentation, the subject recollects its own activities and establishes a relation to its own past separated by a temporal gap. In the case of empathetic de-presentation, the subject finds another subject, someone "over there," separated in space.[45] In both cases, consciousness distances itself from itself, de-presents its own activities, and is thus able to establish a relation to other conscious activities outside itself. Thus Husserl insists that the self and its operations are a necessary methodological starting point for all phenomenology: "Only by starting from the ego and the system of its transcendental functions and accomplishments can we methodologically exhibit transcendental intersubjectivity and its transcendental communalization, through which, in the functioning system of ego-poles, the 'world for all' and for each subject as world for all, is constituted."[46]

In my understanding, Merleau-Ponty did not abandon this methodological guideline.[47] His discourse of anonymity should not be taken as an alternative, non-egological approach but must be seen as part of his phenomenological account of intersubjectivity and generativity. Merleau-Ponty saw clearly the constitutive role that generativity has for transcendental intersubjectivity. His innovation was to use Husserl's concept of de-presentation to pose a phenomenological question about trans-generative reference. In *Phenomenology of Perception,* he argued that we need to explicate and analyze the forms of de-presentations that are operative in the establishment of intentional relations between subjects separated not just in space, but also in time.

"As my living present opens upon a past which I nevertheless am no longer living through, and on a future which I do not yet live . . . it can also open on to temporalities outside my living experience and acquire a social horizon, with the result that my world is expanded to the dimensions of that collective history which my private existence takes up and carries forward."[48]

Neither recollective de-presentation nor empathetic de-presentation alone is able to establish such relations. The first merely relates us to our own past, and the second relates us to contemporary others. We need both types of self-distancing in order to connect intentionally to those who have acted on objects and suffered from their influences already before our own appearance. Only a generative account of intersubjectivity can provide the basis for the phenomenology of sexual difference.[49]

Conclusion

My conclusions concern the conceptual resources of Husserlian phenomenology and the role that Merleau-Ponty gave to these concepts in his account of perception and embodiment.

First, I hope that my explication of Husserl's concept of the transcendental person has removed the worries about voluntarism and intellectualisms. As long as transcendental personhood is taken to be formed exclusively from or by the acts of judgment and will, it certainly seems that Husserl's philosophy is intellectualistic or voluntaristic and that it gives no solid basis for a theory of sexual difference: femininity and masculinity seem to be understood as results of positing acts and acts of will. But we have seen that for Husserl, the transcendental person is the *Gestalt* that is formed in internal time, in the process of living, in the passage from one lived experience to another. Thus understood, the person includes, at least potentially, all kinds of experiences: volitional and judgmental acts, to be sure, but also affective experiences and the sensuous life. It encompasses the positing acts of theoretical consciousness, but also the axiological and practical acts of enjoying, desiring, and willing. And this all is founded on the passive syntheses of sensation.

Second, I hope that my reading of Merleau-Ponty has shown that our sexed bodies carry out and perform operations that lean not merely on our own earlier actions and passions, but also on the actions and passions of our predecessors—perhaps even animal predecessors. This basis can be characterized as "driven" or even "instinctual," but we should not think that the anonymous life of the body is an autonomous system that determines or fixes our sexual identities and differences independently of our personal acts of volition, decision, and judgment. The anonymous is not independent of our ego-activities; it does not determine these acts, nor does it undermine them. Rather, we should see it as intertwined with our acts of cognition, volition, and decision, thus forming a complex dynamic structure of mutual in-forming.

So the anonymous aspects of experience should not be opposed to what first begins with my own acts. The concepts of the anonymous and the personal do not distinguish between two forms of experience or between two concepts of subjectivity or agency, but between two different aspects of concrete human existence.

The fundamental feminist idea of this chapter is that human existence is given to us in two different variations—the masculine and the feminine. Both variations include anonymous and personal elements; both are driven and both are free. Thus the feminine is no more instinctual than the masculine; and the masculine is no more rational than the feminine. "[B]oth live in their different ways the strange ambiguity of existence made body."[50]

Notes

I am grateful to professor Rudolf Bernet, professor Helen Fielding, and doctor Joona Taipale for their critical comments on earlier versions of this chapter that helped me to develop and refine its argument.

1. Cf. Sepp, "Geschlechtsdifferenz—ein Thema für Husserls Phänomenologie," 47–59; Schües, "Generative Phänomenologie in feministischer Perspektive," 46–66. For the background of Schües's argument, see her *Changes of Perception*.

2. Husserl diverges from Brentano in arguing that *genetic* inquiries into the temporal structures of consciousness do not need to proceed in a causal-empirical fashion, but can proceed in an eidetic manner and disclose necessary orderings of development. Compare Husserl's characterizations of genetic phenomenology to Brentano's notion of genetic psychology, as outlined in his *Descriptive Psychology* (*Deskriptive Psychologie* 1887, 1891), trans. Benito Müller (London: Routledge, 1995).

3. For a full account, see Heinämaa, *Toward a Phenomenology of Sexual Difference.* For an illuminative introduction to the phenomenological account of embodiment, see Edith Stein's *Zum Problem der Einfühlung,* in English, *On the Problem of Empathy.* For a broader perspective, see Rudolf Bernet's "Encounter with the Stranger."

4. For example, when I grasp my right arm with my left hand.

5. Beauvoir, *Le deuxième sexe I–II,* 73; *The Second Sex,* 66, translation modified.

6. For a detailed discussion of the problems of the sex/gender framework, see Heinämaa, "Woman—Nature, Product, Style?"

7. Husserl, *Zur Phänomenologie der Intersubjektivität,* 42–44.

8. Husserl, *Zur phänomenologischen Reduktion,* 200–201, my emphasis. I am indebted to Sebastian Luft for pointing out this paragraph. For Luft's interpretation of the paragraph, see his "Husserl's Concept of the Transcendental Person." Compare also the paragraph quoted to what Husserl writes in *Phänomenologische Psychologie,* 294; cf. Merleau-Ponty, *Phénoménologie de la perception,* 487–88; *Phenomenology of Perception,* 426.

9. For a complete account of the phenomenological transcendental concepts of ego-pole, person, and monad, see Sakakibara, "Das Problem des Ich und der Ursprung der genetischen Phänomenologie bei Husserl"; Heinämaa, "Selfhood, Consciousness and Embodiment."

10. Husserl, *Cartesianische Meditationen und Pariser Vorträge,* 100; *Cartesian Meditations,* 66.

11. Cf. Sepp, "Geschlechtsdifferenz," 58–59.

12. Husserl, *Ideen zu einer reinen Phänomenologie und phänomenologischen Philosophie,* 136–37; *Ideas Pertaining to a Pure Phenomenology and to a Phenomenological Philosophy,* 143–45. The phenomenological concept of person differs from the traditional concept, which is defined by the ideas of social roles and role playing. However, it has interesting similarities with the Lockean understanding of personal identity. Cf. Waldenfels, "Fremdheit des anderen Geschlechts," 65.

13. See, e.g., Husserl, *Die Krisis der europäischen Wissenschaften und die transzendentale Phänomenologie,* 222; *The Crisis of European Sciences and the Transcendental Phenomenology,* 218.

14. Husserl, *Cartesianische,* 103; *Cartesian,* 69.

15. Husserl, *Cartesianische,* 100–14; *Cartesian,* 66–81; *Phänomenologische Psychologie,* 208–17; *Formale and transzendentale Logik,* 277–81. For an introduction to genetic phenomenology, see Steinbock, *Home and Beyond;* cf. also the fifth chapter, "Genetic Constitution," in Sokolowski, *The Formation of Husserl's Concept of Constitution.*

16. Cf. Kortooms, *Phenomenology of Time,* 212.

17. Cf. Waldenfels, "Fremdheit," 63.

18. For a detailed argument, see Heinämaa, "On Luce Irigaray's Phenomenology of Intersubjectivity"; cf. Heinämaa, "Feminism."

19. Husserl, *Ideen*, 270; *Ideas*, 283.

20. Butler, "Chapter 15," 255.

21. Butler, *Bodies That Matter*, 7.

22. Merleau-Ponty, *Phénoménologie*, 187; *Phenomenology*, 160.

23. Merleau-Ponty, *Phénoménologie*, 99; *Phenomenology*, 84.

24. Diprose, *Corporeal Generosity*, 89; cf. Stawarska, "Anonymity and Sociality"; Carman, *Merleau-Ponty*, 2. For a critical perspective, see Olkowski, "Corporeal Generosity?"

25. Merleau-Ponty, *Phénoménologie*, 249; *Phenomenology*, 215; cf. Beauvoir, "La phénoménologie de la perception de Maurice Merleau-Ponty," 366; in English, "A Review of *The Phenomenology of Perception* by Maurice Merleau-Ponty," in *Philosophical Writings*, 163.

26. Merleau-Ponty, *Phénoménologie*, 513–14; *Phenomenology*, 451.

27. Merleau-Ponty, *Phénoménologie*, 185; *Phenomenology*, 158.

28. Merleau-Ponty, *Phénoménologie*, 404, my emphasis; *Phenomenology*, 351–52.

29. Cf. Stoller, "(Phänomenologische) Anonymität und (geschlechtliche) Differenz," 244.

30. Merleau-Ponty, *Phénoménologie*, 250, my emphasis; *Phenomenology*, 215.

31. Merleau-Ponty, *Phénoménologie*, 241; *Phenomenology*, 208; *Signes*, 201; *Signs*, 159; cf. Husserl, *Ideen*, 213–15; *Ideas*, 224–26.

32. Merleau-Ponty, *Phénoménologie*, 293–94; *Phenomenology*, 254.

33. Merleau-Ponty, *Phénoménologie*, 250, my emphasis, cf. 399; *Phenomenology*, 215–16, cf. 347.

34. Merleau-Ponty, *Phénoménologie*, 101; *Phenomenology*, 85.

35. Merleau-Ponty, *Phénoménologie*, 253ff.; *Phenomenology*, 219ff.

36. Merleau-Ponty, *Phénoménologie*, 279; *Phenomenology*, 241.

37. Merleau-Ponty, *Phénoménologie*, 250, my emphasis, cf. 503; *Phenomenology*, 216, cf. 440.

38. Merleau-Ponty, *Phénoménologie*, 367; *Phenomenology*, 318.

39. Merleau-Ponty, *Phénoménologie*, 399, my emphasis; *Phenomenology*, 347.

40. Merleau-Ponty, *Phénoménologie*, 404; *Phenomenology*, 351–52.

41. Cf. Schües, "Generative Phänomenologie," 46–66.

42. Merleau-Ponty, *Phénoménologie*, 249; *Phenomenology*, 215.

43. Merleau-Ponty, *Phénoménologie*, 293; *Phenomenology*, 254.

44. Merleau-Ponty, *Phénoménologie*, 417; *Phenomenology*, 363.

45. Husserl, *Die Krisis*, 188–89; *The Crisis*, 185–86; *Zur Phänomenologie der Intersubjektivität*, 588–92.

46. Husserl, *Die Krisis*, 189; *The Crisis*, 186.

47. For an argument to this effect, see Heinämaa, "From Decisions to Passions"; see also Heinämaa, "The Living Body and Its Position in Metaphysics."

48. Merleau-Ponty, *Phénoménologie*, 495; *Phenomenology*, 433.

49. For a full account of the idea of generative phenomenology, see Steinbock, *Home and Beyond.*

50. Beauvoir, *Le dèuxieme sexe II,* 658; *The Second Sex,* 737.

Bibliography

Beauvoir, Simone de. "La phénoménologie de la perception de Maurice Merleau-Ponty." *Les temps modernes* 1 (1945): 363–67. Trans. Marybeth Timmermann: "A Review of *The Phenomenology of Perception* by Maurice Merleau-Ponty." In Simone de Beauvoir. *Philosophical Writings,* ed. Margareth A. Simons with Marybeth Timmermann and Mary Beth Mader, 159–64. Urbana: University of Illinois Press, 2004.

———. *Le deuxième sexe I–II.* [1949] Paris: Gallimard, 1991, 1993. Trans. and ed. Howard M. Parshley: *The Second Sex.* Harmondsworth: Penguin, 1987.

Bernet, Rudolf. "Encounter with the Stranger: Two Interpretations of the Vulnerability of the Skin." In *Phenomenology of Interculturality and Life-World,* ed. Ernest Wolfgang Orth and Chan-Fai Cheung, 89–111. Freiburg, Munich: Verlag Karl Alber, 1998.

Brentano, Franz. *Descriptive Psychology.* Trans. Benito Müller. London: Routledge, 1995. Originally *Deskriptive Psychologie* 1887, 1891.

Butler, Judith. *Bodies That Matter: On the Discursive Limits of "Sex."* New York: Routledge, 1993.

———. "Chapter 15: Gendering the Body: Beauvoir's Philosophical Contribution." In *Women, Knowledge, and Reality: Explorations in Feminist Philosophy,* ed. Ann Garry and Marilyn Pearsall. New York: Routledge, 1991.

Carman, Taylor. *Merleau-Ponty.* London: Routledge, 2008.

Diprose, Rosalyn. *Corporeal Generosity: On Giving with Nietzsche, Merleau-Ponty, and Levinas.* Albany: New York State University Press, 2002.

Heinämaa, Sara. "Feminism." In *A Companion to Phenomenology and Existentialism,* ed. Hubert L. Dreyfus and Mark A. Wrathall, 500–513. Malden, Mass.: Blackwell, 2006.

———. "From Decisions to Passions: Merleau-Ponty's Interpretation of Husserl's Reduction." In *Merleau-Ponty's Reading of Husserl,* ed. Ted Toadvine and Lester Embree, 127–46. Boston: Kluwer, 2002.

———. "The Living Body and Its Position in Metaphysics: Merleau-Ponty's Dialogue with Descartes." In *Metaphysics, Facticity, Interpretation: Phenomenology in the Nordic Countries,* ed. Dan Zahavi, Sara Heinämaa, and Hans Ruin, 23–48. The Hague: Kluwer, 2003.

———. "On Luce Irigaray's Phenomenology of Intersubjectivity: Between the Feminine Body and Its Other." In *Returning to Irigaray: Feminist Philosophy, Politics, and the Question of Unity,* ed. Maria C. Cimitile and Elaine P. Miller, 243–65. Albany: State University of New York Press, 2007.

———. "Selfhood, Consciousness and Embodiment: A Husserlian Approach." In *Consciousness: From Perception to Reflection,* ed. Sara Heinämaa, Vili Lähteenmäki, and Pauliina Remes, 311–28. Dordrecht: Springer, 2007.

———. *Toward a Phenomenology of Sexual Difference: Husserl, Merleau-Ponty, Beauvoir.* Lanham, Md.: Rowman and Littlefield, 2003.

———. "Woman—Nature, Product, Style?" In *Feminism, Science and the Philosophy of Science*, ed. Lynn Hankinson Nelson and Jack Nelson, 289–308. Dordrecht: Kluwer, 1996.

Husserl, Edmund. *Cartesianische Meditationen und Pariser Vorträge. Husserliana, Band I*. Ed. Stephan Strasser. The Hague: Martinus Nijhoff, 1950. Trans. Dorion Cairns: *Cartesian Meditations*. Dordrecht: Martinus Nijhoff, 1960.

———. *Die Krisis der europäischen Wissenschaften und die transzendentale Phänomenologie. Husserliana, Band VI*. Ed. Walter Biemel. [1954] The Hague: Martinus Nijhoff, 1962. Trans. David Carr: *The Crisis of European Sciences and the Transcendental Phenomenology*. Evanston, Ill.: Northwestern University Press, 1970.

———. *Formale und transzendentale Logik, Versuch einer Kritik der logischen Vernunft. Husserliana, Band XVII*. Ed. Paul Janssen. The Hague: Martinus Nijhoff, 1974.

———. *Ideen zu einer reinen Phänomenologie und phänomenologischen Philosophie. Zweites Buch: Phänomenologische Untersuchungen zur Konstitution. Husserliana, Band IV*. Ed. Marly Bimel. The Hague: Martinus Nijhoff, 1952. Trans. Richard Rojcewicz and André Schuwer: *Ideas Pertaining to a Pure Phenomenology and to a Phenomenological Philosophy. Second book: Studies in the Phenomenological Constitution*. Dordrecht: Kluwer Academic Publishers, 1993.

———. *Phänomenologische Psychologie, Vorlesungen Sommersemester 1925. Husserliana, Band IX*. Ed. Walter Biemel. The Hague: Martinus Nijhoff, 1968.

———. *Zur Phänomenologie der Intersubjektivität, Texte aus dem Nachlass, Zweiter Teil, 1921–28. Husserliana, Band XIV*. Ed. Iso Kern. The Hague: Martinus Nijhoff, 1973.

———. *Zur phänomenologischen Reduktion, Texte aus dem Nachlass (1926–1935). Husserliana, Band XXXIV*. Ed. Sebastian Luft. Dordrecht: Kluwer Academic Publishers, 2002.

Kortooms, Toine. *Phenomenology of Time: Edmund Husserl's Analysis of Time-Consciousness*. Dordrecht: Kluwer Academic Publishers, 2002.

Luft, Sebastian. "Husserl's Concept of the Transcendental Person: A Response to Heidegger." *International Journal of Philosophical Studies* 13 (2005): 141–77.

Merleau-Ponty, Maurice. *Phénoménologie de la perception*. [1945] Paris: Gallimard, 1993. Trans. Colin Smith: *Phenomenology of Perception*. London: Routledge, 1995.

———. *Signes*. [1960] Paris: Gallimard, 1998. Trans. Richard C. McCleary: *Signs*. [1964] Evanston, Ill.: Northwestern University Press, 1987.

Olkowski, Dorothea. "Corporeal Generosity? Review of Rosalyn Diprose's *Corporeal Generosity: On Giving with Nietzsche, Merleau-Ponty, and Levinas*." *Hypatia* 20 (2005).

Sakakibara, Tetsuya. "Das Problem des Ich und der Ursprung der genetischen Phänomenologie bei Husserl." *Husserl Studies* 14, no. 1 (1997): 21–39.

Schües, Christina. *Changes of Perception: Five Systematic Approaches in Husserlian Phenomenology*. Frankfurt am Main,: Peter Lang, 2003.

———. "Generative Phänomenologie in feministischer Perspektive." In *Feministische Phänomenologie und Hermeneutik*, ed. Silvia Stoller, Veronica Vasterling, and Linda Fisher, 46–66. Würzburg: Köningshausen & Neumann, 2005.

Sepp, Hans Reiner. "Geschlechtsdifferenz—ein Thema für Husserls Phänomenologie." In

Phänomenologie und Geschlechterdifferenz, ed. Silvia Stoller and Helmuth Vetter, 47–59. Vienna: WUV-Universitätverlag, 1997.

Sokolowski, Robert. *The Formation of Husserl's Concept of Constitution*. The Hague: Martinus Nijhoff, 1964.

Stawarska, Beata. "Anonymity and Sociality: The Convergence of Psychological and Philosophical Currents in Merleau-Ponty's Ontological Theory of Intersubjectivity." *CHIASMI International* 5 (2004): 295–309.

Stein, Edith. *Zum Problem der Einfühlung*. Halle (Saale), 1917 (Inaugural-Dissertation, ersch. in der Buchdruckerei des Waisenhauses Halle). Trans. Waltraut Stein: *On the Problem of Empathy*. The Hague: Martinus Nijhoff, 1964.

Steinbock, Anthony. *Home and Beyond: Generative Phenomenology after Husserl*. Evanston, Ill.: Northwestern University Press, 1995.

Stoller, Silvia. "(Phänomenologische) Anonymität und (geschlechtliche) Differenz." In *Verhandlungen des Geschlechts: Zur Konstruktivismusdebatte in der Gender-Theorie*, ed. Eva Waniek and Silvia Stoller, 238–49. Vienna: Turia + Kant, 2001.

Waldenfels, Bernhard. "Fremdheit des anderen Geschlechts." In *Phänomenologie und Geschlechterdifferenz*, ed. Silvia Stoller and Helmuth Vetter. Vienna: WUV-Universitätsverlag, 1997.

4.

THE POWER OF TIME:
TEMPORAL EXPERIENCES AND
A-TEMPORAL THINKING?

Christina Schües

The question I wish to take up is not whether women and men think or experience differently. Instead, I wish to address a different set of questions, questions such as: Who has his or her own time? What sort of structures of consciousness correlate with what kind of time structures? How differently can time be structured, and in which time structure does one live, experience, or think? Does time have power over consciousness? Do I have power over time?

In order to address these questions I would like to generally thematize the temporal structure of experiences (i.e., intentionality) and the temporal structure of reflective thinking. By way of comparison I try to show that these two acts are grounded in very different time structures and that these structures concern also our relation to temporality. The awareness of these different structures of time and our relation to them is basic to the idea that time is a way to control humans and to expropriate the ego. The length of time a person has for his or her actions determines how s/he can do them, and the way the person structures and fills the time for those who depend on him or her—for example, children—determines, among other things, how the person feels.

First, I address how experiences are temporally structured. Then I turn to the question of the self-constitution of time and its embeddedness in the gendered body and worldly lived experience. In the last part of the chapter, I discuss the concept of thinking and its time structure. I attempt to show that experiences, particularly perceptual experience, and thinking are differently temporally structured and that these differences have consequences for the relation between power and time. A clear understanding of this relation is important for discussions about the themes of gendered activities or gender relations and their structures.

The Temporal Structure of Experiences

Classical phenomenologists such as Husserl, Merleau-Ponty, and Heidegger oppose the idea of a deduction or construction of time on the basis of an a-temporal point or an a-temporal subject. For them, the field of investigation of the phenomenon *time* is the "field of presence" in which time is found neither in things nor in states of consciousness. However, Husserl's conception of time is not based upon one unifying and identical moment fixed in the present, and it is not only bound up *just* with a metaphysics of being as presence, but is also developed in relation to an absolute time-constituting flux that allows for the present as well as for the absent, for relationships as well as for differences. In this section I consider experiences that are directed toward external objects, and, hence, are bound to events in the world and that have the events' temporal structure.

When considering experiences, the most important notion to understand here is *intentionality*. Experiences are intentional: someone perceives something, feels something, thinks something. Intentionality constitutes objects in an act of objectivation by ascribing an ideal identity to a sensible diversity, a manifold, given *across* time: "Temporal consciousness is . . . an objectivating consciousness. Without identification and differentiation, without now-positing, past-positing, future-positing etc., there could be no duration, no rest and change, no successive being etc. That means: without all that the absolute 'content' would remain blind, would fail to mean objective being, duration etc.— Something is in objective time. Something!"[1] What this implies is that the field of presence, that is, the field of appearing appearances, which is the perceptual field of an objectivating consciousness, is intentionally structured in horizons of retention and protention. Hence, experience has a triadic structure.

The idea that time is structured as past, present, and future would not make any sense without the assumption of a subjective standpoint in the world. From such a standpoint every experience has a temporal structure as a formal-transcendental fundamental structure that constitutes itself as well as the temporal experience in consciousness. This fundamental structure shows the concretization of the particular contents of my experience, which are always organized in the triadic perceptual structure of co-presented retention (primal memory), the "now" (presentation), and co-presented protention (anticipation).

According to Husserl, retention is the grip one has on the "just having been"; presentation is the experience at the "now point," which is understood as the border between retention and protention, and protention is the anticipation of that which has-not-yet-been and which is-yet-to-come. Strictly speaking the "now" is made up of impressions; however, impressions do not flash up in the moment of the "now," but rather they flow continuously.[2] Retention is a "sinking down into the past (the pull of death),"[3] "a certain falling off from the greatest peak of sensation in the now to the point of imperceptibility."[4] Thus, sensation, and the whole of perception, goes through a decline of evidence in this flowing from "here" to "there," from "the top downward" in a "cone" of retention. In the end "every perception disappears as an *obscura et confusa perception*,"[5] and can be sedimented in the "dark of consciousness" and brought back to mind in the future.[6]

Protention is the intentional ordering of possibilities with the tendency of continuing the experience just-had. The imaginatively, retentionally, and habitually founded anticipations are directed into the future, which is "an intentional modification of a past" within a field of indeterminacies, possibilities, and probabilities.[7] In other words, it is a *fictionally* anticipated field of possible perceptual objects or of ways of perceiving an object. This description of the temporal structure of experiences presents *only* an instantaneous moment of time. It shows the triadic structure from a subjective standpoint. Therefore, talk about past and future still presumes a standpoint in a "field of presence." However, the perceiver is conscious *of* the perceptual object *in* and *through* retentional and protentional intentionality; therefore, every experience is essentially removed from the moment of presence, which would be the "now." "These retentions are characterized in themselves as modifications of primal impressions which belong to all the remaining, expired temporal points of the constituted durations. Each is consciousness of the past of the corresponding earlier now-point and gives this point in the mode of the before corresponding to its position in the expired durations."[8]

Retention is thought of ambiguously. On the one hand, it is a modification of the impressional "now," which is discrete; on the other hand, it is a differential repetition of the primal impression, which is continuous, and in which a now-consciousness is conscious of itself for the first time.

The temporal structure of experience is built upon two directions of intentionality: a "transversal" and a "longitudinal" intentionality (*Quer- und Längs-intentionalität*). The former intentionality is responsible for "holding on to" the object through all its retentional modifications, and the latter, the longitudinal intentionality, is responsible for the unity of the object throughout the passing time. This characterization of the two intentionalities is particularly apparent in the perception of the motion of a physical object. The transversal intentionality is responsible for the constitution of the same object through its movements and modifications, and the longitudinal intentionality constitutes the linear flow of now points, that is, of the "differences" in the temporal flow. This structure of transversal intentionality means that perceptual experiences are presented in a "juxtaposition" (*Nebeneinander*) of objects and aspects.[9] One can distinguish two directions of temporal constitution:

(1) The objective direction of the constitution of an object where we can phenomenologically distinguish the appearance of an object from the consciousness of experiences itself. The experienced object constitutes itself in its temporal triadic structure.

(2) The subjective direction, the absolute flow of consciousness, which is constantly time-constituting. The inner consciousness as transcendental self-consciousness is not in possession of itself in an objective (*gegenständlichen*) experience. It situates itself in a pre-intentional continuous possession of itself, which means that the inner consciousness lives as a temporal consciousness through its self-temporalization (i.e., it develops its own temporality).

However, the pre-intentional self-possession of the inner time flow (2) is dependent on the experience of intentional objects (1), and vice versa; that is, the continuous time-constituting flow of consciousness is responsible for the constitution of appearances, which takes place in its conscious structures. "The appearing thing is constituted [constitutes itself, my translation] because unities of sensation and homogeneous apprehensions are constituted [constitute themselves, my translation] in the primordial flux; therefore, there is always consciousness of something."[10] The absolute flow of temporality must be continuous because the discontinuity that arises when something is lifted out as a *difference* presupposes continuity, in the form either of constant duration or of constant change.[11]

Temporal Self-constitution, the Unity of the Temporal Flow, and Its Anonymity

The temporal time flow constitutes the unity of itself, and this constituting is anonymous.[12] This is accomplished by its coinciding with that which it constitutes as itself, that is, that which was called longitudinal intentionality, an intentionality that goes through the temporal flux itself and that is, thus, in a "continuous unity of coincidence with itself."[13] Thus, self-constitution means that "the constituting and constituted coincide."[14] Hence, experiences are bound to the world and experiences are temporal. Therefore, temporality *is bound to the world and to the self.*

The transversal and the longitudinal intentionalities are responsible for the self-temporalizing of consciousness. The former grounds the identity of the object throughout any modification, and the other, the longitudinal intentionality, is responsible for the flow of now points that were presented in terms of the actual (phenomenal) "difference" between their pre- and after-actuality.

The constituting temporal flow and the constituted temporal experience do not coincide in every respect, because the self-constitution of the flow is not only the self-appearance but also the essential adumbrating—*differing*—of the flow itself through which it can appear to itself. The coincidence is not total because the original impressions immediately transverse into retentional modification by virtue of which the original impression is then objectified, that is, differentiated, in its immanent unity. Thus, in certain respects the longitudinal intentionality is privileged because it is responsible for the continuous identity of the flow of temporal consciousness. This longitudinal intentionality, which is the continuous temporal flow in its unity, can be brought into a self-appearance only in self-reflection, whose temporal structure I will discuss in a moment.

The appearance of the temporal flow belongs to the immanent structure of the temporal self itself; that is, the ego presentifies itself, that is, appears to itself *as* being temporal. Thus, only *because* the constituting and the constituted do not fully coincide with each other is it possible that the flow of consciousness appears to the self. However, this flow is not something temporally objective; it cannot be objective because it is that original consciousness which is responsible for the flow. We *know* about this flow through the impressions we receive from already constituted objects when, for example, we perceive objects that move or we experience the passage of time in feelings of boredom or attention to the unfolding of music. However, it is not only that we know about the temporal flow; even more, *we are taken* by it, we are taken by the object, the situation, or the action we are experiencing.

I can try to reflect upon my experiences or my action. However, in self-reflection I can grasp my empirical self only as an *anonymous* temporal stream. I can never intentionally objectify my own functioning self or its self-temporalization because I always "come too late." That is, my own functioning self is given for me only retentionally and not in its self-temporalization. Thus, as a constituter of time, I remain anonymous.

> The ego which is the counterpart [*gegenüber*] to everything is anonymous. It is not its own counterpart. [That which I see, for example,] the house is my counterpart, not vice versa. And yet I can turn my attention to myself. But then this counterpart in which the ego comes forward along with everything which was its counterpart is again split. The ego which comes forward as a counterpart and its counterpart (e.g. the house it was perceiving) are both counterparts to me. Forthwith, I—the subject of this new counterpart—am anonymous.[15]

Since the ego cannot grasp itself in its actual functioning, it is anonymous. This fact of anonymity, and the fact that it springs from itself, are one and the same. Thus, the ego in the anonymity of its functioning presence and the constant streaming of time are the same. The self-possessing universal flow of constitution is indicated by the *manifold* appearances of the constituted time structure of the experienced objects. The temporality of consciousness is characterized by a *presence and by an absence* in presence, as also by the unity of the absolute flow of time, which is in principle anonymous.

However, as soon as one realizes that the transcendental ego is also an embodied self and, hence, a generative self that is born, then it is possible to understand that the self does not so much temporalize itself as *it is temporalized by its own ongoing activity in the world.*

Thus, (a) time constitution presumes an embodied self, and (b) the self is temporalized by its ongoing activities in the world.

Time Constitution Presumes an Embodied Self

The notion of intentionality, relevant to Husserl's later texts and to Merleau-Ponty's explorations, is not that of an "act" but rather that of a "functional intentionality" (*fungierende Intentionalität*), an intentionality that bears some resemblance to the notion of the transcendence of human being (*Dasein*) in the Heideggerian sense.[16] And when Merleau-Ponty or the later Husserl speaks of "synthesis," the synthesis in question is no longer an activity effected by a subject, but assumes the form of a "passive synthesis" inherent in being in the world.

The thesis that time constitution presumes an embodied self and its link with lived experience is grounded on three arguments, which are all more or less linked with the insight that time and gender are not to be thought apart. The *first* argument holds that temporality is subjective and personified. In order to illuminate this argument I have to turn to Merleau-Ponty. With him we can understand Husserl's phenomenology of time as an analysis that undermines any idealism of *sense-giving* and accommodates a reformulation of intentionality and constitution that is in harmony with his privileging of the theme of being-toward-the-world. On the other hand, with Merleau-Ponty's approach, we recognize Heidegger not so much in contrast to a Husserlian phenomenology of subjectivity, but rather as a continuation of the latter, a continuation whereby the issue of time is reformulated in an ontological language. This is so because thinking time as a whole is possible only insofar as time is "personified." Therefore, temporality and subjectivity coincide with each other. Merleau-Ponty draws on Heidegger not with a view to setting subjectivity aside, but rather with a view to empowering subjectivity with temporality. *Temporality is subjective* only insofar as *the subject is time.*

My *second* argument for the thesis that time constitution presumes an embodied self is based on the fact that my body is the center of orientation in space and time, and this body is gendered. Thus, I temporally and spatially structure the world around me from a gendered orientation. Perspectival (visual) perception originates from the *"difference"* inherent in the "now" (and the "here"). By virtue of being a gendered body, I am situated in a presence that continuously elapses into my past that remains my past, my personified, gendered past. For both Merleau-Ponty and Husserl, the body is the center of orientation: if I had no body, I would not have any time or space. My own spatial and temporal existence is indispensable for me, for it is "the primary condition of all living perception."[17] My body, being affective, inhabits time and space, perceiving them from an orientation determined by my point of view. Thus, any perception takes place from the particular center of orientation "now" and "here." This situatedness and the free mobility of consciousness are felt within consciousness in the form of kinesthetic sensations. Kinesthetic sensations are embedded in the relativity of perspectival profiles (*Abschattungen*). As a consequence, the perceptual object appears *in* their sensible appearances.

Disparate sensible appearances caught *across* different moments of time can be appearances of different sides of the same object because each is an appearance of the object from a different point of view. Each object has an index of orientation. Each aspect refers to other aspects by referring to a center of orientation that, in turn, refers further to a system of other centers of orientation. The constitution of an object requires an intentionality that is situated somewhere within the space it constitutes. The ascription of a multiplicity of sensible appearances requires the variability of the situatedness of intentionality and, thus, its being incarnated in the body.

Duration, and each temporal point of duration, is unique, even though they might be the same for another object. Any predication of, or attribution to, an object is in principle repeatable—and with regard to its temporal form. Such a duplication would have different time points that themselves *may* have their particular location in the (assumed) spatial reference system. "The thing-bodily shape does indeed remain in movement with the object, but it has its individuality in every temporal point with respect to the absolute singularity of the fullness of the piece of space in which it is mementary."[18] Everything that is constituted through perceptual consciousness is situated in space and has its absolute uniqueness in its spatial position.

The *third* important argument is the following. Experiences, especially perceptual experiences, are sensible because they are located in a temporal field of sensations. The reflection on temporal consciousness reveals that "sensations" as well as the "original presence" are revealed to us by way of retentional intentionality. We can never grasp the functioning present in the pure impression. Objects are intended *across* the materiality of "sensations" (*hyletic data, the psychic matter*), and *across* their "original presence."

In *The Visible and Invisible,* Merleau-Ponty argues that sensations are *dimensional,* thus, they exist in stretches of space and time and in *depth.*[19] They have a certain style and density. Each sensation is a dynamic specific filling of space and time. Space here is understood as lived space and as temporal space. Since the pre-intentional sensitivity of the body exists in a certain space and is given in a temporal spread, "my body is to the greatest extent what every thing is: a *dimensional this. . . .* But, while the things become dimensions only insofar as they are received in a *field,* my body is this field itself, i.e., a sensible field that is dimensional *of itself.*"[20] In other words, objects are experienced as being sensible *because* they are located in a temporal field of sensations, which becomes meaningful only due to intentionality. The felt temporality of an experience, for example, a tone, a mood, or an action, is personal and subjective *and* also pre-determined *from* the experienced object and its contexts. Hence, intentionality is bound to the sensible world in its order and, therefore, binds the ego to the world by means of a gendered orientation.

The Self Is Temporalized by Its Own Ongoing Activity in the World

The self is temporalized by his or her activities and experiences in the world. Activities involve the body; they are, as Silvia Stoller emphasizes,[21] more or less *anonymously* gendered, and they need time and are temporally structured because they are bound to particular series of plots and temporal modes of how it is undertaken; experiences need time and they are temporally structured. Since everything cannot be experienced at once, and since, by way of our bodily orientation, experiences are perspectival, they are temporally structured in the sense of before and after, again or concurrent, quiet or hectic, and so on. Thus, the way experiences and activities are temporally structured results in a temporalization of the self as well. The structuring of time is grounded in the relation of intentionality between the self and the world. My temporal experience is embedded in a world that is itself already temporally structured. Temporal determinations (*Vorgaben*) are given; time forms the body and experiences. If children have no time structures they have difficulties adapting in school and in society. Time connects nature and culture; it structures relations between human beings. Certain time structures are presented by certain needs, and natural ones are intertwined with cultural and social ones; this becomes apparent, for example, when we consider different sleeping behaviors. Women have a monthly cycle, but how they deal with it differs greatly. Babies must be fed, and they need a certain time of caring for their well-being, but how it is done is socially and culturally different. Education is supported by the regime of forming through time; we need to sleep at night, and to take on temporal habits. The order of time becomes like a second nature. Different kinds of experience have different conceptions of time. Experiences are bodily and temporally structured. Time is fundamental to human relations, and the sharing of time is essential for them. For instance, caring for another person means adapting more or less to another person's time structure and time order. A loving relationship can be disturbed if the partners have too different time structures and time feelings. Time is felt through the body. It remains with me all the time: in relation to a day (for example, because I get sleepy), to the time of the year, or to the years that have passed by. Thus, time can be taken as a way to control other human beings and their lives.

Society or individuals structure *power relations* by way of a temporal order. For instance, positions low on the hierarchy are temporally very restricted and controlled in comparison to those that are higher. The question of power is: Who controls whose time? How much time does somebody have? How long does somebody have to wait? Perhaps prisons are the most strictly controlled. Prisoners are not only spatially limited but also temporally controlled at every hour. And when you consider the question of "who controls whose time?" you can determine the hierarchy of a relationship.

Generally speaking, every activity in the world involves a certain temporal order. And every activity and every experience temporalizes the ego in a particular way. So the question may arise, regarding a particular experience, of who decides what sort of experience I have and for how long. In the next section, I will show how the temporalizing of the self can be studied in reference to the process of objectification and socialization of the ego.

Objectification and Socialization

It is not important here whether or not persons relate to one and the same world. What is important is that the world to which they are directed is taken as an objective world. That is, the perceiver needs to *abdicate* her own subjective standpoint in order to be a member of the community and live in a "personal attitude."[22] Being a member of the community and living a personal attitude in a temporal sense presupposes three mechanisms by which I am temporally socialized and culturalized: de-perspectivation, de-presentification, and de-centering. All three aspects are fairly intertwined and work together; they merely emphasize slightly different aspects of the phenomenological description. In assuming my intersubjective identity I have to *de-perspectivize* my own view in reference to an "objective" communal view. A simple example for this aspect is the spatial perception of a coin. Strictly speaking, I see the coin from my subjective standpoint as elliptical. For all that, I refer to it as being round (which is still perspectival) and as having, above all, a monetary function and value within our present society. Already in the perception of material objects we do take into consideration a certain expropriation (*Enteignung*). This expropriation (of my privileged position) in every experience transforms me *locally, temporally, socially,* and *culturally* into a member of a community in terms of "being in accord" with a certain form of life.[23] The form of life contains the communal point of view: "And they agree in the language they use. That is not agreement in opinion but in a form of life."[24] Thus, the expropriation (or de-perspectivation) of my subjective standpoint is a process of socialization that is, however, never homogeneous or totally determined.

Husserl situates the personal ego at the mundane empirical level. However, if we consider that the living course of original consciousness is necessarily a temporalizing course in which the personal ego is taken as an apperceptive form of the pure ego and in which the transcendental ego apperceives itself as a self (in self-reflection), then the personal ego is also understood as being transcendental. In that sense also transcendental consciousness itself becomes personal and thereby social. Thus, the transcendental ego is personalized (i.e., socialized) through its temporalizing self-constitution in the form of a continuous *de-presentification* of the pure ego (through forgetting), and, hence, by a *presentification* of the personal ego by way of retentional and protentional consciousness. The result is that—strictly speaking—the perceptual object includes always a presented and an a-presented (that is, the term "a-presented" refers to the reverse side or the use or value of something). De-presentification and immanent temporal personalization, that is, socialization (presentification of my-self), stand in an analogous relation to each other as well as to the empathic act and the socialization (personalization) process by way of which one becomes one among the (transcendental) others.

Experiencing means, because it is *intentional,* to *put oneself into* over there, "into" the situation and the object of the experience.[25] If I transcend myself by way of a de-presentation, then I situate myself in *another* temporal context, that of the experienced event. This means a *de-centering* of my personal standpoint (of the pure ego), of my "here" and "now." In my de-centeredness, which is an expropriation (*Enteignung),* I am not by myself but in the temporal being of the experience. Thus, in a de-centeredness I make myself one among others in the world experienced. That is, the alteration of my standpoint has a socializing effect on me. In becoming-one-among-others, in constituting myself via the temporal experience, I also adopt a "personal attitude," that is, I *socialize* myself into the "mundane," "objective," "empirical" self that I am in the personal attitude. This goes together with taking myself for granted (*Selbstverständlichkeit*), "forgetting" myself by not self-reflecting on myself. Sometimes, however, this adaption is not possible, for instance in cases when the temporal order is completely alien to me. This phenomenon of temporal disturbance happens, for example, during a journey to another country or another culture. Temporal disturbances may take place also between different social groups or between individuals, as Gail Weiss explains in her chapter, "Sharing Time across Unshared Horizons."[26]

The result of the temporality of experience is a *socialization* of the ego by way of, firstly, an expropriation (or de-perspectivation); secondly, a de-presentation of the "field of presence"; and, thirdly, a de-centeredness: that is, being here (because of my body) and there at the same time. These considerations hold within an epistemo-logical framework; however, they are also reasonable within a social-philosophical realm. Certainly, people have more or less a choice in how they act and, hence, what they experience. Some experiences are voluntary, others accidental, and again others involuntary. When I like an activity and undertake it voluntarily and with joy, then it does not seem to constrain me or to put much force on me, *even though* I am taken up by the time order of that experience. Every experience I have puts me in the time order of *that* experience, sometimes with my will and sometimes against my will, sometimes with joy and sometimes with abhorrence. Particularly when I am forced into an activity or a situation, and hence into an experience, I feel even more strongly the sense of being taken by a time order that is not mine. For example, waiting is often experienced as a loss of (personal) time. Also, work-ing in an assembly line was a new historical factual experience in the 1920s. As Jeffrey Eugenides describes in his novel *Middlesex:* "People stopped being human in 1913. That year Henry Ford put his cars on rollers and made his workers adopt the speed of the assembly line. At first, workers rebelled. They quit in droves, un-able to accustom their bodies to the new pace of the age. Since then, however, the adaption has been passed down: we've all inherited it to some degree, so that we plug right into joysticks and remotes, to repetitive motions of a hundred kinds."[27] In another example, integration is the aim of education. A well-educated child, or a well-integrated "foreigner," is a person who is disciplined and who lives in "our" world of values. One important instrument for breaking the rebelliousness of the child or of anybody who is supposed to be integrated is to control their time and to habituate them to the dominant time order.

These considerations are not to be understood as saying that any experiences imposed on someone are a loss of the self. It is rather *because* experiences inhere epistemologically in a temporal structure that is grounded in the experienced object and activities; *time can be used* as a measure of social control and conditioning. However, if the personal ego were *simply* expropriated, de-presented, and de-centered, then it would be removed from its original presence, which is also the source of its self-temporalization. The result would be the collapse of the ego. Thus, the concept of the protentionally and retentionally expanded presence, linked with the concept of de-centeredness, is central to finding an intermediate position between the two poles of embeddedness in a particular temporally structured community, and it gives the possibility of self-reflection.

Merleau-Ponty summarizes the parallel between the two objective and subjective analyses in this way: "It is the essence of time to be not only actual time, or time which flows, but also time which is aware of itself, for the explosion or dehiscence of the present toward a future is the archetype of the *relationship of self to self,* and it displays an interiority or ipseity."[28] In other words, fundamental to time consciousness is the possibility of a *self-reflexivity* of consciousness, that is, the relation of the self to itself. The possibility of such a self-reflexivity is grounded in an explosion, or dehiscence, that is, an opening power of presence (the "upper limit of sensibility") toward the future and the past. Thus, in this deep sense, temporality and subjectivity interrelate reciprocally: this is so for Heidegger as well as for Husserl; and this is essential for the constitution of experiences and their manifold modifications and possibility of self-reflection and of thinking.

Reflective Thinking

In the context of temporal constitution I have referred to self-reflection. Now, I shall look at it in order to discuss how the ego relates to the temporal structure of thinking. Is the ego taken by the temporal structure of thinking in the same way as it was taken by an experienced object?

The text from Husserl also cited above points to the fact of the splitting up of the object of thinking, and in order to consider the anonymity of the ego. "I can turn my attention to myself. But then this counterpart in which the ego comes forward along with everything which was its counterpart is again split. The ego which comes forward as a counterpart and its counterpart (e.g. the house I was perceiving) are both counterparts to me. Forthwith, I—the subject of this new counterpart—am anonymous."[29]

The possibility of self-reflection is the ground for consciousness both to become aware of its temporal structure and to be aware of a self as it appears. Even though or just because my ego is anonymous, I can confront myself in an inner dialog. The structure of an *inner dialog*—the splitting up of I and self—is the structure of thinking. "Thinking—the two-in-one of the soundless dialogue—actualizes the difference within our identity as given in consciousness."[30] Thus, without self-reflection, the presentification (*Gewahrwerden*) of one's own self, thinking would not be possible; hence, self-reflection is necessary in order to initiate thinking. However, cognitive acts are distinct from thinking; that is, thinking itself has no results. Rather, as Hannah Arendt suggests, judging as the product of thinking realizes thinking and makes it manifest in the world. Thus, thinking *liberates* us from experiences and activities in the world in order to *release* the faculty of judging. Therefore, judging in fact needs thinking. The activity of thinking examines whatever happens to come to pass or to attract attention, regardless of results and specific content. Thus, it is also a condition for acting according to a decision and against "thoughtless" actions.[31]

How does thinking function? Thinking is not intentional but rather *dialectical,* which means that thinking is like a dialogue *about* something. *About something* could mean that thinking means a "flying over," a *"pensée survolante,"* in a neutral way, but this is not how I understand it. *Thinking is bound to the world, yet it destroys boundaries!* It destroys the boundary and the relation toward the world and its temporal order. When I think, then, I have to *withdraw from* the world. I interrupt my activities in the world; thinking is out of order, and I can question positions, opinions, or beliefs which I have. The result is that when I think *I* am by myself, I am able to think about that which I have experienced: I may think about what is right or wrong, activities that I have done or am about to do. I am able to move my thoughts back and forth in time by memory or anticipation, turn them around, think about "things" from different perspectives. Thus, thinking is not de-perspectivation in the sense of bringing me over there; it is rather the destruction of one particular perspective. It opens variations and possibilities of perspectives about something.

Secondly, as Valéry said (and Merleau-Ponty, as well as Arendt, refers to him): "At times I think, and at times I am."[32] Anyone who takes thinking in this way contrasts thinking and reality in an analogy to death and life, as though we are alive only when we are in the world. Others, such as Cartesian rationalists, might take the relation the other way around. Being seems so faded that it does not seem to be alive, but thoughts are clear and, therefore, real and alive. I don't think that either extreme is correct: anyone would feel a kind of death if the world were destroyed, if the world of beliefs and understanding were withdrawn and became unreal, or if the world-belief were destroyed. If such a destructive situation were to occur, the individual would be silenced. But this is not the situation of thinking. In thinking *I* withdraw from the world, and am by myself; that is, *I have* the feeling of the *liveliness* of myself (and liveliness can also be part of our experiences). However, the inability to think about "something" turns a human being into a "sleepwalker."[33]

Thirdly, thinking "deals always with absences and removes itself from what is present and close at hand."[34] This means that reality, which we experience in space and time, is spatially and temporally suspended; it means that we de-sense, or de-materialize, the products of our thinking. These thoughts become meaningful, and they are distillations, but not necessarily abstractions—rather, "essences." The understanding of thoughts as (mostly) meaningful "essences" (and not only as abstract identities, such as, for example, numbers) is grounded on the observation that we can be sensually touched by thoughts. Being touched by thoughts can even result in bodily changes, such as, for instance, the heartbeat changing, or the face turning red. The location of the thinking ego is therefore "nowhere" *but* still located in the sensitivity of the body, which threatens to break into the train of thoughts: "The thinking ego, moving among universals, among invisible essences, is, strictly speaking, nowhere; it is homeless in an emphatic sense (—which may explain the early rise of a cosmopolitan spirit among the philosophers)."[35] When we think we are nowhere, but we are also still in space and time insofar as now, in reference to Kant, time determines the relation of representations to each other. Representations are taken from memory, from anticipations, from present ideas, and so on.

Fourth, if time determines the relation of thoughts, then thinking must transform experiences. The temporal structure of thinking forces representations into the order of a sequence; these sequences become "thought-trains."[36] Thinking is discursive, and, insofar as it follows a train of thought, it could by analogy be presented as "a line of progressing to infinity."[37] Thus, in order to create such a line of thought, thinking must transform the juxtaposition in which experiences are given to us in a succession of words. Thus, we have de-sensed and de-spatialized the original experiences.

The Time Structure of Thinking

Where is the thinking ego located temporally? Arendt illustrates where the thinking ego is located in time by citing a parable by Kafka (out of a collection of aphorisms entitled "HE"):

He has two antagonists; the first presses him from behind, from his origin. The second blocks the road in front of him. He gives battle to both. In fact, the first supports him in his fight with the second, for he wants to push him forward, and in the same way the second supports him in his fight with the first, since he drives him back. But it is only theoretically so. For it is not only the two antagonists who are there, but he himself as well, and who really knows his intentions? His dream, though, is that some time in an unguarded moment—and this, it must be admitted, would require a night darker than any night has ever yet been—he will jump out of the fighting line and be promoted, on account of his experience in fighting, to the position of umpire over his antagonists in their fight with each other.[38]

This parable describes the "inner state" of the thinker in regard to time and, especially, in regard to being captured by the governance of time. The previous argument concerning the description of the temporal experience was that the experiencing ego *is taken* by the structure of the time of the experience. Thus, thinking means jumping out of the determination of a time structure (but only for the moment of thinking). Now, when the ego turns to thinking, then the experience of the past is transformed into something that lies *behind* us, and the expectation of the future is transformed into something that *approaches us from ahead* (German: *Zukunft*; French: *avenir*). The forces are "his" antagonists; they are not simply in opposition, and they fight only because "he" is there.[39] The in-between is the "he," the now, the eternal moment, the battleground where the thinking ego is at home. This time construct is totally different from that of experiences in ordinary life. Thinking is interruption, and interruption is beginning. Thus, in this thinking the three senses do not simply nor smoothly follow one by one; rather, the thinking ego is a presence that is surrounded, pushed, and attacked by the past and future. This ego withdraws from daily life, from "business as usual," or from any worldly surroundings or bodily necessities. The thinking ego debates with itself; it is a hungry ego, hungry for meaning and making sense.

The thinking ego in the parable is not our self as it appears; it seems ageless, nowhere, liberated from concrete contents, timeless (?), yet it is real: the thinking ego senses as his dual antagonists time itself. The ego is time, is temporal, and, therefore, is constantly transformed from being into becoming. In its fight it constantly destroys its own present: "As such, time is the thinking ego's greatest enemy because—by virtue of the mind's incarnation in a body whose internal motions can never be immobilized—time inexorably and regularly interrupts the immobile quiet in which it is active without doing anything."[40] But Kafka's "HE" wants to jump out in an unguarded moment. Does he become the uninterested, undisturbed spectator and judge outside of life? I do not think that the lonely spectator above the world would make much sense.

"He" does not fight against some indifferent antagonist, but against *his* antagonists: it is his past that fights against the future (and "he" is in between), and it is his future that fights against his past. He is needed to make the difference between past and future; without him there would be *only* change. His fight is in the present; it is now. The antagonistic forces and the thinking effect the clash between past and future, and thereby they are transformed into my *personal, gendered* behind and ahead. *She has her past and future and he has his past and future.* Thinking emerges out of the clash between (the gendered) past and future, almost as though it would be timeless. But thinking is certainly not timeless; rather it takes the not-anymore and the not-yet, the behind and the ahead, in its own presence.

Thus, time is the "antagonist" of the thinking ego in a double sense. The positive sense is the following one: time constrains the ego from the past and from the future, from my "behind" and from my "yet to come"; they force me onto the battlefield of the in-between and initiate thinking. And here we have to understand that my past and my future are generated and gendered in a very concrete sense. I have lived as a girl, then as a woman in a particular context, with particular experiences, feelings, and thoughts. I have grown up in my family and in a particular generative context; I have my female and male friends and colleagues, and so on. The force and style, how the behind and the yet to come "attack" my ego and the present depends *also* on my gendered being. Not that the thinking itself can be regarded as "typically" male or female, but the battleground between past and future is personal, and hence female or male in its concrete sense. Thus, "he," in the aphorism, can be a "she"; I remember my past and I anticipate my future. The act of remembering and anticipating are fundamental to feeling the antagonism of the behind and ahead. In particular, the remembering, but also the anticipating are specifically gendered; when I remember myself I cannot remember just a neutral person. I always remember myself as a girl or as a woman in a particular context and in specific relations.

The negative sense of the "antagonist" of the thinking is the following: if an order of time is forced upon me by the external world or by the other who interrupts my train of thought, then the activity of a thinking ego is hindered. This happens also if one of the antagonists is too strong, that is, if the ego is captured by, for instance, past experiences. Then thinking may be disturbed, go in circles, or not even "take place." This happens if my time is controlled by a strict order. If I cannot even have a "battlefield," if I cannot reflect upon myself, if the dialectical principle, which is fundamental to thinking, is destroyed because time is controlled, then the plurality of the world is reduced to one understanding, one opinion, and one dimension. The one-dimensionality of a monological consciousness destroys the ability to think and to experience, and it eliminates the possibility of considering other perspectives and horizons. Hence, it would be the elimination of the being of human beings.

Yet, time is not only the antagonist; it must be made to be our friend because *thinking needs leisure time,* spare time; this is a time that is not controlled, valued with money, or interrupted by worldly necessities. If thinking is like a dialog, then it must be construed in open horizons of time. Thinking withdraws the thinker from the world: it disrespects given time orders; it liberates; it destroys doctrines. Therefore, the time in which we think means the empowerment of our own time and an entering into the world of thought, which is different from the world of facts. Most dictators know about this force of thinking, and thus know they have to control space and time—and this holds true, I believe, for all power relations.

It is my goal to lay some basis for the idea that reflective thinking (with its necessary leisure time) is necessary as one source for finding "our" paths in the world and in the future. The ability to think, and its liberating aspect on judging, brings about a multidimensional reality. It refers to the different perspectives of different human beings; it is open to making sense of the world. Without thinking we are lost in experience; we are lost in time without having our own time. And without experiences we have lost the world. Having the power over one's own time order is based on the freedom of choice and is necessary for reflective thinking.

Notes

1. Husserl, *Zur Phänomenologie des inneren Zeitbewußtseins (1893–1917)*, 297. "Das Zeitbewusstsein ist also ein *objektivierendes* Bewusstsein. Ohne Identifizierung und Unterscheidung, ohne Jetzt-Setzung, Vergangenheits-Setzung, Zukunfts-Setzung etc., kein Dauern, kein Ruhen und Sich-Verändern, kein aufeinanderfolgendes Sein etc. Das heißt: ohne all das bleibt der absolute 'Inhalt' blind, bedeutet nicht objektives Sein, nicht Dauern etc. . . . *Etwas* ist in der objektiven *Zeit. Etwas!*"

2. See ibid., 324–26. Some of these descriptions I have formulated in my *Changes of Perception*, 165–97.

3. Husserl, *Zur Phänomenologie des inneren Zeitbewußtseins*, 365. "Herabsinken in die Vergangenheit (Zug des Todes)."

4. Husserl, *The Phenomenology of Internal Time-Consciousness*, 86. The English translation of *Zur Phänomenologie des inneren Zeitbewußtseins* does not include all appendixes and supplements.

5. Sommer, *Lebenswelt und Zeitbewußtsein*, 157.

6. Husserl, *The Phenomenology of Internal Time-Consciousness*, 161. "When a primal datum, a new phase, emerges, the preceding one is not lost but is 'retained in concept' ["in a grip," my revision] (i.e., 'retained' exactly), and thanks to this retention a looking back to what has expired is possible. Retention itself is not an act of looking back which makes an Object of the phase which has expired. Because I have the phase which has expired in hand, I live through [*durchlebe*] the one actually present, take it—thanks to retention—'in addition to' and am directed to what is coming (in a protention)."

7. Cairns, *Conversations with Husserl and Fink*, 84.

8. Husserl, *The Phenomenology of Internal Time-Consciousness*, 105.

9. Arendt, *The Life of the Mind,* 202.

10. Husserl, *The Phenomenology of Internal Time-Consciousness,* 120. Original version: *Zur Phänomenologie des inneren Zeitbewußtseins,* 92. "Das erscheinende Ding konstituiert sich, weil sich im ursprünglichen Fluß Empfindungseinheiten und einheitliche Auffassungen konstituieren, also immerfort Bewußtsein von etwas."

11. See Husserl, *The Phenomenology of Internal Time-Consciousness,* 113.

12. For the anonymity in the structure of temporal experiences, see Silvia Stoller's chapter in this volume.

13. Husserl, *The Phenomenology of Internal Time-Consciousness,* 107.

14. Ibid., 109–10.

15. Edmund Husserl, *Ms. C 2 1,* p.2, Aug., 1931, quoted in Mensch, *Intersubjectivity and Transcendental Idealism,* 220.

16. For example, Husserl, *Analysis Concerning Passive and Active Synthesis;* or *Cartesian Meditations.* For Heidegger, the notions of "transcendence" and transcendental are related neither to subjectivity nor to consciousness; rather they are determined from the ecstatic temporality understood by "Dasein." See Heidegger, *Sein und Zeit,* § 69 b, c.

17. Merleau-Ponty, *Phenomenology of Perception,* 109.

18. Husserl, *Analysis Concerning Passive and Active Synthesis,* 589.

19. Merleau-Ponty, *The Visible and Invisible,* 260.

20. Ibid.

21. See Stoller, "Gender and Anonymous Temporality," in this volume.

22. The "personal attitude" (or natural attitude) is seen in contrast to the "naturalistic attitude" of science (physics, chemistry, etc.), in which the scientist analyzes an "objective" world. We are in the personal attitude when we see our environment as replete with cultural objects and persons to whom we speak. See Husserl, *Ideas Pertaining to a Pure Phenomenology and to a Phenomenological Philosophy.*

23. Spatial perception is perspectival because of my local position, and vice versa; the spatiality and social determinations and the meaningfulness of the sphere of experiences (*Erfahrungsraum*) determine my local position.

24. Wittgenstein, *Philosophical Investigations,* §241.

25. ". . . to put oneself into" could also be construed as Bergson's notion of a "leap" (which resembles Kierkegaard's notion of a "leap of faith"). See Bergson, *Matter and Memory,* chs. 2, 3.

26. In this volume.

27. Eugenides, *Middlesex,* 95.

28. Merleau-Ponty, *Phenomenology of Perception,* 426.

29. Edmund Husserl, unpublished manuscript, *C 2 1, 2,* Aug. 1931, quoted in Mensch, *Intersubjectivity and Transcendental Idealism,* 220.

30. Arendt, *The Life of the Mind,* 193.

31. Ibid., 5.

32. Ibid., 198; See Merleau-Ponty, "The Philosopher and His Shadow," 174.

33. Arendt, *The Life of the Mind,* 191.

34. Ibid., 199.
35. Ibid.
36. Ibid., 201.
37. Ibid., 202.
38. Ibid., 202–12.
39. Remember also the allegory in Nietzsche's *Zarathustra*.
40. Arendt, *The Life of the Mind*, 206.

Bibliography

Arendt, Hannah. *The Life of the Mind*. San Diego: Harcourt Brace Jovanovich, 1978.
Bergson, Henri. *Matter and Memory*. Trans. Nancy M. Paul and W. Scott Palmer. New York: Zone Books, 1991.
Cairns, Dorion. *Conversations with Husserl and Fink*. Ed. Husserl-Archives in Louvain. The Hague: Martinus Nijhoff, 1976.
Eugenides, Jeffrey. *Middlesex*. London: Bloomsbury, 2003.
Heidegger, Martin. *Sein und Zeit*. 15th ed. Tübingen: Niemeyer, 1979.
Husserl, Edmund. *Analyses Concerning Passive and Active Synthesis. Lectures on Transcendental Logic*. Trans. Anthony J. Steinbock. Dordrecht: Kluwer Academic Publishers, 2001.
———. *Cartesian Meditations*. Trans. Dorion Cairns. The Hague: Martinus Nijhoff, 1950.
———. *Ideas Pertaining to a Pure Phenomenology and to a Phenomenological Philosophy*. Second book: *Studies in the Phenomenology of Constitution*. Trans. Richard Rojcewicz and André Schuwer. *Collected Works*, vol. 3. The Hague: Kluwer Academic, 1989.
———. *Zur Phänomenologie des inneren Zeitbewußtseins (1893–1917)*. Ed. Rudolf Bernet. Husserliana X. The Hague: Martinus Nijhoff, 1966. Trans. James S. Churchill: *The Phenomenology of Internal Time-Consciousness*. Bloomington: Indiana University Press, 1964.
Mensch, James. R. *Intersubjectivity and Transcendental Idealism*. Albany: State University of New York Press, 1988.
Merleau-Ponty, Maurice. *Phenomenology of Perception*. Trans. Colin Smith. London: Routledge and Kegan Paul, 1962.
———. "The Philosopher and His Shadow." In *Signs*. Trans. and ed. Richard C. McCleary. Chicago: Northwestern University Press, 1964.
———. *The Visible and Invisible*. Trans. Alphonso Lingis. Evanston, Ill.: Northwestern University Press, 1968.
Schües, Christina. *Changes of Perception: Five Systematic Approaches in Husserlian Phenomenology*. Frankfurt/M.: Lang, 2003.
Sommer, Manfred. *Lebenswelt und Zeitbewußtsein*. Frankfurt/M.: Suhrkamp, 1990.
Wittgenstein, Ludwig. *Philosophical Investigations*. Trans. Gertrude H. M. Anscombe. Ed. Gertrude H. M. Anscombe and Rush Rees. Oxford: Blackwell, 1969.

5.

GENDER AND ANONYMOUS TEMPORALITY

Silvia Stoller

In order to examine time in the framework of "feminist phenomenology," it is vital to address gender in relation to temporality. In this chapter I consider the interrelation between phenomenology and gender, concentrating on a specific aspect of temporality in phenomenology: the idea of anonymity, and link it to the issue of gender. Merleau-Ponty is my main reference, since it is in his work that the idea of anonymity is so clearly formulated. My main interest lies in introducing an aspect of temporality that seems to be widely underdeveloped not only in feminist philosophy but also in theories of time in general: the anonymous aspect of temporality. I would like to introduce the concept of anonymous temporality to feminist theory and gender studies, arguing that the anonymous dimension of time experience in general may also illuminate gendered time experience.[1]

The first part of this chapter introduces a certain concept of female temporality in feminist theory. The second deals with a phenomenologically based concept of an anonymous temporality of gender. While the first part depicts the filmmaker Maya Deren and her concept of female temporality, the second part refers to the concept of anonymity in Merleau-Ponty's phenomenology. The third part sums up the conclusions reached from a critical reading of the theory of "female temporality" aided by phenomenology.

Female Temporality

I would like to begin by introducing a key idea of the filmmaker Maya Deren in the documentary film *In the Mirror of Maya Deren* from the Austrian filmmaker Martina Kudláček.[2] In this documentary film, Deren claims that women have a specific time experience due to their female existence, a specific "time sense" as she calls it.

What I do in my films is very . . . oh, I think very distinctively . . . I think they are the films of a woman, and I think that their characteristic time quality is the time quality of a woman. I think that the strength of men is their great sense of immediacy. They are a now creature and a woman has the strength to wait—because she had to wait, she has to wait nine months for the concept of a child.[3] Time is built into her body in the sense of becomingness. And she sees everything in terms of a being in the stage of becoming, she raises the child knowing not what it is in any moment but seeing always the person that it will become. Her whole life from a very beginning is built into her, is the sense of becoming. Now, in any time form this is a very important sense. I think that my films putting as much stress as they do upon the constant . . .—one image is always becoming another that is . . . it is what is happening that is important in my films not what it is in the moment. This is a woman's time sense, and I think it happens more in my films than in almost anyone else's.[4]

Men are "now creatures" having no sense of duration. Women do have a specific experience of temporal duration. Deren calls it "strength." She argues that it is due to their biologically specific reproductive bodies that women have this different "time sense." It is due to a woman's awareness of pregnancy that they hold another gender-specific time experience. The pregnant woman experiences carrying somebody in her body for nine months, *waiting* for the birth of her child, being *patient,* continually recognizing the *changes* in and of her body, the *growing* of her child, living an intense double life *for a certain time period.*

I believe that Deren is right—at least in a certain sense. Women do indeed have a specific sense of temporality due to their female bodies. In order to demonstrate what this means, I will give you two examples:

(1) The first example refers to Deren herself and her view of female temporality. Pregnancy most often means waiting for a period of nine months for an event to occur. This is a time that usually changes the life of a woman, and prepares her for a different role. So long as only women give birth to children, this bodily experience is restricted to the existence of women. Experiences always have consequences. They determine our behavior as well as our thinking, and often they have a very strong effect upon our worldview in general. The same is true with bodily changes that might also change our everyday lives. Just as weak eyesight, as a bodily defect, can change our common orientation in the world and our view of others, pregnancy too may effect a different quality of being. As with every experience that is taken up and incorporated into our habitual body, so too is this the case with pregnancy. Thus, it is the female body, and the potential of our embodied existence to incorporate bodily experiences, that allows us to say that women have a specific time sense.

(2) The second example refers to human biology, namely to female menstruation. It seems without any doubt that female menstruation influences a woman's experience of time. These experiences vary from woman to woman. Some women feel themselves strongly handicapped when they menstruate. Many women who experience menstruation as painful are forced to change their timetables. They have to lie down for a while; they cannot go to work as usual; they walk more slowly; they can even lose consciousness, and some even break with their social environment as is typical for patients in pain. On the other hand, some women feel stronger at a certain point in their menstruation and become more productive during this period of time. As is the case with pregnancy, this also points to bodily experiences influencing the experiences of women in general. This not only affects the female body but also the life of a woman.

However, the claim that women have a different time sense due to their bodily experiences is a false generalization and almost a form of biological essentialism. If we take into consideration the diversity of women and their experiences, the claim of a gendered time experience must be called into question. This seems evident if we consider the case of childless women. Put differently, do women who have not had the experience of pregnancy also have no strength to wait, no sense of becoming, as Deren's claims suggest? Is the assertion that women have a certain sense of time true only for those women who were once pregnant? If this is the case, then Deren cannot maintain that all "women" have a specific time sense. If she wants to claim that women have a specific time sense independent of the fact of pregnancy, then her claim that "women" have a specific time sense has a false premise. In both cases, Deren's claim suffers from false essentialism as well as from false generalization.

Deren's underlying *biological* gender essentialism is even more problematic. In my opinion, the debate over female temporality should not be reduced to biology in general or the biological bodies of women in particular. Although bodily facts and bodily experiences may influence the existence of women, including their sense of time, something else must be taken into consideration: the cultural factor. In other words, there are numerous cultural facts that obviously have an influence on women's experience of temporality. In order to demonstrate what this means, I would like to mention two examples that should show how culture influences the temporal experience of women.

(1) Until recently, being first or being ahead of others, at least in the public sphere, was not a particularly female experience (e.g., the first Olympic women's marathon took place in Los Angeles only as recently as 1984). Or another example: it was only in 1897 that women were allowed to study at Austrian universities.

However, women were not allowed to study at the Catholic-theological faculty until 1946.[5] In 1907, for the first time in the Austrian history, a woman, Elise Richter, received the *venia legendi,* the academic right to teach. Richter was also the first woman in Austria and Germany to receive the title of professor, in 1921. Being first or being last, being something or somebody for the first time, must be understood as temporal parameters deriving from cultural affairs. That women had to wait in order to be allowed to do something for the first time, as the example of studying philosophy as a woman demonstrates, doubtlessly must have had an influence on women's "sense" of time. Or to put it in terms of Deren: since women had to wait to be allowed to study philosophy or to participate in Olympic women's marathons, they do indeed have a specific "time sense." The difference is that it is not the body but the culture that has an impact upon women's sense of time.

(2) More generally speaking, women were *historically* trained to wait: to wait until they were allowed to appear: to appear in the public sphere, to appear among men, to appear prior to men, to speak in front of men, to speak before a man speaks, to have the first or the last word, and so on, and so on. Waiting, however, is a fundamental element of temporality. It is duration in the temporal field. It means a certain *time quality.* It means a different attitude to time, a different sort of interaction with time, and it also means a different "knowledge" of time. I think that the historical fact of women's waiting is one of the strongest experiences women have endured and still endure.

I started my paper with Maya Deren's claim that women have a specific time sense. I argued that the body does indeed play a central role in determining a women's sense of time, but I also cautioned that the issue of a specific female temporality should not solely be discussed in terms of biology since it falls into the problems that accompany arguments dependent on biological essentialism. I share the more general implication of Deren's argument, that temporality is not a universal but a particular experience because of the fact of gendered experiences. Thus, up to this point I do agree with her. However, I do not believe that femaleness in itself is a very good or convincing ground for her argument. In particular, I am skeptical of the more biological argumentation of Deren's view about female temporality.

Hence, I would like to continue by deepening my criticism of Deren's thesis, that women do have a specific time sense. In particular, I will radicalize my criticism in arguing that it is not true that only women have such a specific time sense. Taking Deren's starting point, I doubt that only women have this "strength to wait." Let me introduce the following consideration: Deren's biological argument is based on woman's self-experience; this means the state of being pregnant and its effects on her own experience of time.

(1) My first argument refers to the principle of self-experience. Deren seems to overemphasize self-experience in relation to the experience of the other (*Fremderfahrung*), in other words, the experience of another person's experience. I argue that in my experience of the experience of another, in the participation of the experience of another person, I take over, at least partly, the experience of the other person. In psychoanalysis this process of taking over is called "introjection": I take over certain characteristics, habits, or feelings of another person (a person with whom I have a close relationship), for example, I emulate her worldview or her way of walking or speaking. If we take this sort of co-experience into consideration, then one must admit that a woman's pregnancy influences not only the pregnant woman herself but also her social field, that is, her immediate partner. If the partner takes part sufficiently in this exciting gestational process, then she or he might also be influenced by these nine months of pregnancy. The partner is not wholly separate from the beloved person. He or she is not a neutral observer who is left untouched by the experiences of this other person, but rather is emotionally bound and maintains a powerful interest in the other person; he or she feels empathy with her, and the stronger the interest and the empathy are, the more the experiences of the other might be shared.[6] This sort of *Fremderfahrung* seems to be responsible for the fact that the other's experience does not belong solely to the subject of this experience. Thus, not only the pregnant woman herself, but also her partner, is placed in a situation of being influenced by this specific time experience. Certainly, the experiences of time they both seem to share are not exactly the same. In the one case, it is the experience of the pregnancy, and in the other, the experience of participating in the experiences of his/her partner. Nonetheless, they participate in the same event of pregnancy. As a consequence, one must argue that it is not only the woman who has to wait for the birth of the child but so too does her partner. The strict separation of female and male temporality is called into question.

(2) A second example might demonstrate the difficulties with the claim of sexually differentiated time senses. In addition to the claim that women have the strength to wait, as Maya Deren contends, it has often been said that women have a specific *cyclic* knowledge as, for example, Julia Kristeva thoroughly describes in terms of "cyclical time."[7] Deren's argument follows the same logic. Women's time is cyclical because of her specific bodily experiences, an argument I do not find at all convincing. To say that women have a particular

knowledge of "cyclicity" means that men miss out on such an experience. I would like to argue that men also have cyclic experiences, perhaps less due to their bodies than to their cultural heritage, experiences such as waking up, drinking coffee, picking up a briefcase, leaving the house, working in an office, having meetings, coming home again in the evening, having dinner, going to bed, and doing the same thing the next morning. What can be more cyclic than such a regulated working day? As a consequence, I would venture to say that such a working day can also be incorporated by men. It is fully regulated and cyclic insofar as the man's line of action begins with leaving a place in the morning and ends with a return to the starting point in the evening. So, I wonder how Deren could ever claim that men are "now creatures," individuals who live in the now, spontaneously and fully deregulated. Although I admit that the case I mention describes an extreme stereotype, it is intended to clarify how the experience of the incorporation of "cyclicity" is not solely an experience that pertains to women. Moreover, the rhythms of awakening and falling asleep, according to some biological principles, could be cited as evidence for the existence of powerful cyclic experiences that women and men both share.

The Anonymous Temporality of Gender

The introduction of the aspect of anonymity into the issue of gender and time has been motivated by this question: From where do differentiations, as in the case of different time senses, stem? If such a "strength of time" experience indeed exists in one or the other person/gender, then where does it come from? To put it differently, does "difference" not presuppose something else in its origin? In order to avoid any sort of essentialism, which has already been called into question, it must be possible to explain from where such a difference as female or male temporality originates by way of a more philosophical standpoint. I argue that phenomenology provides a helpful tool for answering this question since it is *lived temporality* that underlies "difference" and that makes any "differentiation" with respect to female or male temporality possible. Following Merleau-Ponty's phenomenology, lived experience, however, is mainly characterized by anonymity.

Interestingly, Merleau-Ponty has emphasized his idea of anonymity in his chapter on sexual being (*être sexué*) in his *Phenomenology of Perception,* arguing that sexual being is based on an anonymous sexuality. However, since anonymity is not restricted to the issue of sexuality and sexual being, it might also be applied to the issue of temporality, that is, to the issue of gender and temporality. In the chapter on temporality in his *Phenomenology of Perception,* he explicitly states that what he had elaborated for sexuality is also true for temporality: "We can now say of temporality what we said earlier about sexuality and spatiality."[8] So my starting point is the following: if there is an anonymous sexuality, then we may also claim an *anonymous temporality.* What would such an anonymous temporality look like? If we understand what anonymous temporality is, then it should be possible to relate it to the issue of gender.

I have shown elsewhere how the phenomenological idea of anonymity is linked to sexuality, and how the concept of anonymous sexuality contributes to current debates in feminist philosophy and gender studies.[9] I argued that the idea of anonymous sexuality helps us to understand that sexual difference is an ongoing process of differentiation. As such, it stands for a strict non-essentialist theory since it does not presuppose difference. Similar to Judith Butler's claim in *Gender Trouble* and *Bodies That Matter,* the sphere of anonymous sexuality is a sphere that enables the development of specificities but without having any guarantees for the "right" development. In *Gender Trouble,* for example, Butler emphasizes how difficult it is to deliver a full account of one's subject determination. The fact that we very often add an "etc." at the end of a list of characterizations, she argues, illuminates the principle of incompleteness of such an effort. Importantly, she claims: "The theorists of feminist identity that elaborate predicates of color, sexuality, ethnicity, class, and able-bodiedness invariably close with an embarrassed 'etc.' at the end of the list. Through this horizontal trajectory of adjectives, these positions strive to encompass a situated subject, but invariably fail to be complete."[10]

Instead of proposing that this incompleteness is a failure, Butler argues that we can learn from it, and that it is even a starting point for a non-essentialist gender concept, if not a new concept for thinking the political from a feminist perspective. "This failure is instructive: what political impetus is to be derived from the exasperated 'etc.' that so often occurs at the end of such lines? This is a sign of exhaustion as well as of the illimitable process of signification itself. It is the *supplément,* the excess that necessarily accompanies any effort to posit identity once and for all. This illimitable *et cetera,* however, offers itself as a new departure for feminist political theorizing."[11]

I have always been fascinated by Butler's sensibility of the "illimitable process of signification," and from the very beginning I was convinced that her claim could easily be linked to what phenomenologists have said about the quality of the horizon within the phenomenological structure of figure before horizon, in particular, Husserl's claim in his *Analysis Concerning Passive and Active Synthesis* that the horizon cannot be fully determined, because in the very moment we try to name or describe the horizon a new horizon arises. When Husserl wanted to demonstrate the idea of the indeterminate horizon, he let the things speak for themselves, calling for determination. "There is still more to see here, turn me so you can see all my sides, let your gaze run through me, draw closer to me, open me, divide me up; keep on looking me over again and again, turning me to see all sides. You will get to know me like this, all that I am, all my surface qualities, all my inner sensible qualities, 'etc.'"[12]

However, as Husserl's "etc." here indicates, since the horizon can never fully be grasped, the determination can never come to an end. There will also be something else that could be looked at or seen. So what characterizes the horizon is a sort of "indeterminable indeterminacy."[13] The process of determination is an endless determination, since one can *always* add another quality by way of perception. For this reason, Husserl, in addition to his "etc.," also speaks of "*in infinitum.*"[14] While Butler and Husserl both speak of the Latin "etc." indicating that there is always something more, Husserl clearly emphasizes the endlessness of the effort of determination, in his use of the Latin *in infinitum.*

The fact that the horizon can never fully be grasped stands for the *overdetermination* of the horizon and for experience in general. This characteristic of overdetermination is crucial for the following considerations about anonymous temporality.[15]

Merleau-Ponty argues in his *Phenomenology of Perception* that anonymous sexuality represents a *surplus* that makes different time experiences possible. Following Merleau-Ponty on this point, I have often compared this sort of overdetermined sexual sphere with Freud's "polymorphously perverse" sexuality that represents an early stage of sexual development in which female or male identities are not yet developed but face the opportunity to develop.[16] I argue, with the help of Merleau-Ponty, that sexual difference presupposes an anonymous sexuality that underlies all our sexual experiences, and also the differentiation between gender identities. As in Freud, female and male sexuality are later developments, also "men" and "women" and whatever signifying gender identities are second-order terms, as Merleau-Ponty would argue with Freud. Anonymous sexuality is a sphere where sexuality is lived without division, and in particular, without designated gender identities. That means, *there is* sexuality, *il y a sexualité,* but it is not yet named or analytically differentiated.

Finally, we can turn to anonymous temporality. According to Merleau-Ponty, "there is" temporality that is not yet named or determined, but that underlies all our specific temporal experiences, women's and men's. Merleau-Ponty calls this "primordial temporality," which is a kind of temporality that "is not juxtaposition of external events, since it is the power which holds them together while keeping them apart."[17] Like anonymous sexuality, anonymous temporality is a latent sphere of temporality that underlies the different time experiences of genders. It is a sphere of temporal generality in which genders do share even as they have their specific time experiences. It is an underlying sphere of temporality that makes gender-specific time experiences possible since they arise from it. Just as Freud's polymorphous sexuality is not without sexuality, the anonymous temporality in Merleau-Ponty's phenomenology is not without temporality. However, this sort of temporality is different from that which can be identified as the temporality of women or men. Since it is defined as anonymous, by definition it resists a conceptual identification or determination in terms of time. Since it is a temporality "not yet named," it remains indeterminable. Anonymous temporality is what Merleau-Ponty, in his *Phenomenology of Perception,* has identified as "primordial experience" that, as lived experience, precedes any intellectual analysis or reflection and serves as the basis upon which analysis and reflection are built. One might also say, with the help of Freud's vocabulary, that anonymous temporality is a polymorphous temporality, characterized by a surplus of temporality that stands for a horizon against and from which any specific temporality derives, including the time experiences of women as well as of men and other gendered beings.

From a more practical perspective and to make the concept of "anonymous temporality" more concrete, I would like to distinguish between three forms of anonymous temporality. First, there is one on the side of the "subject," that is to say, that I am not always aware of my own "temporality" in a strict sense. In order to reflect upon my own age, for example, or to make myself aware of the very fact that I am mortal, a shift from the lived perspective to the reflective perspective, in which I start to reflect upon my previously lived temporality, must take place. Anonymous temporality is transformed into a determined temporality. Second, there is one on the side of the "object." In my lived experience toward the other I do not always know how old the other is. I may have a certain sense of her or his aged being, but it remains anonymous, that means not yet named or determined, up to the point where I start to consciously reflect upon her or his age and finally end up with a reflective judgment: "She is forty-five years old." Third, there is an anonymous sphere of temporality on the level of sociality. Our social relations are not only deeply shaped by generational structures that remain mostly unconscious to us while relating to each other (e.g., the relation of a daughter to her mother), our interactions also take place within a certain time and they are always part of a historical epoch. However, while operating in the world we can speak only of a latent knowledge we have from this specific time and epoch. Time is there, but only in an unconscious, latent, or anonymous way. This anonymous temporality can be characterized as polymorphous since it remains a resource for the acts of determination with regard to time.

Conclusions

Theorists of female temporality are right in claiming that there are sexually differentiated time experiences. However, such an approach falsely universalizes gender experiences. It does not take into account that certain experiences can be shared by other genders in one way or another. For this reason, we are confronted with the old and well-known problem of claiming female identity without taking differences among women into account. Moreover, biological argumentations ignore the influence of culture over temporal experiences. Here we are confronted with the problem of biological determination and the inability to explain cultural differences and changes within culture. Finally, theorists of female temporality cannot explain from where this "sense" of femaleness with respect to temporality comes. If we do not want to claim that gendered temporality exists from the very beginning, and if we do not want to claim that the sexual differentiation of female and male temporality takes place outside of time, then the assumption of an underlying respectively anonymous temporality becomes necessary.

Phenomenology provides us with a tool for reflecting upon the very ontological conditions of gendered temporalities. The concept of anonymous temporality enables us to understand where the differentiations of femaleness/maleness or female/male temporality, or, returning to our starting point of Maya Deren, different "time senses," stem from. Moreover, the fact of anonymous temporality resists the issue of two distinct gendered temporalities. Since anonymous temporality, by definition, designates an open field of temporality that is not yet determined, it becomes possible to think of time experiences that exceed the narrow field of sexual difference, as a difference between two, and consequently, as a difference conceived in terms of heterosexuality. It is at this point that the phenomenological notion of anonymity can open the field for the *political* in terms of a plurality of gendered experiences of time, which means a plurality of gendered time experiences that is not restricted to the difference between man and woman.

Notes

I would like to thank those who have commented on my paper at the conference in Vechta. My special thanks go to my friend Ida Černe as well as to Helen Fielding, who helped me with the English language, and to Dorothea Olkowski for her helpful remarks.

1. Anonymity is a key concept in phenomenology, especially in Husserl, Merleau-Ponty, and Levinas. In the past I have applied the concept of anonymity to the issue of gender and sexual difference (see, e.g., my "(Phänomenologische) Anonymität und (sexuelle) Differenz"; "Phänomenologie der Geschlechtlichkeit"; and "Anonymität als Bestimmung von Welt." For further efforts that take up Merleau-Ponty's notion of anonymity in the framework

of feminist philosophy, see Olkowski, "Only Nature Is Mother to the Child," and Kruks, "Merleau-Ponty and the Problem of Difference in Feminism."

2. Maya Deren (1917–61) was a famous and legendary filmmaker, a key figure of the American avant-garde in the 1940s and 1950s. She became famous for her film theory and her films on the Haitian Voudoun.

3. This quote is a transcript of the documentary film *In the Mirror of Maya Deren*. Deren speaks of the "concept of a child" but presumably means "birth of a child."

4. Cited from the film *In the Mirror of Maya Deren,* made by Martina Kudláček (2001). I would like to thank the Austrian society Sixpack for making a VHS video of this documentary film available for the conference in Vechta where this paper was first presented in 2006.

5. Cf. Stoller and Waniek, "Universität, Bildung und Politik. Eine Bestandsaufnahme aus feministischer Sicht."

6. It might be interesting to note that pregnancy might also influence the male partner on a biological level. Expectant fathers often gain weight during their partner's pregnancy, and even go through a kind of pregnancy themselves (participating in birth classes, they may take on an actual attitude of waiting, which might even have effects on their bodies). Studies have shown that men's hormonal levels also change during their partner's pregnancy (see, e.g., Wynne-Edwards, „Why Do Some Men Experience Pregnancy Symptoms Such As Vomiting and Nausea When Their Wives are Pregnant?"). I thank Ida černe for drawing my attention to this phenomenon.

7. Kristeva, "Women's Time." Kristeva distinguishes between three different sorts of times: the linear, the cyclical, and the monumental time. I would like to thank Gertrude Postl for reminding me of this early paper of Kristeva.

8. Merleau-Ponty, *Phenomenology of Perception,* 410.

9. Stoller, *Existenz, Differenz, Konstruktion*, ch. 7.

10. Butler, *Gender Trouble,* 143.

11. Ibid.

12. Husserl, *Analysis Concerning Passive and Active Synthesis,* 41.

13. Ibid., 42. Gail Weiss touches on the idea of indeterminacy and its various forms presented in French philosophy ("Ambiguity, Absurdity, and Reversibility: Responses to Indeterminacy").

14. Husserl, *Analysis Concerning Passive and Active Synthesis,* 60.

15. Gail Weiss rightly has made me conscious of the fact that indeterminacy and overdetermination, strictly speaking, are not exactly the same. While indeterminacy means something is *in*determined, *over*determination refers to something that has several or many determinations. As I understand the argument, in indeterminacy there is a lack (in German, *Leere*), whereas in overdetermination there is a richness (in German, *Fülle*). While I am very grateful for this lucid consideration, I must, nevertheless, point out that what is overdetermined is, at the same time, not determined in form of distinctiveness or predication. The overdetermined has no name yet; it remains unclassified, and it is there only in vagueness. This is what, incidentally, "anonymity" shares with "indeterminacy," since the Greek "an ònyma" means "unnamed" or "not yet named."

16. See Freud, *Three Essays on the Theory of Sexuality.*
17. Merleau-Ponty, *Phenomenology of Perception,* 422.

Bibliography

Butler, Judith. *Gender Trouble: Feminism and the Subversion of Identity.* London: Routledge, 1990.

Freud, Sigmund. *Three Essays on the Theory of Sexuality.* Trans. James Strachey. New York: Basic Books, 2000.

Husserl, Edmund. *Analyses Concerning Passive and Active Synthesis: Lectures on Transcendental Logic.* Trans. Anthony J. Steinbock. Dordrecht: Kluwer Academic Publishers, 2001.

Kristeva, Julia. "Women's Time." In *The Continental Philosophy Reader,* ed. Richard Kearney and Mara Rainwater, 378–401. London: Routledge, 1996.

Kruks, Sonia. "Merleau-Ponty and the Problem of Difference in Feminism." In *Feminist Interpretations of Maurice Merleau-Ponty,* ed. Dorothea Olkowski and Gail Weiss, 25–47. University Park: Pennsylvania State University Press, 2006.

Kudláček, Martina. *In the Mirror of Maya Deren.* Austria, Switzerland, Germany. 103 minutes, 2001.

Merleau-Ponty, Maurice. *Phenomenology of Perception.* Trans. Colin Smith. London: Routledge, 1962.

Olkowski, Dorothea. "Only Nature Is Mother to the Child." In *Feminist Interpretations of Maurice Merleau-Ponty,* ed. Dorothea Olkowski and Gail Weiss, 49–70. University Park: Pennsylvania State University Press, 2006.

Stoller, Silvia. "Anonymität als Bestimmung von Welt." In *"Welten": Zur Welt als Phänomen,* ed. Günther Pöltner and Martin Wiesbauer, 51–68. Frankfurt/Main: Peter Lang, 2008.

———. *Existenz—Differenz—Konstruktion: Phänomenologie der Geschlechtlichkeit bei Beauvoir, Irigaray und Butler.* Munich: Wilhelm Fink, 2010.

———. "(Phänomenologische) Anonymität und (sexuelle) Differenz." In *Verhandlungen des Geschlechts. Zur Konstruktivismusdebatte in der Gender-Theorie,* ed. Eva Waniek and Silvia Stoller, 238–49. Vienna: Turia + Kant, 2001.

Stoller, Silvia, and Eva Waniek. "Universität, Bildung und Politik. Eine Bestandsaufnahme aus feministischer Sicht." *IWK-Mitteilungen* 4 (1996): 1–5.

Weiss, Gail. "Ambiguity, Absurdity, and Reversibility: Responses to Indeterminacy." *Journal of the British Society for Phenomenology* 26, no. 1 (1995): 43–51.

Wynne-Edwards, Katherine E. "Why Do Some Men Experience Pregnancy Symptoms Such As Vomiting and Nausea When Their Wives Are Pregnant?" *Scientific American,* June 28, 2004. http://www.sciam.com/article.cfm?id=why-do-some-men-experienc&print=true (accessed February 19, 2007).

6.

GENDERING EMBODIED MEMORY

Linda Fisher

> *I take up a field and invent myself (but not without my temporal equipment),*
> *just as I move about in the world (but not without the unknown mass of*
> *my body). Time is that "body of the spirit" Valéry used to talk about.*
>
> —*Signs, 14–15.*

Although in the everyday frame of mind (when our deeper awareness is often parenthetical), we tend to think of our bodies as primarily distinguished by their mass and volume and tangibility—in other words, their spatial qualities—our bodies are, of course, eminently temporal. Indeed the temporality of our bodies might well be even more primordial than their spatiality, at least from the perspective of the lived body. Our embodied being is drenched with temporality, from the moment we appear in time to our fading out, our leaving time; when we are, in all senses, out of time. In between, temporality colors, conditions, and etches our experience and being by situating us, while simultaneously moving us along, structuring, regulating, "timing" us, and finally propelling us through life's stages, phases, and shadings as we age and proceed toward our own end of time, inexorably.

In what follows I engage these themes of embodied time and temporal bodies from the perspective of feminist phenomenology. Specifically, with the notion and category of gender in view, I consider how temporal embodiment could be gendered, or alternately put, how embodied temporality could be read through the lens of gender. To be sure, analyses of gender and temporality are not unknown. However, within the intertwined approach of feminist phenomenology I wish to look at how phenomenologies of time and temporality might be amenable to and enhanced by a gendered analysis, and in turn accounts of gender extended by incorporating insights from phenomenologies of time and temporality.

The focus of my phenomenological analysis is Merleau-Ponty's discussion in his *Phenomenology of Perception* of the spatiality of the body and motility. It appears at first glance to confirm my observation above about the priority often placed on the spatiality of the body, along with being a seemingly odd choice for an analysis of embodied temporality. But as will become clear, temporality runs through his discussion as a persistent, albeit somewhat fleeting and unacknowledged, theme—but realized most notably, I will argue, in his culminating account of habit, and what, drawing on this account, I will elaborate as embodied memory. Before embarking on my examination of Merleau-Ponty's account, however, I begin by discussing the relation of phenomenology and gender and in particular the task and way of gendering phenomenology. As such, in the first section I lay out how we might think phenomenologically about gender and gendered lived experience and subjectivity, and what a gendered analysis might bring to phenomenology. I then turn to my discussion of Merleau-Ponty's account of the spatiality of the body and motility, and his analysis of habit. In the final section I explore how, in light of the foregoing discussions, we can begin to think about gendering embodied memory, as well as gender as embodied memory.

Gendering Phenomenology

My point of departure is simply this: gender is a fundamental component of social existence and subjective lived experience, and as such, phenomenology, as the descriptive science of subjective lived experience, must undertake and incorporate an analysis of gendered lived experience.

That is, our lived experience is not merely incidentally gendered, with our gender just a trait or characteristic among others. Rather, gender, or more importantly the situation of *being gendered,* permeates and frames that experience such that gender is more than a mere trait or property, but a fundamental conditioning feature of lived experience. As such a feature of our experiencing, of our situation and how we have the world, the category of gender calls out for a phenomenological treatment, and relevant phenomenological analyses need to be gendered. Moreover, to the extent that gender, as a complex specification of both our natural embodiment and cultural being, conditions how we are in the world, it is constitutive of our subjective experience and being and can be seen, I argue, as a modality of our subjectivity. In other words, the embodied subject, who as embodied interacts in a social surrounding world with other subjects, is more fundamentally a gendered subject, pointing to the sense of our subjectivity as gendered. Thus phenomenologies of subjectivity and subjective experience must also examine gender as both feature and constituent of that subjectivity.

First, a brief word about the term "gender" itself. One of the earliest initiatives of feminist theorizing was to counter the conventional understanding of the origins of the differences between the sexes as grounded in biological givens. Feminist critics targeted such received views as the naturalized source and justificatory discourse of the oppression of women (as encapsulated in the much-cited Freudian axiom of "Biology is Destiny"). Concerns about a biological determinism and reductionism potentially implied in any focus on "sex characteristics" prompted feminists and women's studies scholars to renounce the use of "sex" and "sex differences" in favor of the term "gender." "Gender" not only avoided the problematic connotations of biology, but emphasized the character and origins of such traits, roles, and behaviors in socialization. In keeping with this terminological shift, the sex/gender distinction was instituted by feminists (as well as other scholars in social science doing similar research),[1] where sex denoted the bio-physical aspects of our being, and gender the social or acculturated aspects.

To be sure, many gender dimensions and ideologies could be traced to long-standing conventional sex-based attributions—the base, as it were, upon which gender had been "built"—but the category of gender was quickly seen to comprise an extensive and systemic network of sociopolitical relations and symbolic systems that clearly went beyond the mere acculturation of biological properties. Accordingly, gender could no longer be seen as simply a given set of traits, roles, and behaviors, much less just a regular sociological or anthropological category, but now also designated complex and interwoven structures of entrenched asymmetry, hierarchy, and power. As such, gender was now seen as a political category, a significant organizing principle of sociopolitical relations and forces, and importantly, a key concept in analyses of political and socioeconomic systems of hierarchy and power distribution.

These frameworks, along with the related growth and development of gender theory, including formulations of the intricate amalgam of agency, representation, and performance in gender identity, are the current prevailing frameworks for gender research. However, some of these analyses have come under criticism (particularly from feminist philosophers) for being too heavily reliant on social constructionist models, and neglecting the material and embodied, not to mention the subjective, psychic, and interpersonal, dimensions of sexed and gendered existence,[2] while the sex/gender distinction itself was increasingly questioned, then mostly abandoned, now seen as overly binary and oppositional.

While mindful of all these considerations, I propose to use the terms "gender" and "gendered" for the most part, by which I do not mean simply sociocultural products or discursive effects, but a synthetic and dialectical relation whereby gender and gender attributions are intertwined with lived embodiment, and this embodiment is always read in a particular sociocultural context—gender as acculturated corporeality *and* embodied and naturalized social ontology. In short, gender is both cultural product and organizing principle of sociopolitical relations and forces and lived, bodily, experiential category; both conditioning horizon of experience and phenomenal datum and modality of subjective experience.[3]

The foregoing is clearly bound up with the claim that gender is experientially relevant. Extensive psychological, historical, anthropological, and sociological studies, along with feminist analyses concerning gender, have documented and underscored the role that gender plays in shaping and conditioning our experience, social circumstances, and history. So that, for example, depending on our determined biological sex, at birth we are given a name that (usually) reflects and specifies a particular gender, and our subsequent gender socialization encodes particular tasks and activities, appearances, roles, and expectations for us—such prescriptions increasingly being challenged, certainly, but by virtue of being in a position *to be* challenged, still having a hold nonetheless.[4] From a sociological perspective gender begins as a marker, conventionally predetermined and fixed, of our social definition and status; our sex socialized, as noted above, in a complex sociocultural symbolic system that extends far beyond anatomical properties or biological capacities. However, the intersubjective dimension is immediately imposed: in interactive social situations always already delineated and framed according to given gender attributions, those respective attributions suggest, if not mandate, guidelines and rules for conduct, communication, and the ensuing dynamics of the situation—how we perceive, define, behave toward, and interact with others, and they with us. This is true of the various possible sexed and gendered combinations in such sociality (i.e., women and men, women and women, men and men), but a further complexity is the dimension of sexuality and various intentionalities of desire, bound up to be sure with dynamics of sex and gender, and as such often (some would argue always) further layering and conditioning, and complicating the already complex nature of sociality.[5]

Theorists of race, class, and sexuality will point out that in numerous contexts and circumstances, one's race or class or sexuality can equally dictate prescribed roles or treatment; and indeed, many question the legitimacy of even discussing any one of these categories in isolation from the others, arguing that they coexist and are codetermined in an entangled sociopolitical dynamic in which these interlocking identities are not reducible to singular categories. As such, many theorists advocate adopting approaches such as the "intersectionality" approach, exploring the interaction and intertwining of multiple social positions and identities.

It is undeniable that other categories and social positions are also extremely significant and influential. I would like to argue nevertheless that it is possible to analyze these various categories individually, and moreover, that gender occupies a distinctive position in our experiencing and apprehension of the world. It does not necessarily take priority over other categories or have primacy, for example from a sociopolitical standpoint,[6] but gender does seem to possess a singular character that can justify a more specific focus, particularly in phenomenological terms. Consider, for instance, the evident importance of knowing the gender of the person we are dealing with in terms of proceeding to interact with that person. Cases of *not* knowing, or not being sure of, a person's gender are usually regarded as confusing or disorienting experiences. On the other hand, while in some contexts knowing that a person is one race rather than another may influence the nature of the interaction, in other circumstances it may not be a crucial item of knowledge or significant determining factor. In other words, while a racist may always need to know, for racist reasons, the race of the person he or she is dealing with, for a non-racist, in many neutral circumstances, it would presumably be irrelevant.

While clearly gender can also be less relevant in given circumstances, it still seems to have deeper—perhaps we can even say ontological—dimensions. Our habitual need to ascertain and establish the gender of the other person in a given situation or interaction determines in turn a wide spectrum of accordingly adjusted intersubjective behaviors, ranging from modes of address to bodily comportment, especially in view of the often attendant matrix of gender/desire/sexuality. A salient example of the importance of definitive gender determination in many cultures can be found in the increasingly controversial cases of intersex babies—babies born with underdetermined or "ambiguous" genitalia/sex characteristics.[7] In many such cases, following consultations with the parents and relevant medical personnel, the baby undergoes "corrective" surgical procedures to bestow a clear sex designation one way or the other. In many respects this response is perhaps an understandable reaction to the normative societal mandates regarding gender identity—that it be unambiguously defined as one or the other—while cognizant of the difficulties awaiting the child who does not conform to this. But at the same time what is also being corrected in such instances is a culturally unacceptable (in most Western or European societies at least) sex and gender ambiguity. On the one hand, Western cultures are often intolerant of such ambiguity—or, it is tolerated as a lurid voyeuristic spectacle, in forms of carnivalesque exoticism, such as past freak-show exhibitions of "hermaphrodites."[8] On the other hand, on a more fundamental psychological and experiential level (admittedly conditioned by sociocultural prescriptions), such ambiguity seems to be extremely disconcerting or unsettling—think, for example, of the reaction transgender or transsexual individuals are sometimes subject to.

Given the vast array of acculturated gender traits and behaviors, the extensive and pervasive symbolic systems and regimes of socialization, enforced in processes of sociopolitical and hierarchical relations, not to mention a variety of interpersonal and psychosexual dynamics, the pressing question truly seems to be whether gender is *ever* irrelevant. As such, while acknowledging the importance of other categories, and their interrelations and intersectionality, I maintain nevertheless that there is something experientially distinctive and significant, if not irreducible, about the category of gender.[9] Gender is a fundamental constitutive factor in our lived situation, which is always, even within the social context, also the situation of a subject: having a gender, being gendered, being *this* rather than *that* gender, conditions and layers our everyday experiences as we live them and our personal lived history. We are the subjects of these experiences and history; they are conditioned by the fact that we are gendered, and we are thus gendered subjects.

Gendered experience is therefore the proper subject of a phenomenology of such lived experience, and this makes the gendering of phenomenology imperative, in a twofold sense: (1) a developed analysis of gender and gendered experience from a phenomenological perspective, as a fundamental experiential modality; and (2) the gendering of phenomenological analyses, in investigating which accounts or experiential phenomena would benefit from, if not require, gendered analyses or specifications. To take a well-known example, Merleau-Ponty's accounts of embodiment and sexuality in his discussions of the "body-subject" have been criticized by feminists for the absence of sexed or gendered specifications, among others, thematizing instead a generic embodied experience (which, they argue, is in fact a default male one).[10] Such earlier omissions do not mean that gendered analyses are not viable phenomenologically, nor do they preclude the gendered phenomenological analysis; rather, phenomenology provides precisely the frame and mode of investigation in which such further relevant variations and particularities might be delineated and thematized, even if previous phenomenologists did not always pursue such analyses.[11]

Furthermore, to the extent that there is validity in the critiques of those phenomenological analyses that present an ostensibly generic or neutral mode of embodiment or subjectivity, but one that actually bears male or masculine characteristics or overlooks pertinent female ones—the traditional feminist critique that such masculine modes are taken as default and universal—then with respect to such analyses, phenomenology is already gendered. That is, analyses that evince specifications of male modes of being or experiencing are already gendered analyses. What is needed, then, is to supplement these with analyses of specifically female modes of being and experiencing, not just to supply hitherto missing accounts or modalities, but to ensure that particularized women's experiences are also thematized and their meanings examined—in short, that they are also given their phenomenological due. Such thematizations of women's experiences have certainly already been undertaken—Beauvoir's groundbreaking discussions in *The Second Sex* and Iris Marion Young's early work on female embodiment[12] being notable examples—but much still remains to be done.

The Spatiality of the Body, Motility, and Habit

At the end of the third chapter of the section on "The Body" in his *Phenomenology of Perception*,[13] in which, as promised by the title, he discusses the spatiality of the body and motility, Merleau-Ponty states that in sum, "what we have discovered through the study of motility, is a new meaning of the word 'meaning'" [*un nouveau sens du mot "sens"*].[14] The sense, as it were, of the word "*sens*" will prove especially significant for this analysis, given that along with signifying meaning, "*sens*" denotes direction or sense. Acknowledging that the strength of intellectualist psychology and idealist philosophy was the demonstration that perception and thought have "an intrinsic significance" and cannot be explained in the terms of associationist or empiricist accounts, Merleau-Ponty notes, however, that in such rationalism all meaning is conceived as an act of thought, "as the work of a pure *I*."[15] And while this is capable of refuting empiricism, it is itself unable to account for the variety of experience, Merleau-Ponty says, for the element of senselessness and the contingency of contents.

The earlier analysis of bodily experience, on the other hand, has led us to recognize an "imposition of meaning" that is not the work of a universal constituting consciousness, but rather adheres to the contents of experience. The meaning "clings to" the content, but is not "in" the content as such, but instead is enacted through my bodily involvement with the world. As such, "my body is that meaningful core which behaves like a general function."[16] Thus, the "new meaning of the word 'meaning'" is a meaning that, in the characteristic Merleau-Pontian eschewal of the familiar conventional alternatives, is neither intellectualist and cognitivist nor realist and empiricist, but a corporeally mediated meaning, an intertwining of bodily meaning and meaningful body.

This "meaningful functioning" that is our body lends an additional layer and deepens the well-known formulation that "the body is our general medium for having a world."[17] Read initially in terms of the body as our situation in, our opening and mode of access to, the world—in short, in multiple respects our modality for "having the world"—what is now also suggested is an existential hermeneutics of the body as interpreter of the world and enactor of meaning; the deepening mediated by the doubled (and dialectical) sense of "medium," as mode and intermediary. This hermeneutics of the body is similarly unfolded in a twofold sense, that of the bodily and embodied nexus of world-meanings, and the body as mediator and interpreter of the world and world-meanings, in the sense of hermeneutic intermediary. The "body as our medium" thus has the interwoven senses of situation, mode, and manner, along with mediator and facilitator of experience, meaning, and significance. Together, this is what having the world consists in.[18]

Merleau-Ponty arrives at this culminating account of the meaningful body in the course of the chapter's examination of motility, the bodily enactment of and relation to movement and spatiality, and this is mediated in turn by the penultimate analysis of habit. That is, the analysis of habit is itself the medium whereby the examination of movement and spatiality is able to disclose the meaningful body in its implications for existence and perception generally. Habit is the mediator between bodily space and spatiality, enacted through motility and bodily meaning; it is the body that "understands" in the cultivation of habit [c'est le corps qui "comprend" dans l'acquisition de l'habitude].[19] In a variety of ways, the meaningful body performs, Merleau-Ponty says, a "function which is to endow the instantaneous expressions of spontaneity with 'a little renewable action and independent existence,'" borrowing a phrase from Valéry.[20] Habit is a form of this "fundamental power," and "the body has understood and habit has been cultivated when it has absorbed a new meaning, and assimilated a fresh core of significance."[21]

This process of taking in new meaning and fresh significance underscores the sense of bodily enactment and incorporation of meaning ("absorbed"; "assimilated"), while signaling additionally a temporal character. Time and temporality are, in this chapter on spatiality, a persistent if somewhat elusive theme. Yet insofar as the body clearly inhabits both space and time, and these are inseparably intertwined, bodily time and temporality are also very much at play throughout the analysis of bodily space and motility. Indeed, I want to suggest that in the concluding discussion of habit, temporality comes into its own, as it were, insofar as the mediating function of habit for bodily space and bodily meaning is temporal: in terms of the fundamental temporality of any action or movement and the temporal character of intending and performing meaning, in its dialectic of possibility and actuality, as well as the character of repetition and renewal in habit. Finally, the mediation of spatiality/motility and meaning cannot take place on strictly intellectualist or associationist/mechanistic terms; nor, I would argue, on spatial and motor terms, even in consideration of the situational and meaningful bodily space that Merleau-Ponty articulates. Rather, in habit we see the sedimentation—itself a temporal notion—of meaning and significance, attained and (re)enacted through bodily action and motility, in the form of the habitual body and embodied memory. That is, the body that understands, that acquires and enacts meaning, is the body that remembers.

Merleau-Ponty's analysis of the spatiality of the body and motility opens with an examination of the relation of intent to meaning with respect to the mediating and enacting function of the body in this relation—again, not only how the body is meaningful, but also, how meaning is bodily—and specifically how the mediation of meaning will be enacted in bodily motility and motor capacity. In asking about the body image, as corporeal schema, Merleau-Ponty notes that psychologists often say that the body image is dynamic. What this means is that "my body appears to me as an attitude directed towards a certain existing or possible task."[22] This has implications for the body's spatiality, which, as it turns out, is not like that of external objects, insofar as it is not a spatiality of position, but a spatiality of situation. A subsequent discussion of the relation of bodily space and external space surmised that the two form a "practical system," the first being the background against which the object as the goal of our action stands out. As such, "it is clearly in action that the spatiality of our body is brought into being," and the analysis of our movement will enable a better understanding of this spatiality. As Merleau-Ponty states: "By considering the body in movement, we can see better how it inhabits space (and, moreover, time) because movement is not limited to submitting passively to space and time, it actively assumes them, it takes them up in their basic significance which is obscured in the commonplaceness of established situations."[23] By way of elucidating the fundamental relations between the body and space, Merleau-Ponty proceeds to an analysis of an example of "morbid motility" [*motricité morbide*].[24] This is in keeping with his characteristic analytical strategy of examining the irregular, atypical, or in some manner impaired case, as a counterpoint to illuminate the more typical or regular occurrence. Morbid motility manifests as motility or motor disturbances, and Merleau-Ponty focuses his reflection on the celebrated case of Schneider, a war veteran who sustained a head injury and as a result suffered from what was termed "psychic blindness" by traditional psychiatry. Schneider is unable to perform "abstract" movements with his eyes shut, that is, movements that are not relevant to any actual situation, such as moving his arms or legs when requested. He can manage the abstract movements only if he is allowed to watch the limb needed to perform them or to go through some preparatory movements involving the entire body. Yet at the same time, even with his eyes closed he is able to quickly and precisely carry out the movements needed in "living his life, provided that he is in the habit of performing them," for example, taking a handkerchief from his pocket and blowing his nose, or taking a match from a box and lighting a lamp.[25] He can even perform these "concrete" movements on order, and without any preparatory movement. By the same token, although he is able to grasp something, he is unable to point on order to something. Merleau-Ponty notes that in many such cases there is a dissociation of the act of pointing from the actions of taking or grasping, leaving him to posit that "'grasping' or 'touching,' even for the body, is different from 'pointing.'"[26] Schneider, says Merleau-Ponty, is "conscious of his bodily space as the matrix of his habitual action, but not as an objective setting; his body is at his disposal as a means of ingress into a familiar surrounding, but not as the means of expression of a gratuitous and free spatial thought."[27]

Speaking of the capacity for a kind of "potential movement," Merleau-Ponty observes that in the case of the normal subject, the body not only is available in real situations into which it is drawn, but also can turn aside from the world and apply its activity to stimuli that affect its sensory surfaces, and generally take its place in the realm of the potential. But because of its "confinement within the actual" an impaired sense of touch requires special movements designed to localize stimuli.[28] As such, "whereas in the normal person every event related to movement or sense of touch causes consciousness to put up a host of intentions which run from the body as the centre of potential action either towards the body itself or towards the object, in the case of the patient, on the other hand, the tactile impression remains opaque and sealed up."[29]

In the case of patients who understand an order but have difficulty executing the requested movement, in looking to the body to perform the movement, the patient is, says Merleau-Ponty, like a speaker who cannot utter a word without following a previously prepared text. The order given is not meaningless, but it has an *intellectual significance* for him, and not a *motor* one, and it communicates nothing to him as a mobile subject: "What he lacks is neither motility nor thought, and we are brought to the recognition of something between movement as a third person process and thought as a representation of movement—something which is an anticipation of, or arrival at, the objective and is ensured by the body itself as a motor power, a 'motor project' (*Bewegungsentwurf*), a 'motor intentionality' in the absence of which the order remains a dead letter."[30] As such, Merleau-Ponty's exhaustive analysis of the various disturbances leads him to frame motility as "basic intentionality," and in the well-known formulation he thus states that consciousness is not in the first instance a matter of "I think that," but of "I can," drawing on terminology from Husserl.[31] A page earlier Merleau-Ponty had indicated that the life of consciousness is subtended by an "intentional arc" that projects around us our past, future, context, and our various situations, enabling us to be situated in these respects. Moreover, the intentional arc ensures the unity of the senses, of intelligence, sensibility, and motility. And it is this, says Merleau-Ponty, that "goes limp" in the case of illness.[32] Schneider's motor difficulties cannot be reduced to a failure of the function of representation. That is, consciousness is not representation, movement is not thought about movement, and bodily space is not space thought of or represented. Accordingly, we can think of disturbances or breakdowns in motility as thereby connected to a breakdown in intentionality, or at least as impaired intentionality—in this case, the "I can" compromised, "gone limp" in an "I cannot."

In sum, then, "Consciousness is being towards the thing through the inter-mediary of the body. A movement is learned when the body has understood it, that is, when it has incorporated it into its 'world', and to move one's body is to aim at things through it."[33] Thus, it is not that our body is *in* space or *in* time, but rather that it *inhabits* space and time. As Merleau-Ponty notes, "I am not in space and time, nor do I conceive space and time; I belong to them, my body combines with them and includes them."[34] Intention is intricately connected to motility and spatial being, and in turn motility has a direct relation to meaning; it possesses the basic power of giving a meaning.[35] Meaning is bodily enacted in motility; the meaningful body is the body of movement.

This brings us back once again to the phenomenon of habit as a "rearrangement and renewal" of the body image. Habit, says Merleau-Ponty, presents difficulties to traditional philosophies, which tend to conceive synthesis as intellectual synthesis. By the same token, the synthesizing process in habit of actions, reactions, and "stimuli" is not an external procedure of association of individual movements and individual stimuli. Rather, Merleau-Ponty says, the subject "acquires the power to respond with a certain type of solution to situations of a certain general form."[36]

There is a manner of organization of elements in the acquisition of a habit, and as such what takes place is indeed the grasping of a significance. But as Merleau-Ponty points out, it is the motor grasping of a motor significance, in keeping with the notion of a body that "understands" movement. Our bodily space is extended to a situational orientation, whereby, for example, someone just knows the safe distance between the feather in his hat and objects that might break it off, or when driving knows without needing to calculate whether or not she can fit the car through a given opening. The blind man's cane is no longer an object for him and perceived for itself, but rather an extension of his touch.[37] More than a mere interrelation or interlacing, there is in this instance a fundamental incarnation. To develop a habituality with such objects in this manner is, Merleau-Ponty states, to be transplanted into them, or conversely to incorporate them into our own body.[38] "Habit expresses our power of dilating our being in the world, or changing our existence by appropriating fresh instruments."[39]

The typist knows how to type without being able to specify the precise loca-tion of the letters on the keyboard; the musician can play her instrument without needing to represent to herself the correct position of the keys or stops. To know how to type is not to know where each letter is among the keys, nor to have a conditioned reflex that is triggered by the letter as we see it. Habit is not a form of knowledge, nor is it an involuntary action, so, Merleau-Ponty asks, what is it then? The answer is that it is knowledge in the hands, forthcoming only when bodily effort is made. In contrast to the view that would characterize typing as a process whereby the perception of a letter on paper gives rise to the representation of this letter, which in turn gives rise to the representation of the movement required to produce it on the typewriter, Merleau-Ponty asserts that patterns are formed as we look, which are endowed with a typical or familiar physiognomy: "When I sit at my typewriter, a motor space opens up beneath my hands, in which I am about to 'play' what I have read."[40] The question is how these "visual" patterns evoke a motor response, that is, how intent is actualized, translated into performance, and how this relation is enacted. Reiterating the notion that it is the body which "understands" in the cultivation of habit, Merleau-Ponty now frames understanding as the harmony between "what we aim at and what is given, between the intention and the performance—and the body is our anchorage in a world."[41] The typist's movements are governed by an intention, but that intention does not posit the keys as objective locations, says Merleau-Ponty. Rather the subject who knows how to type has incorporated the space of the keys into his or her bodily space. We can see even better how habit resides neither in thought nor in the objective body, but in the body as mediator of a world, when we consider the example of instrumentalists. Taking the example of an organist, Merleau-Ponty notes that an experienced organist is fully capable of playing a new organ with different configurations than the organist's usual instrument after only a short preparation. During this preparation the organist acquaints himself or herself with the instrument, the pedals, the stops, and so on, incorporating within herself or himself the relevant elements. Between the musical score and the actual notes from the organ, a direct relation is established such that "the organist's body and his instrument are merely the medium of this relationship."[42]

This unfolds the character of the body as expressive space, as well as intention and purpose enacted through motility. One issue here is the question of how the body enacts in motility a given intention, such as walking to the window or picking up an object. It is a similar, though possibly more complex, issue of how the body translates a collection of words or notations on a score into typed text or performed music. There is a process of translating these that is still bodily, but also involves a comprehension of the "idea" to be actualized in text or music. This is where the phenomenon of habit, as the possibility of a habitual action, but also as a recurring and embedded practice, comes into play, as it were. The origin of all meaning and significance is the body, as we know; and habit is a particularly interesting example of the mediation and enactment of this meaning in a manner that draws on previous enactments, while carrying them through into further, and in some respects transformed, enactments. Merleau-Ponty says that the body "understands," that "knowledge is in the hands"; however, this does not seem to be sufficient to account for how these processes can take place.

This is where I think a more developed notion of embodied memory can prove helpful. Within the living system of meanings the dynamic body image moves and acts as "an attitude directed towards a certain existing or possible task."[43] Striving for and attaining meanings, the body is not only a temporal enacting, that is, an enacting in time and through time, but also a process of recognizing and enacting relations between thought and action, intent and meaning. Enacting these relations in which the body somehow recognizes and understands is not an intellectualist procedure of applying concept to contents of experience, let alone mechanistically reacting through reflex to stimuli. It is, rather, a complex interaction between bodily motility and motor capacity, intent and aim, each mediated by a temporal flow. This flow is, to be sure, not a linear movement from point A to point B and so on, but rather a movement "forward" or toward, which entails a casting back and then a revitalized movement onward and outward again within an action that has been at most renewed and refreshed. It is a banality by now to say that movement is temporal and temporality is a movement. The deepened sense revealed here is that temporality is not only embodied; it is also enacted in motility and motor capacity, as movement is enacted through the temporal understanding of the body, facilitated specifically through the bodily memory of the habitual body.

Merleau-Ponty says at various points that it is not a question of "memory" per se, if by that is meant an intellectualist or mechanistic memory, let alone a kind of behaviorism. There is something in the phenomenon and experience of playing an instrument, for example, that entails a kind of embodied memory, not only of the external aspects such as the position of keys or pedals, or which keys produce which notes. So there is a sense in which the capacity to play and to play a certain piece of music, especially from memory (often termed in both English and French "play by heart," suggesting the corporeal aspect), does seem to point toward a memory process: not a stored memory, or the "warehouse" notion of memory, but a remembering process. For example, when I used to play the piano, from time to time when playing something "by heart" I would forget how a sequence went, or lose track of what came next. It was no good to attempt to think about the written music, let alone try to conceptualize or mentally represent to myself what the sheet music looked like, or the notation of the missing or lost phrase. What did work, however, was to play until I came to the memory lapse, and if necessary play the preceding part a number of times, until the lapsed sequence, and thereby the rest of the piece, came back. The remembering was like that of a retrieved memory—but unlike other instances of suddenly remembering something, where it can feel like retrieving a thought from some place in the mind it had been housed, in this case it was a distinctly bodily experience. The sensation here was of a memory contained—better yet, embedded—in my hands, which for some reason had become blocked or disrupted, or had faltered momentarily. And then, in that moment something happened, something triggered or relaxed, and the memory was "released" and came pouring out through my fingers. Long before I studied philosophy or had heard of Merleau-Ponty, I had this experience, which I used to think of as my hands remembering the piece for me. Indeed, music teachers will advise students to play or sing a piece over and over until it is ingrained and incorporated into the body and the muscles. This is not merely muscle memory, but the body learns it, and "remembers" it. In this manner the bodily memory will participate, if not lead, in performing the music even if the score is being used. Such an analysis of bodily memory seems to fit very well into an analysis of habit in the context of the body's spatiality and motility, although in this particular discussion, Merleau-Ponty does not pursue it.

Habit is a spatial as well as temporal phenomenon, mediated through the motility of the body. Unfolding the mediating role of habit as habitual and embedded practice clarifies the interlacing and correlative nature of spatiotemporal corporeal existence and being. It also underscores the manner in which our bodies not only move, act, feel, have intent, and so forth, but in complex and important ways that we still have not fully grasped, our bodies also remember.

Gendering Embodied Memory, Gender as Embodied Memory

We can now cast back to our point of departure, to our inquiry into gendering phenomenology, and draw it through the analysis of motility, habit, and the understanding, meaningful body. It is clear that there is much space, as it were, in such analyses for gendering, as well as for other possible specifications. Once again, this is not an implied critique of Merleau-Ponty for not having carried out more of these particularized analyses himself. Merleau-Ponty's body-subject is always a body-subject in situation. And this situation is formed and conditioned by a wide variety of factors: cultural, political, medical, historical, and so on. Gender as yet another modality is an obvious addition to the variables in any given situation, and can therefore be addressed and thematized within such a phenomenology. The body, as we have seen, is for Merleau-Ponty a meaningful body, a body imbued with meaning. While in a more theoretical sense Merleau-Ponty's body is that of a generality, it is also important to remember that embodied meaning for Merleau-Ponty is both general and particular, with specificities and individualities intertwining with the general sense of the body as the more generic mode of having a body. We are all embodied beings. That is, we share the situation of having a body as a possibility for living and for having the world. There are certainly commonalities that we all share with respect to having a body or being embodied, but there is also ample room for the myriad of variations and specifications that will characterize my particular body and embodiment, and everyone else's. We all have a body, and I have *my* body.[44]

As such, thematizing the particularities of my embodiment, or of any given individual's embodiment, is not only a phenomenological possibility, but a mandate. And as I have argued, gender is preeminently such a particularity and modality of our lived subjectivity, and as such must be integrated into and thematized within phenomenological analyses. Turning to the theme at hand of embodied temporality, and specifically embodied memory, how might such embodied memories be gendered? To the extent that both gender and embodiment are always already read in a temporalized sociocultural context, the layers of specification are seemingly endless when we begin to contemplate the multivalent ways that our lived temporalized activities and projects are gender coded, how our gendered experience and being is inextricably tied to our temporal and contextualized horizons. Themes ranging from embodied temporal experiences such as pregnancy to gendered traumatic memory to countless examples of body memory and place memory and embodied dwelling—in multiple cases inflected by gender—are rich potential areas of phenomenological inquiry. What of the embodied memory or habit memory I unfolded in my discussion of Merleau-Ponty? On one level, of course, such learned habit memory has its own generality. The bodily practice of the typist and the organist are quite probably similar enough in respect of sex and gender, although there are always, to be sure, possibilities for differentiation based on relative embodiment, such as hand size, extension, or the length of the legs (in the case of playing an organ). But such differentiated specifications can also apply within a given sex, and therefore are not necessarily indicative of a gendered experience.

To be sure, some habitual practices will be more gender-specific; for example, knitting is arguably practiced more by women while carpentry is done more by men, but in this day and time, I would immediately pull back from what is in all probability an archaic generalization (as it is, I reversed the genders of the hat wearer and the driver in my discussion of Merleau-Ponty's account of habit, with no appreciable effect). But I would continue to maintain the possibility nevertheless of specifying sex and gender particularities when it comes to body memory and habitual practices. There has already been a great deal of work, particularly in the social sciences, on the gendered dimension of embodied practices such as dance and sports, and insofar as these involve habitual bodily practices—the body remembers a particular gesture, style, or technique—they are clearly instances of embodied memory and are eminently suitable for a thoroughgoing phenomenological analysis.

I can offer an example from my own experience of a learned and habitual embodied practice that I was able to thematize only recently as a gendered embodied memory. Since I began using a wheelchair several years ago, my excursions into the outside world now involve being accompanied by someone, usually my husband, to handle the wheelchair. Making the transition from being ambulatory and self-propelling to a reliance on such a device is never easy, and modern urban landscapes can present any number of difficulties and challenges. But at a certain point I began noticing that at times when we would be on our way somewhere or traveling along certain routes I would begin to experience a vague uneasiness. Upon reflection I realized that the source of the uneasiness was the proximity to various groups or entities that our path took us. That is, we would go far closer to large, somewhat boisterous dogs than I ever would have in the past (although admittedly I have a certain phobia due to an unfortunate dog-bite incident when I was a child). Or upon encountering a group of loud and raucous and possibly even inebriated individuals ahead of us, we would forge right along and pass within a few feet of them. I should add that, in these instances, there was no real danger, yet I realized that in the past, when moving about more independently and able to chart out my own route, I would have either avoided such close passing by or endeavored to give a wider berth. And while years and years ago I might have thought consciously about doing so (or been instructed by my parents at some point), such considerations had long since been internalized into an embodied practice—one I daresay I share with many others—and this was now effectively an embodied memory. My body, when confronted with certain situations, remembered to react in a certain way. This is not an embodied memory that my husband, raised with and accustomed to a different public bodily comportment, manifests in most circumstances. Arguably my unease could be explained by a sense of vulnerability occasioned by being a wheelchair user. This is a valid consideration, and I have also experienced that sense of uneasiness. But in the case of my example here I believe the uneasiness is distinct, and more fundamentally connected to the already instilled embodied practice that predated my wheelchair use. As such, I would still claim this as an example of gendered embodied memory. I would not argue that such responses are ideal or even necessarily justified, although it is arguably often the prudent course (for anyone) given some circumstances. It is also not the most felicitous enactment of gendered being, insofar as it denotes a wary, cautious, and arguably tentative embodiment in certain contexts, but I was raised in a certain era, and had occasion to be on my own and travel alone quite a bit, and so such embodied practices developed. I offer this as but one example of a putative gender difference in learned embodied practices and embodied memory. There are many more to be uncovered and analyzed, and this is the task that awaits us as feminist phenomenologists.

There is a final element in these analyses of gendered body memory and habitual practices, hinted at in the foregoing discussions, which can be unfolded more explicitly. We have seen how embodied memory is mediated and facilitated by habitude; or rather, as I have argued, the analysis of habit leads us to a developed notion of embodied memory. Habit, as we saw, is both the possibility of habitual action and also a recurring and embedded practice, and these features are further synthesized with respect to memory and embodiment as the bodily memory of the habitual body and the habitual bodily remembering. In the further step of gendering embodied memory the connection between gender and habitude is unfolded. Reading gender through all of the foregoing reveals a sense of gender as an embodied habitual practice. In other words, gender is a bodily habitude and embodied memory and practice.

This is not to suggest that gender is hereby conceptualized as a fixed and static category, locked in an ongoing and pre-delineated reiteration of the same. As we know from other theories of repetition, repetition and reiteration do not have to entail the continuous (re)enactment of the same. Rather, with each reiteration there is a difference, thus constituting a new iteration. Habit is no different. As we have seen, habit is an enactment of meaning that draws on previous enactments, all the while carrying them forward into new and different enactments. As such, gender as embodied habitude does not have to be seen as static, but rather can be viewed as a recalled and continually transformed process. The conceptualization of gender as embodied memory and habitual bodily practice captures, therefore, the intertwined sense of lived embodiment and sociocultural enactment, while furnishing a frame, through the notions of memory and habit, for a retained yet fluid basis and a recalled and transformed enactment.

Through these discussions of embodied time, memory, and gender we can begin to see the way and tasks of feminist phenomenology. There are a myriad of possibilities for phenomenological analyses of gendered temporality, temporal embodiment, and embodied memory. At the same time, phenomenological analyses of embodied memory and habit reveal a rich conception of gender as habitual bodily practice. Taken together, these possibilities point to the potential for phenomenologies of time and temporality to be deepened and enhanced by a gendered analysis, while accounts of gender can be expanded and enriched through insights from phenomenologies of time and temporality. This is indeed the time for feminist phenomenology.

Notes

Research for this article was supported by the Central European University.

I am deeply grateful and thankful to Christina Schües, Dorothea Olkowski, and Helen Fielding for their continued support and encouragement during the writing of this paper. Without them it would not have come to fruition in its present form.

1. See Robert J. Stoller, *Sex and Gender,* generally acknowledged to be one of the earliest and most authoritative analyses and groundings of the distinction between sex and gender.

2. For example, in many historical gender analyses where, in the face of fears of any formulation that might be "ahistorical," there is no datum, no concept, no system of relations, that is not reducible to historical circumstances and processes.

3. In other words, the framework I have in view is a theoretical merging of the sociocultural analyses of gender hierarchies and asymmetry of Foucauldian, poststructuralist, and various social science discussions, with the perspectives and conceptions of philosophies of embodiment and sexual difference, incorporating a developed phenomenology of gendered lived experience.

4. For the present discussion I will operate within a two-gender model of female and male. There are cases to be made for the claim that there are more than two genders—for example, the Muxes of the southern state of Oaxaca in Mexico, whom some consider to be a "third gender"—or that many people are not simply one or another gender but an admixture of two (or more). Nevertheless, for my programmatic purposes here I will remain within the more conventional, albeit binary, version.

5. Analyzing sexuality and the nature of sexual being and experience is one of the tasks of a phenomenology of gendered experience. There have been, to be sure, phenomenological analyses of sexuality, eros, and sexual desire, but I would argue that the more traditional phenomenologies are often insufficiently, if at all, informed by a gender perspective, while many gendered analyses, even if phenomenological in orientation, are not enough of a thoroughgoing phenomenology.

6. Although this might be argued within a non-intersectionality perspective.

7. Other examples of corrective surgery in relation to the baby's sex have involved cases of anatomical anomalies or damage. See for example, John Colapinto, *As Nature Made Him: The Boy Who Was Raised as a Girl,* which deals with the much-publicized story of David Reimer.

8. People with disabilities, especially visible disabilities, have also been subject to this intolerance/lurid fascination dynamic. What underlies both reactions, of course, is the identification as "freak."

9. At any rate, some feminist theorists argue that even in race- or class- or sexuality-determined contexts, the additional gender dimension—especially, given the political dynamics, when the individual is a woman—constitutes a significant, perhaps even more fundamental, factor.

10. For critical analyses of Merleau-Ponty, see, for example, Butler, "Sexual Ideology and Phenomenological Description"; Grosz, *Volatile Bodies;* and Sullivan, "Domination and Dialogue in Merleau-Ponty's *Phenomenology of Perception.*"

11. For more on the potential of phenomenology for gendered and feminist analysis see my "Phenomenology and Feminism."

12. See Young, *Throwing Like a Girl and Other Essays in Feminist Philosophy and Social Theory.*

13. Merleau-Ponty, *Phenomenology of Perception* (originally published as *Phénoménologie de la perception*). Page references are to the English translation, except where the French text is specifically cited. The third chapter of the section on "The Body" is titled "The Spatiality of One's own Body and Motility."

14. Merleau-Ponty, *Phenomenology,* 146/172.

15. Ibid., 147.

16. Ibid.

17. Ibid., 146.

18. For more on the hermeneutic dimension of Merleau-Ponty's thought see my "Merleau-Ponty's Hermeneutics of Philosophical Engagement."

19. Merleau-Ponty, *Phenomenology,* 144/169.

20. Ibid., 146.

21. Ibid.

22. Ibid., 100.

23. Ibid., 102.

24. Ibid., 103/119.

25. Ibid., 103.

26. Ibid.

27. Ibid., 104.

28. Ibid., 109.

29. Ibid.

30. Ibid., 110.

31. Ibid., 137.

32. Ibid., 136.

33. Ibid., 138–39.

34. Ibid., 140.

35. Ibid., 142.

36. Ibid.

37. I don't completely agree that the cane is no longer an object for him. I think the issue with such assistive devices is more complex—they do become more integrated with the body, but they don't entirely lose their sense of being an objectivity, as a necessary but still somewhat alienated (and alienating) device. The relationship to the device has a tension that belies the uniform interaction that Merleau-Ponty claims.

38. Merleau-Ponty, *Phenomenology,* 143.

39. Ibid., 144. For a wide-ranging discussion of habit in Merleau-Ponty, see Casey, "Habitual Body and Memory in Merleau-Ponty."

40. Merleau-Ponty, *Phenomenology*, 144.

41. Ibid.

42. Ibid., 145.

43. Ibid., 100.

44. Ibid., 143. For a detailed discussion of difference, including gender difference, with respect to Merleau-Ponty's thought, as well as a defense of Merleau-Ponty against some of his feminist critics, see Kruks, "Merleau-Ponty and the Problem of Difference in Feminism."

Bibliography

Butler, Judith. "Sexual Ideology and Phenomenological Description: A Feminist Critique of Merleau-Ponty's *Phenomenology of Perception*." In *The Thinking Muse: Feminism and Modern French Philosophy*, ed. Jeffner Allen and Iris Marion Young, 85–100. Bloomington: Indiana University Press, 1989.

Casey, Edward S. "Habitual Body and Memory in Merleau-Ponty." *Man and World* 17 (1984): 279–97.

Colapinto, John. *As Nature Made Him: The Boy Who Was Raised as a Girl.* New York: HarperCollins, 2000.

Fisher, Linda. "Merleau-Ponty's Hermeneutics of Philosophical Engagement." In *Chiasmi International 6: Merleau-Ponty – Between Art and Psychoanalysis* (2005), 173–190.

———. "Phenomenology and Feminism: Perspectives on Their Relation." In *Feminist Phenomenology*, ed. Linda Fisher and Lester Embree, 17–38. Dordrecht: Kluwer Academic Publishers, 2000.

Grosz, Elizabeth. *Volatile Bodies: Toward a Corporeal Feminism.* Bloomington: Indiana University Press, 1994.

Kruks, Sonia. "Merleau-Ponty and the Problem of Difference in Feminism." In *Feminist Interpretations of Maurice Merleau-Ponty*, ed. Dorothea Olkowski and Gail Weiss, 25–47. University Park: Pennsylvania State University Press, 2006.

Merleau-Ponty, Maurice. *Phenomenology of Perception.* Trans. Colin Smith. London: Routledge and Kegan Paul, 1962. Originally published as *Phénoménologie de la perception.* Paris: Éditions Gallimard, 1945.

Stoller, Robert J. *Sex and Gender.* London: Hogarth Press, 1968.

Sullivan, Shannon. "Domination and Dialogue in Merleau-Ponty's *Phenomenology of Perception*." In *Hypatia: A Journal of Feminist Philosophy* 12, no. 1 (1997): 1–19.

Young, Iris Marion. *Throwing Like a Girl and Other Essays in Feminist Philosophy and Social Theory.* Bloomington: Indiana University Press, 1990.

7.

THE TIME OF THE SELF:
A FEMINIST REFLECTION ON RICOEUR'S
NOTION OF NARRATIVE IDENTITY

Annemie Halsema

Time affects the understanding of ourselves. Our bodies grow older, and we adapt our prospects accordingly; our life experiences accumulate and influence our self-perception and self-definition. But not only our self-understanding, also the notion of "the self" itself incorporates time, that is, includes constancy as well as change. My aim in this essay is to exemplify the notions of time that inhere in "the self." I will start from the concept of the self that Paul Ricoeur develops in *Oneself as Another* (1992)—which explicitly builds upon the relationship between time and the self.

Ricoeur develops a narrative and ethical notion of the self that is characterized by a dialectics between sameness and self, *idem* and *ipse*. In feminist theory, his thought is not considered very often,[1] unlike that of other continental thinkers in contemporary history, such as Merleau-Ponty, Sartre, Derrida, and also Husserl and Heidegger. To illustrate the relevance of his notion of the self, I will show how it is interrelated with time, and compare his "self" with the limits of narrative identity that Judith Butler develops in *Giving an Account of Oneself* (2005), and with Luce Irigaray's notion of sexual difference.[2]

Time and the Self

Personal identity in the philosophical tradition is often understood in terms of constancy, as that which remains the same. We understand personal identity not so much in terms of numerical identity (A=A), or qualitative identity (as in: person X and Y are wearing the same coat), but rather as the uninterrupted continuity between the first and last stages of development. Personal identity, in other words, refers to permanence in time. Ricoeur in *Oneself as Another* aims at a notion of permanence in time that makes the self understandable not only as something that remains relatively the same, but also as changing.[3] For he does not consider the self to be identical: its experiences change; its self-definition changes; its body changes over time. He claims that in order to understand this self we need a notion that incorporates both constancy and mutability. With the notion of narrative identity we have such a model for dynamic identity. For narrative identity mediates the extremes of the course of time: sameness and change.

Narrative identity includes the identity we grant to someone about whom we speak, as well as the identity that we call our own. It involves both the sameness that we refer to when we say of someone that he or she is one and the same person, and the self-same that we refer to in speaking of our own identity. In short, it pertains to the third-person as well as to the first-person perspective. The self-sameness of the self is worked out by Ricoeur as *idem,* sameness, or in French *mêmeté;* the "selfhood" as *ipse,* in French *ipséité.*[4] Both *idem* and *ipse* are aspects of personal identity that stand in a dialectical relationship, and both in a different sense relate to permanence in time. *Idem* relates to constancy, to what remains the same; *ipse* is closer to change, yet also incorporates something that remains constant. In the next section, I will first work out the temporal consequences of the conception of the self as *idem* and as *ipse.* In these reflections, I understand the self in the first-person perspective, that is, as marker for designating ourselves. After that, I will turn to the temporality of the narrative.

Constancy and Mutability: Idem *and* Ipse

In contrast to philosophers who understand personal identity as that which remains the same, Ricoeur does not seek for a principle of permanence in time in the sense of "what," but rather one that answers the question: who? "Is there a form of permanence in time that is a reply to the question 'Who am I?'" he asks.[5] He finds that principle in a notion of narrative identity that expresses the dialectic between two models of permanence in time that we use in speaking about ourselves: character and keeping a promise. For Ricoeur, narrative identity forms the mediator between these two poles that both in different ways give articulation to permanence in time. The first one, character, is close to self-constancy, and includes an almost complete overlapping of *idem* and *ipse.* Keeping one's promise is closer to mutability and change, and implies the almost total irreducibility of *idem* and *ipse* to each other; it is the pole where "selfhood frees itself from sameness."[6]

Character is "the set of lasting dispositions by which a person is recognized."[7] It describes persons from the third-person perspective, but we also use it to designate our own identity. It is something we do not choose, but to which we consent. In his earlier work, Ricoeur describes it under the heading of "the involuntary," as opposed to voluntary decision.[8] It forms the pole where *idem* and *ipse* coincide because it is "the same" *of* the self.

Ricoeur works out the notion of character by associating the dispositions that make us recognize a person with the notions of habit and acquired identifications. Both elucidate the temporal nature of character. Habit points at the sedimented nature of dispositions, and clarifies why *idem* is central in character. *Ipse*, however, is not completely effaced because of the fact that my character does not coincide with me: my character is mine, but I am not (only) my character. There remains a dialectic between *idem* and *ipse*, but one in which *ipse* announces itself as *idem*. Acquired identifications show that the nature of character not only implies that we can be recognized *by* characteristics, but also that we recognize ourselves *in* them. There is an element of acquisition in identity and of internalization of characteristics that are ascribed to someone, or that someone ascribes to herself.

Altogether, character for Ricoeur designates the "what" of the "who." It indicates one pole of the dialectic of *idem* and *ipse* that characterizes narrative identity, namely the pole in which the question "Who am I?" is answered by means of an answer to the question "What am I?" This answer is given in the form of a narrative, which has the advantage of preventing the complete and everlasting identification of the self with its character (because the narrative can be told differently on different occasions).

The other model of permanence in time that Ricoeur distinguishes is "keeping one's word." It expresses a self-constancy that can be inscribed only in the dimension of "who?" and has nothing to do with the permanence of time that characterizes character. The self-constancy of the promise means that even though one's opinions, values, desires, inclinations, and so forth change—in other words, notwithstanding the fact that one is no longer the same—one does hold firm. The promise thus has nothing to do with the permanence of *idem*. Keeping one's promise is described by Ricoeur as a challenge to time, a denial of change: "even if my desire were to change, even if I were to change my opinion or my inclination: 'I will hold firm.'"[9] As such, the promise indicates the split of *idem* and *ipse*, for at this end of the continuum there is no sameness anymore, only the constancy of the self that holds on to its promise.

Narrative identity forms the mediator between *idem* and *ipse*, between self-sameness, where time forms a relative threat to identity because identity seems to fall apart in the course of time, and the promise, in which time is denied. Ricoeur distinguishes narrative identity from the self. The self is the reflexive subject that he aims at in the course of *Oneself as Another*.[10] Narrative identity is the identity created in the life story. The self thus falls apart in the I that tells its life story and the protagonist of the story told. The first "I" is expressible only by the second, but will never be completely articulated. But the second, the narrative I, also runs across the limits of what is expressible, as we will see when we contrast Ricoeur with Butler.

The self is thus, by means of its narrative, situated in the interval of *idem* and *ipse*. It is the constructed self of the I that tells its life story. This life story in itself also incorporates time.

The Time of the Narrative: Concordance and Discordance

Ricoeur's notion of personal identity includes time not only because it points out the dialectic between change and constancy, but also because it is in telling a narrative about ourselves that we acquire an identity. For Ricoeur the narrative is "the guardian of time": "there can be no thought about time without narrated time."[11] "The narrative allows us a privileged mode of access to human time," explains Kathleen Blamey.[12] The narrative in all of its forms, from the novel to fairy tales and nonfiction genres such as historical accounts, biographies, and chronicles, brings time to expression. In the case of telling the story of a life, the relationship between the recounted life and the narrative incorporates time in several ways. In the first place, the self can tell different stories about itself in the course of its life.[13] Thus, the narratives about one's life can change over time. In the second place, the narrative itself is something that articulates time in such a way as "to give it the form of human experience."[14] Time is, Ricoeur says, "the referent of the narrative." The narrative itself develops in time: it "uses" time, and also narrates about the progress of time. It is especially this last aspect that interests me here.

The narrative about one's life is a story that weaves a thread between specific events. In telling the story, we constitute the connectedness of our personal lives. The narrative places these events into a particular order. Ricoeur refers to the Aristotelian notion of "emplotment" to designate that order of events. For Aristotle, in the *Poetics* the plot forms the structuring and integrating process that gives an identity to the story. It is not a static structure, but a process that composes the story and makes it into a complete story that, in the end, can be finished only by the reader.[15]

Ricoeur redefines the Aristotelian notion of emplotment as the synthesis between heterogeneous elements. That means in the first place that the plot synthesizes multiple events or incidents into one completed story. The events or incidents recounted are not simply occurrences, but receive a necessity because they form the elements that compose the progress of the narrative. Moreover, the story itself is not simply a serial or successive enumeration of the events, but connects them to each other in a specific way. Furthermore, the events, incidents, and persons referred to, among which the plot weaves a thread, are heterogeneous: planned and unplanned actions, coincidental or intended encounters, interactions ranging from conflict to collaboration, persons that suffer from actions and persons that commit them, and so on. The plot puts these heterogeneous elements into a dynamic unity that we, as readers or listeners, are able to follow. The heterogeneity of the events or incidents means that we can always ask: what happened then, and then, and then? This structure, which is typical for emplotment, means that the narrative is at once a discrete succession that is open and indefinite, *and* an integrated, closed, particular composition.

With respect to time, the narrative contains both time as passing, flowing away, and time as enduring, remaining.[16] It also includes time as discrete succession that is unfinished, and it integrates the various events and makes the succession of events into a configuration. The configuration contains the sort of time that endures: it is that which remains in the course of the events that pass away.

Thus, the specific model of the interconnection of events that emplotment constitutes integrates permanence in time with variability, discontinuity, and instability. Ricoeur specifies the configuration that characterizes emplotment with the notions of concordance and discordance. Concordance refers to the principle of order "that presides over the arrangement of facts"; discordances are the reversals of fortune that make the plot of the story of one's life "an ordered transformation from an initial situation to a terminal situation."[17] Thus, discordances disturb the unity of the plot; they threaten its identity. Ricoeur understands the narrative composition as a specific dialectic between both, that is, as discordant concordance, which is similar to "the synthesis of the heterogeneous." The result of this dialectic is that contingency and necessity become related; in other words, in one's life story the contingent (i.e., the events that could have happened differently or that might not have happened at all) is incorporated into a larger configuration that makes it necessary or at least probable. The unity of one's life story creates a necessary structure out of contingent events, in that way converting the contingent into what is necessary, or to be more precise, into a narrative necessity (which of course is not the same as a necessary event in one's life).

Ricoeur thus understands narrative identity as the creation of a coherent life story, in which breaks within one's life, for instance the death of a child or partner, or other traumatic events, are taken up into the story of one's life. Indeed, discordant events such as these can sometimes be accounted for and articulated within language, and as such be woven into one's life story. However, it is questionable whether they make the life story into a coherent one. Rather, they keep existing as breaks within the story. In other cases, for instance in a situation where a traumatic event is not recollected and (partly) escapes from memory, it remains unaccounted for, but nevertheless continues to exist within someone's life as an influential and unarticulated event. Thus, the notions of "synthesis of the heterogeneous" and "discordant concordance" suggest a harmony of one's life story that is illusory. The narrative notion of identity, and especially the centrality of the Aristotelian conception of emplotment, makes identity into a too-harmonious category. For Ricoeur, even though discordances are part of the story and disturb the order, in the end they become part of the story. They are taken up and represented in the plot. The possibility for creating a unity out of a series of events for him lies in the fact that the story is partly based on fiction. We imagine the line that we draw between the events in our lives. Ricoeur understands narrative identity as that which integrates historical and fictional narrative. The narrative draws both on the events in one's life and on fiction, thus "turning the story of a life into a fictional story or historical fiction."[18] Yet, in holding on to the centrality of the notion of "emplotment," he gives priority to the creation of a coherent narrative.[19]

But there is more. Apart from not always being able to account for the events within one's life, there is, in Judith Butler's words, also "that in me and of me for which I can give no account."[20] In *Giving an Account of Oneself,* she points out that not everything about lives and experiences is narratable. She indicates the aspects that obstruct the coherence of the narrative and that show the limits of the possibility of narrating the self. Bodily experiences, for instance, are not precisely narratable; the unconscious is not explicitly part of our life story. Even though I can explain what I feel bodily, there is always a part of my bodily history of which I have no recollection, and to which I cannot give a narrative form. The unconscious consists of the representations of the drives, phantasms, and imaginary scenes upon which the drive becomes fixated.[21] It cannot be uttered (entirely), but influences our experiences, thoughts, feelings. Thus, the narrative that the self tells is limited: the self is never completely narratable. And the self that tells its life story cannot be completely identified, nor can it completely identify itself, with its life story.

The Self and Its Character

With respect to time, the notion of narrative identity implies variability as well as constancy, and as such fits human self-understanding. But for Ricoeur, the self that tells its life story does not necessarily coincide with the character in the narration. In "Life in Quest of Narrative" he explicitly addresses the question of the relationship between life (the I that narrates) and narrative (the character in the narrative). The relationship between both is exemplified, firstly, in the hermeneutical sense that the life story is completed only by its reader: "the sense or the significance of the narrative stems from *the intersection between the world of the text and the world of the reader.*"[22] This implies that stories are not only recounted but also lived "in the mode of the imaginary."[23] Our life stories influence the sense of who we are. But also, for Ricoeur, life *needs* narration because it exceeds being a biological phenomenon only if it is interpreted. This means it is possible to narrate it because of its pre-narrative quality: life has a pre-narrative capacity; it is prefigured narratively. We understand action and passion through the entire network of expressions and concepts that are offered us in language. Human action is embedded within a semantics of action that makes it understandable. We thus understand our lives in the same sense as we understand narratives. Next, human action is symbolically mediated; it is articulated in "signs, rules, norms."[24] Ricoeur claims: "Our life, when then embraced in a single glance, appears to us as the field of a constructive activity, borrowed from narrative understanding, by which we attempt to discover and not simply to impose from outside *the narrative identity that constitutes us.*"[25]

We need to narrate who we are in order to understand ourselves. But that does not imply that our narrative identity and "self" overlap. Ricoeur exemplifies that we, firstly, are not the author of our life story—which would be an argument for the overlap of self and narrative identity—but co-author of its meaning. Secondly, "we need the help of fiction to organize life retrospectively"[26] because of the elusive character of real life. Life exceeds narrative identity, but is also not recognizable and cannot be constructed without the narrative.[27]

The Body of the Narrative Self

Is the distance between the self and its narrative an effect of the embodiment of the self? Does the body, because it is not fully narratable, exceed narrative identity, ensuring that the self and its narrative identity do not coincide? In this part of the essay I will claim that it is not the case that the body as some sort of constancy underlies the variability of the self. Even though bodily experiences are not completely narratable and the body thus exceeds narrative identity, in the end the structure of embodiment resembles the structure of the self and is only to a certain extent narratable.

Idem *and* Ipse: Körper *and* Leib

At first sight, it is tempting to associate the body with that which remains the same, in distinction to the self. The self then would be psychological or spiritual while the body would be material. But Ricoeur objects to identifications of the self with the psyche or mind and the body with the constancy of the self. He writes that he does not want to enter into discussions like those in the analytical tradition over the best criterion for identity: psychological or corporeal.[28] He does not associate the psychological criterion with *ipse* and the corporeal criterion with *idem*. In other words, the *idem-ipse* distinction does not pertain to the body-mind split. For the body does not form the permanent part of our being. It does not even resemble itself: "One only has to compare two self-portraits of Rembrandt," writes Ricoeur.[29] Secondly, the body is not foreign to selfhood, and the reason for that is not that it is the remaining material side of the self, but rather that the self can claim: "this is my body." The mineness of the body that Ricoeur assumes in following the phenomenologists forms "the most overwhelming testimony in favor of the irreducibility of selfhood to sameness."[30] The selfhood of the body is constituted by its belonging to someone who is capable of designating herself as the one whose body this is. Here we come across a double structure similar to that seen in the discussion of character: the body is the what of a who *and* constitutes "who" this is.

Both aspects, the whatness and the whoness of the body, go together with the two orders to which the body belongs: the order of things as well as the order of the self. In correspondence with Husserl, Ricoeur distinguishes two sorts of experience of the body: *Körper* and *Leib*.[31] For this distinction he departs from the Fifth Meditation of Husserl's *Cartesian Meditations,* which addresses the question of the constitution of a shared nature, of an intersubjectively founded nature.[32] Husserl introduces the distinction between *Leib* and *Körper* on the way from ego to other. Yet, otherwise than Husserl, in the *Cartesian Meditations,* with this distinction Ricoeur answers not to the objection of solipsism, but aims at showing the ontological passivity of the body, its openness for otherness.[33]

Husserl's problem in the Fifth Meditation is how such a thing as a body is originally constituted in one's experience. He discusses the primary awareness of my body that is presupposed by any external perception of it, namely as perceptual origin, as active, and as sensitive body. In order to understand the possibility of the constitution of another body with the same characteristics, he suggests that we perceive a *likeness* between the other body and our own. What the intersubjective constitution of nature obliges us to think, according to Husserl, is ourselves as *Leib,* before the constitution of the alter ego. Ricoeur concludes his reading of the Fifth Meditation by stating that Husserl considers what Ricoeur now calls "flesh" as implicating its own "proper" otherness. The otherness of the flesh precedes the otherness of the stranger. It consists in the "I can" that precedes any design and the will. "The flesh is the place of the passive syntheses on which the active syntheses are constructed," elucidates Ricoeur. "It is the origin of all 'alteration of ownness.'"[34]

Ricoeur wants to isolate this distinction between *Leib* and *Körper* from Husserl's transcendental phenomenology and the problem of constitution, and claims that it is possible to do so. Only when the ontology of the flesh breaks free from the problematic of constitution that required it can we think the body as at once my body, flesh, *and* as body among bodies. Whereas Ricoeur finds the mineness of the body to be missing in the analytical tradition, he concludes that Husserl has difficulties thinking the body as part of the world. Husserl has no answer to the question: "How am I to understand that my flesh is also a body?" Ricoeur here runs up against the limitations of phenomenology, at least in intending to derive the objective aspects of the world from a non-objectifying primordial experience. Husserl has difficulties in understanding the materiality of our own bodies (i.e., that they are *Körper*) on the basis of the solipsistic constitution of our bodies, and specifically perceiving external material objects (other bodies) as "like" our own.[35] Husserl's "solution" for the body to appear as body among bodies is to make the flesh part of the world (*mondaneiser*), writes Ricoeur. At that point the otherness of others as foreign is "interconnected with the otherness of the flesh that I am" *and* "held in its way to be prior to the reduction to ownness." Ricoeur elucidates: "For my flesh appears as a body among bodies only to the extent that I am myself an other among all others, in the apprehension of a common nature, woven, as Husserl says, out of the network of intersubjectivity—itself, unlike Husserl's conception, founding selfhood in its own way.[36] While Husserl faced difficulties in thinking the body as *Leib* and as *Körper,* Ricoeur, on the basis of Husserl's meditations and unpublished manuscripts, claims that being *Körper* is as much part of selfhood as being *Leib,* and that the first is no less primordial than the latter.[37]

In understanding embodiment explicitly as being a body among other bodies, Ricoeur understands the body's appearing in the world as of similar importance to self-intimacy and feeling one's body. As such, Ricoeur's perspective on embodiment offers interesting leads for feminist theorizing. A strictly phenomenological account of embodiment, in which it appears as primordially one's own, is limited from a feminist perspective.[38] For a feminist account of embodiment should include a perspective on what it implies to be situated in the world.

In the next part of this essay, I will further work out such a feminist account of embodiment with the help of Luce Irigaray and Judith Butler. But before going into that, a return to the self: for how does the body as *Leib* and *Körper* relate to the self? Earlier I mentioned that the body concerns the what of a who, *and* constitutes its whoness. I furthermore connected this distinction with *Leib* and *Körper,* implying that the whatness of the body coincides with its being *Körper* and its whoness with being *Leib*. Both aspects of embodiment are narratable, and thus can be part of narrative identity. We can recall bodily experiences, explain what we feel and how it feels, which are *Leib*-aspects; and we can objectify our body, speak about its characteristics, what it shares with others, in short, exemplify its *Körper*-aspects. What is articulable about, and is articulated of, the body can be a component of narrative identity, which thus incorporates its body. But the self cannot express its body entirely; for it also articulates itself by means of this same body upon which it does not reflect. The latter shows itself in hesitations, slips of the tongue, and emotions. And as mentioned before, not everything of the body is narratable. The body also exceeds narrative identity.

Irigaray's Body as Relationship-with

Ricoeur, in claiming that being *Körper* is as much part of selfhood as being *Leib*, understands embodiment as being a body among other bodies as well as one's own. As pointed out earlier, this is why Ricoeur's perspective on embodiment offers interesting leads for feminist theorizing. For feminist notions of the body, just like Ricoeur's, understand the body as lived experience, as well as body among other bodies, which implies among other things that the body receives social meanings and is understood as the point where normative social structures cross. It at once situates the individual socially and influences its self-perception. In this and the next section, drawing on both Irigaray's and Butler's later works, I will further work out this notion of the body. Both, from different angles, put Ricoeur's notion of the embodied narrative self into perspective. Irigaray questions the sexual neutrality of Ricoeur's account of embodiment, and Butler draws attention to the limits of narrativity and to the social normative context in which the narrative self tells its life-story.

Luce Irigaray in *To Be Two* explicates a notion of the body that shows that embodiment allows us to participate in a community and that emphasizes relationality. In some aspects, namely in considering embodiment as that which requires us to participate in the community of our *genre*,[39] this notion resembles Ricoeur's body among other bodies. In other aspects, it is very dissimilar, notably in sexualizing Ricoeur's neutral account of embodiment. As I will show, Irigaray, by elucidating the sexually differentiated character of embodiment, brings in difference, and as such, enlarges the ethical potentiality that the notion of embodiment in Ricoeur's account already has.

In a comment on Sartre, Merleau-Ponty, and Levinas in *To Be Two*, Irigaray speaks of the body as at once subjectivity and objectivity. The subjectivity of the body can be associated with the body as *Leib* (which is translated by Sartre as *corps-sujet*—note that in this text Irigaray starts from Sartre). The body as objectivity (in Sartrian terms *corps-object*) is brought in relationship to gender, or in French, *genre.* Irigaray especially develops the objective side of embodiment in writing: "In so far as I belong to a gender, my body already represents an objectivity for me. . . . Belonging to a gender allows me to realize, in me, for me—and equally towards the other—a dialectic between subjectivity and objectivity which escapes the dichotomy between subject and object."[40] In this passage, Irigaray aims at an alternative dialectics between subjectivity and objectivity than the one she envisions in the works of Sartre and Merleau-Ponty.[41] Embodiment already in itself incorporates a dialectics between subjectivity and objectivity for her. It is not because of the relationship to the other outside of us that we enter into a dialectics, but because of having and being a body itself. The body represents an objectivity because of belonging to a *genre.*

In *I Love to You* Irigaray considers belonging to a *genre* in the context of the relationship between singularity and universality: "I belong to the universal in recognizing that I am a woman. This woman's singularity is in having a particular genealogy and history. But belonging to a gender represents a universal that exists prior to me. I have to accomplish it in relation to my particular destiny."[42]

One's *genre* forms a universal that figures as a sort of horizon against which we can develop as particular beings. In belonging to a *genre* our body already incorporates the potential for its individual development, but it is still one that must be accomplished. Our identities thus should be developed in correspondence with our bodies. Irigaray claims, "I am born a woman, but I must still become this woman that I am by nature."[43] One's belonging to a gender helps the individual to develop itself according to the limitations and potentials that one's *genre* includes.

The concept of "the negative in sexual difference" in *I Love to You* elucidates in what sense embodiment for Irigaray includes both limitations and potential: "The negative in sexual difference" means "an acceptance of the limits of my gender and recognition of the irreducibility of the other."[44] It makes us aware of the limit imposed on us by our *genre,* and it inscribes finiteness in embodiment because of belonging to a gender. Sexual difference represents a negative within each individual: "Being sexuate implies a negative, a not being the other, a not being the whole, and a particular way of being: tied to the body and in relationship with the other."[45] This limitation is not a restriction, but a constitutive or affirmative limit that helps us to develop into beings that realize their "perfection."

The development of a gender identity starts from recognizing that we belong to a gender, which entails being part of something that is larger than oneself, being part of a community, or "the universal" of one's gender. Every individual has to accomplish that belonging in relation to her or his particular destiny. Irigaray, in this respect, also speaks of "accomplishing one's gender's perfection."[46] This is not an ideal that is similar for all women, but rather something that every woman (and every man) has to achieve by gathering her- or himself within her- or himself, and that every individual has to do for her- or himself. It is an individual task that everyone has to perform starting from her (or his) individual history and genealogy.

For Irigaray, embodiment includes finiteness, or passivity. Her notion of passivity resembles Ricoeur's passivity of the body in the sense that it allows us to participate in a community and that it calls for an ethical attitude toward the other that is different from us. Ricoeur considers the body in *Oneself as Another* as one of three passivities that constitute the cogito as broken cogito—the other ones are the relationship to other people and our conscience. He distinguishes a triad of passivities, of phenomenological experiences of otherness, which relate to three ontological faces of otherness that are constitutive for the self. This triad ensures that the self can no longer be taken as self-foundational, and thus radically distances it from the Cartesian cogito, and gives way to a broken cogito. The triad consists of, firstly, "the passivity represented by the experience of one's own body—or . . . the *flesh*"—as the mediator between self and world; secondly, "the passivity implied by the relation of the self to the *foreign*," that is the other (than) self; and thirdly, "the most deeply hidden passivity, that of the relation of the self to itself, which is conscience."[47] Ricoeur does not aim at articulating the full range of possible experiences of otherness, but rather exemplifies three modes of passivity that confront the self with different alterities.

Irigaray connects passivity to sexual difference: it includes respecting your body for what it is *and* respecting the other that is different from you. She ethically calls on us to take up the body's passivity, include it in our sense of self, to develop an identity accordingly, and to relate to others on the basis of this passivity. She, accordingly, sexualizes Ricoeur's neutral account of embodiment, and brings about difference. Whereas in Ricoeur's perspective all bodies are similar to each other, or rather, differences between bodies are not accounted for, in Irigaray's perspective the body is two, either male or female. Even though her naturalization of sexual difference is questionable,[48] I think it opens an enhanced ethical perspective on embodiment. In a sense, Irigaray further elaborates the body-notion that for Ricoeur, in his triad of phenomenological experiences of otherness, forms our "first" encounter with otherness.[49]

Irigaray's perspective on embodiment is ethical not only because she works out an attitude of relating to the finiteness of embodiment and of developing one's identity accordingly. More importantly, ethics for her includes a relationship to the other as not reducible to the self. Ethics implies recognition of the other's transcendence.[50] Her ethics is based on self-limitation, which implies acknowledging the gender of our bodies. Hence, it is an ethics built upon the phenomenological limitations that embodiment includes.

Irigaray's ethics is elucidated by the relationality that belonging to a gender implies for her. She claims that the gendered body is "relationship-with." That means that "in so far as I am a sexuate being, I represent a meaning for the other and I am, in a way, destined to him." Embodiment as such implies relationships "with me," "with my gender," and "with the other gender."[51] Being sexuate, in other words, implies that our bodies have a sexuate meaning, for ourselves, in describing to which part of humanity we belong and how we can accordingly develop ourselves, *and* for the other half of humanity, which is different from us. If we relate to our *genre* as the negative and acknowledge the limitation that embodiment implies, we become aware of being part of only half of humanity, and can perceive the other (*genre*) *as* other (*genre*). In this way, sexual difference, which for Irigaray is the first difference we encounter familially, is the first encounter with difference. If we are able to deal with that, we are capable of engaging with other differences as well.[52]

While Ricoeur shows that embodiment refers not only to the body as one's own, but primarily to the body among other bodies, Irigaray further elaborates "the objectivity" of the body, namely its belonging to a gender. With concepts such as "the negative" she elucidates that embodiment includes limitations that have an ethical value in giving way to recognizing the other. However, "the objectivity" of the body, its being a body among other bodies, implies not only that it is part of a community, but also that it is socially located. In the last section, I will return to language, that is, to narrative identity, in order to show that the embodied self's belonging to a world includes that it can never be "one's own." Butler's concept of performativity in *Bodies That Matter* and her account of narrative identity in *Giving an Account of Oneself* will help me do so.

The Addressed Self

While recognizing that embodiment implies objectivity as well as subjectivity and basing an ethics of self-limitation upon that insight, Irigaray does not explicitly reflect upon the fact that it is within a social order that our bodies receive a sexuate meaning.[53] The concepts "performativity" and "social existence," that Judith Butler develops in *Bodies That Matter* (1993) and *The Psychic Life of Power* (1997), do indicate that, contrary to Irigaray's thinking in which "nature" plays a part, subjectivity and embodiment receive their meaning in a social, normative context.

"Performativity" indicates the reiteration of a norm or set of norms that is cited. In the process of citation not only is the subject created as a social subject, but also its body receives its gendered significance. Regulatory norms for Butler "materialize," and produce gender. She reformulates the concept of gender: it no longer implies the cultural significations ascribed to the sexed body, but it includes the construction of that body as sexed. Thereby, Butler does not understand norms as socially stable, but shows the double constitution of norms and subject. Not only are the subject and its body constituted by citing dominant norms, but these norms themselves are installed because of being cited: "the norm of sex takes hold to the extent that it is 'cited' as such a norm, but it also derives its power through the citations that it compels."[54] The process by which the subject becomes a socially recognizable subject implies that it cites norms, and at the same time, by citing these norms, contributes to the dominance of those norms. Construction for Butler is not only taking place *in* time, but is itself a temporal process operating through the reiteration of norms.

The notion of "social existence," in *The Psychic Life of Power* (1997), in an even more compelling way, shows that there is no subject prior to the norms that it cites and that the subject brings its subordination to the norms to itself. The subject is both the "effect of a prior power" and "the condition of possibility" for agency.[55] As Butler elucidates, a specific temporality inheres in power: at once it both is *before* the subject *and* creates the subject, and is thus present and takes a futural form (because the subject is its effect). Power is reiterated, and therefore the process of subordination in which the subject is constituted is dynamic. Butler further works out how norms operate as psychic phenomena, and not only govern the formation of the subject, but also circumscribe the domain of a livable sociality. In this way, she persuasively reveals the power structures that are part of the social domain and that exclude some and include others as viable subjects.

The performativity of subjectivity and the subject's social existence imply that self-understanding, or in Ricoeur's words, self-interpretation, is not based upon introspection, but arises within a social context that prescribes who is a recognizable subject and who is not. It means that our life story is not so much constituted by us, but rather is constituted in advance by that which is socially understandable. Consequently, we do not "own" our life story, but it is principally addressed.

Butler, in *Giving an Account of Oneself* (2005),[56] explicitly shows that the story of our life, narrative identity, is embedded within normative societal structures. Narrating the self takes place under conditions. She claims that the narrative self, the "I" that tells a story, "can only tell it according to recognizable norms of life narration."[57] Telling the story of a life is not something we do outside of a context, but there is a "you"—which can also be imaginary—that is addressed in the story. She says: "if I can address you, I must first have been addressed, brought into the structure of address as a possibility of language before I was able to find my own way to make use of it."[58] This is so not only because language belongs to the other, and I do not choose the language that is my own, but because telling a story means being addressed by the other. Before articulating myself, I am already spoken to by that which differs from me. Prior to my individuation, I am addressed by another. Otherness is installed in the subject even before it is able to give an account of itself, that is, before telling its life story.

Also, to Ricoeur the thought that we are addressed and conditioned by otherness is not strange. As already indicated, he understands the self as symbolically mediated. The narrative self is, as he writes, "instructed by cultural symbols."[59] It is in language and culture that we narrate our life stories, and the cultural symbols that are available to us for a large part determine how the story is told. The mediation of the self by cultural signs implies at once that the self does not have immediate access to itself *and* that the self as that which we understand ourselves to be is not constant, but subject to change. The self is subject to change not only because it can tell a different life story in different periods of its life, but also because the available language and culture from which it draws are engaged in processes of transformation. Cultural mediation means that narrative identity is not "ours," so that the self does not know itself, but can only interpret itself. Like Butler, Ricoeur thus understands the self as passive, and interrupted by the other. But unlike Butler, he does not think through the social and political consequences for the "self" of this interruption by the other, of the address of the other.

Butler does make us aware of the consequences of the notion of narrative identity that are connected with its being articulated in a language that belongs to the other. Firstly, norms condition what counts and does not count, as a recognizable account of oneself. Every account of myself must in some way or another conform to norms that govern "the human recognizable."[60] This means that in articulating myself I am always addressing the other and that I am constituting myself *as* address of the other. Secondly, Butler points out that not everything of our life and experience is narratable. As indicated earlier, Butler questions the coherence of the life story, and exemplifies the limits of the possibility of telling one's life story, such as bodily experiences, as well as the unconscious. In this way, she not only points out that there are white spaces in the story, margins and missing links, but draws the radical consequences of the dispossession of one's life story: "If I try to give an account of myself, if I try to make myself recognizable and understandable, then I might begin with a narrative account of my life. But this narrative will be disoriented by what is not mine, or not mine alone."[61]

Conclusion: The Time of the Embodied Self

I started this essay by elucidating the different notions of time that inhere in the notion of narrative identity. Not only the aging self—with its body that grows older and the perception and interpretation of the self that change in correspondence or in dissonance with it—but also the concept of the self itself includes time. Ricoeur shows that the notion of narrative identity moves in between *idem* and *ipse,* between self-sameness and constancy on the one hand and the flux of time on the other. The narrative itself contains a notion both of time as passing and of time as enduring. Butler exemplifies that it is not only in narrating our life story that we refer to time and use time, but that also the construction process itself includes time, or rather *is* time. With Irigaray we turned to the body of the narrative self. She elucidates that embodiment includes both subjectivity and belonging to a *genre.* This "objectivity" of the body is not something that *is,* but it has to be developed, and therefore takes time. Identity, or more specifically, sexuate identity, is a construction that implies an appeal to us as embodied subjects to develop ourselves. Butler in the end, however, makes clear that this appeal is not something that we are able to take up and develop strictly individually, but that we are bound to the societal possibilities and restrictions for understanding ourselves. The embodied self articulates itself within a social context for which it cannot account. The time of the social world and the time of the self, in other words, do not coincide. The self, thus, forms only a temporary nonconstant stand in the flux of time.

Notes

1. With the exceptions of Morny Joy (*Paul Ricoeur and Narrative*), Nel van den Haak (*Metafoor en filosofie*), and Shari Stone-Mediatore (*Reading across Borders*).

2. See also Halsema, "Reflexionen über Identität in einer multikulturellen Gesellschaft—Ein Dialog zwischen Ricoeur, Irigaray und Butler."

3. Ricoeur uses the concepts "I," "ego," "subject" interchangeably and "self" as an alternative. He writes: philosophies of the subject "formulate the subject in the first person—*ego cogito*—, whether the 'I' is defined as an empirical or a transcendental ego, whether the 'I' is posited absolutely . . . or relatively. . . . In all of these instances the subject is 'I'" (Ricoeur, *Oneself as Another,* 4). However, the self includes the reflexive subject that acts and evaluates its own acts, and that is mediated by signs, symbols and texts (see Ricoeur, "On Interpretation," 191).

4. Ricoeur, *Oneself as Another,* 116.

5. Ibid., 118.

6. Ibid., 119.

7. Ibid., 121.

8. Ricoeur, *Freedom and Nature,* 355–73, especially 366–71 ("The Significance of My Character").

9. Ricoeur, *Oneself as Another,* 125.

10. The sameness of the self, its *idem*-aspect, is worked out with the help of analytic philosophy, but in the course of the book, Ricoeur's perspective upon the self becomes more and more phenomenological-hermeneutical. The person that is spoken about becomes a subject that is part of the world, considers that world to be his or her own, and in the end evaluates his or her acts. Ricoeur furthermore develops the narrative self as an ethical self, and takes up the question of self-esteem and self-respect in relationship with others and institutions within society. In this essay, because of its focus on time, the ethical aspect of the self is not central, but I mention it here because it forms an inextricable component of Ricoeur's notion of the self.

11. Ricoeur, *Time and Narrative* III, 241.

12. Blamey, "From the Ego to the Self," 574.

13. Ricoeur speaks of several plots composed around the same incidents, and of different plots woven about our lives (Ricoeur, *Time and Narrative* III, 248).

14. Ricoeur, "Intellectual Autobiography," 40.

15. Ricoeur, "Life in Quest of Narrative," 21.

16. Ibid., 22.

17. Ricoeur, *Oneself as Another,* 141.

18. Ricoeur, "Narrative Identity," 188.

19. Ricoeur does not deny that. In "Life in Quest of Narrative" he confronts Augustine, for whom discordances win over concordances ("whence the misery of the human condition," Ricoeur, "Life in Quest of Narrative," 31), and Aristotle, for whom concordance wins over discordance because the narrative forms a synthesis of the heterogeneous. With his notion of narrative identity Ricoeur decides for Aristotle, but he stresses that there remains a tension between concordance and discordance.

20. Butler, *Giving an Account of Oneself,* 40.

21. Laplanche and Pontalis, *Vocabulaire de la psychanalyse,* 197–99.

22. Ricoeur, "Life in Quest of Narrative," 26 (italics in original).

23. Ibid., 27.

24. Ibid., 28.

25. Ibid., 32.

26. Ricoeur, *Oneself as Another,* 162.

27. Ricoeur uses these arguments in order to argue that literary narratives and life histories are complementary, and not mutually exclusive. Apart from the mentioned arguments, he claims that, thirdly, our narrative is intertwined with the life histories of others, but that it doesn't prevent us from speaking of the narrative "unity" of a life. And lastly, narrative identity may seem to limit itself to a retrospective organization of life, which would mean a limitation of what we are to the past, but in fact includes projections, plans, dreams, anticipations, and expectations (Ricoeur, *Oneself as Another,* 162–63).

28. Ricoeur, *Oneself as Another,* 128. Ricoeur mainly mentions works from the seventies by Amelie Rorty, John Perry, Sidney Shoemaker, and Bernard Williams (see note 19 in Ricoeur, *Oneself as Another,* 128–29).

29. Ibid., 129.

30. Ibid., 128.

31. Ricoeur translates the German *Leib* and *Körper* into French as respectively *chair* and *corps*. In the English translation, Blamey speaks of "flesh" and "body." Even though the German *Leib* is commonly translated into English as "lived body," I will hold on to the terminology that Ricoeur uses.

32. Ricoeur, *Oneself as Another,* 322.

33. Note that Ricoeur takes a distance from Husserl's fundamental intention of the constitution of all reality by consciousness. He claims that his ontology of the flesh is closer to Heidegger's being-in-the-world and specifically to the notion of "thrownness." Ricoeur considers thrownness, in the sense of "being delivered over to oneself," the existential category most appropriate to an investigation of the self as flesh, for it implies an opening that includes self-intimacy as well as appearing in the world (Ricoeur, *Oneself as Another,* 327). Heidegger, however, did not "allow an ontology of the flesh to unfold" (Ricoeur, *Oneself as Another,* 322), which is why Ricoeur turns to Husserl.

34. Ricoeur, *Oneself as Another,* 324.

35. See also Smith, *Husserl and the "Cartesian Meditations,"* 222.

36. Ricoeur, *Oneself as Another,* 326.

37. Ricoeur further expands his sympathizing critique of Husserl by showing that otherness is always presupposed, and thus that there is not a sphere of ownness that is not already infected by otherness (see Ricoeur, *Oneself as Another,* 331–35).

38. I do not mean to say that phenomenological accounts of embodiment, such as Husserl's and Merleau-Ponty's, do not offer rich potential for the study of embodiment and for the further elaboration of notions of gender and sexual difference (see for instance Heinämaa, *Toward a Phenomenology of Sexual Difference*), and Stoller, "Phänomenologie der Geschlechtlichkeit"; see also for a more general study of the relationship between phenomenology and feminism Fisher, "Phänomenologie und Feminismus." What I do mean is that the phenomenological perspective is not able to account for social-cultural differences, which are crucial for a feminist analysis of embodiment.

39. I have translated the French *genre* in this essay as "gender," without thereby alluding to the sex/gender distinction. The French *genre* refers to grammatical gender, a style of discourse, or *genre humain* (humankind), and is broader than the sexual dichotomy. In her early works Irigaray often uses the word *sexe* (sex) instead of *genre* in order to avoid the traditional connotations associated with the latter (Irigaray, *Je, tu, nous,* 31n3), but in her later works, starting with *Sexes and Genealogies,* she uses *genre* more often than *sexe*. Note that in her most recent works, she prefers to speak of sexuate difference instead of sexual difference, in order to avoid the confusion of sexuality and sex (Irigaray, *Key Writings*). In the texts that I refer to in this essay, however, she still writes *genre*.

40. Irigaray, *To Be Two,* 21.

41. See Halsema, "Phenomenology in the Feminine," for a further elaboration of this notion of objectivity in relationship to Sartre and Merleau-Ponty.

42. Irigaray, *I Love to You,* 39.

43. Ibid., 107.

44. Ibid., 13.

45. Ibid., 34.

46. Ibid., 27.

47. Ricoeur, *Oneself as Another*, 318.

48. Sexual difference consists of two categories that are inscribed in what Irigaray calls "nature" (see for her notion of nature, Irigaray, *I Love To You*, 35–42, and also Stone, "The Sex of Nature").

49. I do not mean to say that Ricoeur, in naming the body as the first of the phenomenological experiences of otherness, implies that this experience is first in time. But I do wonder why he starts the triad with the body and ends it with conscience? Does that imply that the body forms a sort of foundation for the other experiences of otherness? And is the relationship to the body already part of ethics for him, or does ethics only start with the other outside of us? The triad seems to imply that the relationship to our body *paves the way* for relating to others outside of us. For Irigaray, embodiment, and more specifically sexual difference, without doubt seems our first encounter with otherness (see Irigaray, *I Love To You*, 47; *Democracy Begins between Two*, 129).

50. See for the notion of transcendence Irigaray, *I Love To You*, 103–108; *To Be Two*, 17–29; *Between East and West; Key Writings*, 171–85 .

51. Irigaray, *To Be Two*, 33.

52. For Irigaray, sexual difference forms the privileged encounter with otherness. The question is whether we could expand this thought to other bodily differences. Perhaps not to the same extent as sexual difference, but still age, physical (dis)ability and health, and skin color also form differences that at once limit the possibilities of becoming for the self, and show the potentials for development. Irigaray's sexualization of the phenomenological notion of the body in that case could be seen as a starting point for acknowledging differences between bodies. See also Deutscher, *A Politics of Impossible Difference,* for the relationship between sexual difference and other differences, especially race and ethnicity, in Irigaray's later work.

53. Irigaray does criticize phallocentrism, but does not in a broader sense reflect upon the social constitution of meaning, as Butler does.

54. Butler, *Bodies That Matter*, 13.

55. Butler, *The Psychic Life of Power*, 14–15.

56. In this work, originally given as Spinoza-lectures at the University of Amsterdam in 2002, Butler reflects upon the question whether a poststructuralist subject that is not self-grounding, "whose conditions of emergence can never be fully accounted for, undermine[s] the possibility of responsibility, and, in particular, of giving an account of oneself" (Butler, *Giving an Account of Oneself,* 19). She refutes the critique that poststructuralist critical reconsiderations of the subject do away with responsibility, and claims that theories of subject-formation that acknowledge the limits of self-knowledge can indeed serve ethics.

57. Butler, *Giving an Account of Oneself,* 52.

58. Ibid., 53.
59. Ricoeur, "Life in Quest of Narrative," 33.
60. Butler, *Giving an Account of Oneself,* 37.
61. Ibid., 37.

Bibliography

Aristotle. *Poetics.* Trans. and ed. Stephen Halliwell. In *Aristotle in Twenty-Three Volumes.* Vol. 23. Loeb Classical Library. Cambridge, Mass.: Harvard University Press, 1995.

Blamey, Kathleen. "From the Ego to the Self: A Philosophical Itinerary." In *The Philosophy of Paul Ricoeur,* ed. Lewis Edwin Hahn, 571–603. Chicago: Open Court, 1995.

Butler, Judith. *Bodies That Matter: On the Discursive Limits of "Sex."* New York: Routledge, 1993.

———. *Giving an Account of Oneself.* New York: Fordham University Press, 2005.

———. *The Psychic Life of Power: Theories in Subjection.* Stanford, Calif.: Stanford University Press, 1997.

Deutscher, Penelope. *A Politics of Impossible Difference: The Later Work of Luce Irigaray.* Ithaca, N.Y.: Cornell University Press, 2002.

Fisher, Linda. "Phänomenologie und Feminismus." In *Phänomenologie und Geschlechterdifferenz,* ed. Silvia Stoller and Helmut Vetter, 20–46. Vienna: WUV-Universitäts Verlag, 1997.

Haak, Nel van den. *Metafoor en filosofie: Studie naar de metaforische werking in de filosofie aan de hand van Julia Kristeva en Paul Ricoeur.* Best: Damon, 2001.

Halsema, Annemie. "Phenomenology in the Feminine: Irigaray's Relationship to Merleau-Ponty." In *Intertwinings: Interdisciplinary Encounters with Merleau-Ponty,* ed. Gail Weiss, 63–84. Albany: SUNY Press, 2008.

———. "Reflexionen über Identität in einer multikulturellen Gesellschaft—Ein Dialog zwischen Ricoeur, Irigaray und Butler." In *Feministische Phänomenologie und Hermeneutik,* ed. Silvia Stoller, Veronica Vasterling, and Linda Fisher, 208–34. Reihe Orbis Phaenomenologicus. Würzburg: Königshausen & Neumann, 2005.

Heinämaa, Sara. *Toward a Phenomenology of Sexual Difference: Husserl, Merleau-Ponty, Beauvoir.* Lanham, Md.: Rowman and Littlefield, 2003.

Husserl, Edmund. *Cartesianische Meditationen.* Hamburg: Felix Meiner, 1977.

Irigaray, Luce. *Between East and West: From Singularity to Community.* Trans. Stephen Pluhacek. New York: Columbia University Press, 2002.

———. *Democracy Begins between Two.* Trans. Kirsteen Anderson. New York: Routledge, 2001.

———. *I Love to You: Sketch of a Possible Felicity in History.* Trans. Alison Martin. New York: Routledge, 1996.

———. *Je, tu, nous: Toward a Culture of Difference.* Trans. Alison Martin. New York: Routledge, 1993.

———. *Key Writings.* London: Continuum, 2004.

——. *To Be Two*. Trans. Monique M. Rhodes and Marco F. Cocito-Monoc. London: Athlone Press, 2000.

Joy, Morny, ed. *Paul Ricoeur and Narrative: Context and Contestation*. Calgary: University of Calgary Press, 1997.

Laplanche, Jean, and Jean-Bertrand Pontalis. *Vocabulaire de la psychanalyse*. Paris: Quadrige/PUF, 1967.

Ricoeur, Paul. *Freedom and Nature: The Voluntary and the Involuntary*. Trans. and intro. Erazim V. Kohák. Foreword to the new ed. by Don Ihde. Evanston, Ill.: Northwestern University Press, 2007.

——. "Intellectual Autobiography." In *The Philosophy of Paul Ricoeur*, ed. Lewis Edwin Hahn, 3–53. Chicago: Open Court, 1995.

——. "Life in Quest of Narrative." In *On Paul Ricoeur: Narrative and Interpretation*, ed. David Wood, 20–33. London: Routledge, 1991.

——. "Narrative Identity." In *On Paul Ricoeur: Narrative and Interpretation*, ed. David Wood, 188–99. London: Routledge, 1991.

——. *Oneself as Another*. Trans. Kathleen Blamey. Chicago: University of Chicago Press, 1992.

——. "On Interpretation." Trans. Kathleen MacLaughlin. In *Philosophy in France Today*, ed. Alan Montefiore, 175–97. Cambridge: Cambridge University Press, 1983.

——. *Time and Narrative* III. Trans. Kathleen McLaughlin and David Pellauer. Chicago: University of Chicago Press, 1988.

Smith, Arthur D. *Husserl and the "Cartesian Meditations."* London: Routledge, 2003.

Stoller, Silvia. *Phänomenologie der Geschlechtlichkeit*. PhD diss., Radboud University Nijmegen, 2006.

Stone, Alison. "The Sex of Nature: A Reinterpretation of Irigaray's Metaphysical and Political Thought." *Hypatia* 18, no. 3 (2003): 60–84.

Stone-Mediatore, Shari. *Reading across Borders: Storytelling and Knowledges of Resistance*. New York: Palgrave Macmillan, 2003.

Part 2

ETHICAL AND POLITICAL PERSPECTIVES ON TIME

8.

CONTINGENCY, NEWNESS, AND FREEDOM: ARENDT'S RECOVERY OF THE TEMPORAL CONDITION OF POLITICS

Veronica Vasterling

It is uncontroversial, even a cliché, to state that freedom is an important value in the modern Western tradition of political theory and practice. The question of what freedom means, and what its realization requires, however, has never received a unanimous answer. This question has animated the two rival doctrines that have shaped the Western political landscape of the nineteenth and twentieth centuries: liberalism and socialism. It has also been central to the modern history of feminist ideas, from Mary Wollstonecraft to Simone de Beauvoir, and from Harriet Taylor and John Stuart Mill to Susan Moller Okin. From Wollstonecraft's (1792) indictment of the exclusionary politics of the Enlightenment's universal declaration of the rights of man[1] to Okin's (1989) incisive critique of the gender blindness of Rawlsian liberalism,[2] feminist thinkers have provided critical analyses of overly abstract notions of freedom and argued for better and more realistic conceptions. Though she is not a self-identified feminist thinker, Hannah Arendt's work offers a unique contribution to this feminist tradition of critical inquiry into established notions and practices of freedom. It is unique because Arendt is, as far as I can tell, one of the few philosophers in the Western tradition who examines the metaphysical conceptions of time that condition and constrain Western ideas of freedom. In this chapter I will argue that Arendt's deconstruction of the metaphysical hierarchy of necessity and contingency, and her rehabilitation of contingency as a key feature of human existence, enable an existential phenomenology of freedom that recovers the lived experience of freedom.

Arendt a Phenomenologist?

A quick survey of the by now extensive body of secondary literature on Arendt's work shows that it is still unusual to regard it as belonging to the tradition of phenomenology.[3] So the first question that needs to be addressed is what makes her work phenomenological.

The sources, method, and content of Arendt's work bear quite clearly an existential and hermeneutic phenomenological signature. She has been influenced by the early hermeneutic phenomenological work of Martin Heidegger and the humanist *Existenzphilosophie* of Karl Jaspers. Her work can be characterized as a phenomenology of the human condition with a special emphasis on political phenomena and experiences. Similar to the early Heidegger, Arendt foregrounds worldliness and temporality as the two most important aspects of the human condition, but unlike Heidegger, she brings out the political aspects and the underlying contingency of human existence. Like Jaspers, Arendt considers freedom and plurality the specifically human qualities of human existence, qualities that can be realized only as a worldly reality through political action. Though Arendt doesn't profile herself as a phenomenologist—but then, she doesn't even consider herself to be a philosopher[4]—her way of philosophizing is, in an unconventional and nontheoretical fashion, hermeneutic and phenomenological. It is organized by a set of interdependent and substantial principles, derived from or associated with the tradition of hermeneutic phenomenology that I will review in broad outline.

In the first chapter of *The Human Condition,* Arendt argues that the human condition shouldn't be mistaken for human nature.[5] There are many answers to the question "What is human?": for instance, that humans are a species that evolved from the *Australopithecus afarensis* who inhabited Africa 3 million years ago, or that humans are endowed with *logos* as the ancient Greeks said. Though true and sensible, these answers will never be sufficient because they don't, and never can, do justice to human plurality. According to Arendt, human plurality is "the paradoxical plurality of unique beings," a uniqueness that manifests itself in speech and action, because no two speak and act alike.[6] Plurality is paradoxical because, on the one hand, human beings are similar as members of the same species, but on the other hand, they individuate into unique beings through speech and action. This conjunction of similarity and difference recurs in Arendt's distinction between "who" and "what," that is, individual (unique) identity and collective identity. What I am—a woman, a Dutch person, a philosopher—I share with numerous other people; who I am is the irreplaceable result of a meaningful life. In order to answer the question of human nature one would need, strictly speaking, the biographies of the billions of people who have lived and will live, assuming that biographies do succeed in revealing the uniqueness of the person. Instead of the question of human nature, it is therefore the question of the conditions of human life that is Arendt's point of departure. The conditions of human life—earth and life itself, natality and mortality, worldliness and plurality—determine human life while at the same time being determined by humans, since the development of modern technology.

The distinction between "who" and "what" human beings are is related to another important distinction: between human reality and natural reality. As members of the species *Homo sapiens* we are part of nature in the sense that we need oxygen, water, and nourishment in order to survive; but what makes us human beings is a specifically human reality. Analogous to Dilthey's distinction between the natural sciences (*Naturwissenschaften*) and the humanities (*Geistes-wissenschaften*), Arendt assumes that natural reality can be objectified without loss, whereas human reality can't.[7] Though useful and inevitable in the process of knowledge production, generalizing objectivations and conceptualizations—like the conception of human beings as an evolved species or as creatures endowed with speech—are inadequate for understanding and determining the specific features of human life and human reality. The basic feature of human reality is its worldliness, that is, its inherent dimension of meaning resulting from human speech and action.[8] It is because of this inherent meaningfulness that human reality can't be objectified without a loss. To understand the meaning of actions, words, events, and facts, the external objectifying perspective needs to be exchanged for a participatory position that allows one to be addressed by what one sees and hears. The meaningfulness of human reality also entails that generalizations can never do justice, for the meaning of human interaction is context-dependent and therefore variable—the same action can be an act of heroic resistance in Nazi Germany and an act of conformist cowardliness in Germany in 2007.

In accordance with these principles, Arendt rejects the usual empirical, scientific, and (abstract philosophical) conceptual approach to human reality. Though she makes selective use of scientific and philosophical sources, the usual scientific and philosophical approaches do not fit her project. The objectifying methods and causal explanations of the sciences and the generalizing theories and concepts of philosophy are incapable of addressing and grasping the inexhaustibly variable and context-specific meaningfulness of human reality. Her aim is not to draw up a theory of human reality but to uncover and articulate the forgotten experiences—including their inconsistencies and paradoxes—that underlie concepts pertaining to human existence. For lived experience and (effects of) human action, as a rule, lack the conceptual and argumentative consistency characteristic of scientific and philosophical theories. Based on an array of sources, consisting of literary, historical, political, scientific, philosophical, and other texts, Arendt presents narrative interpretations of historical situations, events, and persons that reveal in exemplary fashion the significance of diverse aspects of human life. Arendt's work also offers original phenomenological analyses of the so-called *vita activa,* to wit, labor, work, and action, in *The Human Condition,* and of the activities of the mind, that is, thinking, willing, and judging, in *The Life of the Mind* (1978).[9] The two books together make for a full-fledged philosophical anthropology in the hermeneutic phenomenological tradition of the early Heidegger, Scheler, Jaspers, and Merleau-Ponty. The phenomenological analyses and descriptions are original because they are based on an unraveling of metaphysical fallacies that distort the philosophical and everyday conception of human existence. Among these, it is the fallacious metaphysical hierarchy of necessity versus contingency that is of particular importance with respect to the political aspect of human existence.

Contingency and Necessity

Arendt's account of metaphysical fallacies in *The Life of the Mind* is very illuminating for at least two reasons. First, it provides a deconstruction of metaphysical presuppositions overlooked by Heidegger and Derrida, and second, it throws more light on Arendt's own previous work, especially *The Human Condition.* Arendt is not given to reflection on her own work, methodological or otherwise, but much of what she says in the context of the discussion of the metaphysical fallacies can be read as a reflective elucidation of the implicit method and viewpoint of *The Human Condition* and other earlier work. The deconstruction of the metaphysical fallacies explicates more fully what remains implicit in *The Human Condition,* namely that contingency is the temporal condition of the phenomenon of the new and the possibility of freedom.

The most fundamental metaphysical fallacy, Arendt contends, is the Platonic two-worlds doctrine, which pits the timeless world of ideas against the temporal world of phenomena. Whereas ideas refer to abiding and eternal being, phenomena refer to changing, that is, appearing and disappearing, being. The timeless world of ideas connotes truth and necessity, whereas the temporal world of phenomena connotes contingency in the sense of blind chance and meaningless change. The age-old hierarchy of timelessness and time, of eternity and change, has mainly been manifest and played out through the related hierarchy of necessity and contingency. Necessary being is conceived as enduring, full, perfect being without any lack of being. As the paradigm of necessary being, God, makes clear, necessary being possesses an ontological fullness and dignity that contingent being can never have. As that which is but could also not be, and that which appears and then disappears again, contingent being is merely incidental and always lacking and, therefore, incapable of ontological integrity and stability. The ontological inferiority of contingent being entails an epistemological inferiority as well. The ontological hierarchy underpins an epistemological hierarchy of reliable knowledge enabled by eternal, necessary being, as opposed to the unreliable and deceptive sensory impressions garnered from changing phenomena. Since Leibniz, modern philosophy has consolidated this epistemological hierarchy in the distinction between, on the one hand, necessary truths, or truths of reason, and on the other hand, contingent truths, or truths of fact. Whereas necessary truths, for instance the law of noncontradiction, are deemed to be self-evident and certain, contingent truths are always questionable and contestable because they are not self-evident, and hence not certain.

Arendt's deconstruction of the hierarchy of the necessary and the contingent is not only, and not primarily, aimed at contemporary philosophy, science, and humanities, pointing up the ways in which they are still inscribed in the onto-logical and epistemological hierarchy. The primary focus of her deconstruction is the lived experience of necessity and contingency in human life. It is against this anthropological backdrop that she argues that the force of necessity is an utterly compelling force, far stronger than the force of violence, which may leave your mind free whereas necessary truths compel human reason.[10] Once you have understood or learned the necessary truths of reason, you never go against them, you don't question them; they leave you, as it were, no space to maneuver. Somebody who questions whether two plus two makes four either is a fool or has very limited mental capacities. The point Arendt wants to make is that contingency completely lacks the compelling force of necessity. Referring to what might or might not be, and what might change any time, contingency, in existential terms, connotes the boundless open space and time of possibility, which, from a political viewpoint, is the space and time of freedom.

In an interesting passage in *The Life of the Mind* Arendt concisely articulates her conception of the way necessity, contingency, and freedom are related: "The opposite of necessity is not contingency or accident but freedom. Everything that appears to human eyes, everything that occurs to the human mind, everything that happens to mortals for better or worse is 'contingent,' including their own existence."[11]

This is a remarkable reinterpretation of necessity and contingency. What is remarkable is not that human reality is presented as contingent throughout—

there are many such statements in Arendt's work—but that necessity is opposed to freedom instead of contingency, as is commonly done.[12] Underlying Arendt's succinct formulation are two very important insights. First, the insight that human reality is a specific ontological realm to be distinguished from, especially, the realm of nature, in which necessity figures prominently. Insofar as humans are also an animal species, we live an animal life according to the dictates, the necessities, of nature. Like other animals we have to eat and drink and procreate in order to survive as species. Though nature has an evolutionary history that is very contingent, the natural conditions of survival of the species of *Homo sapiens* do not leave many options. We have to breathe oxygen, we have to eat and drink, otherwise we die, and so on. From a scientific viewpoint the natural conditions of survival may be thoroughly contingent; from the phenomenological viewpoint of human experience, however, they are the paradigm of necessity. Arendt's second insight concerns the relation between contingency and freedom. Though both human reality and natural reality are contingent, only human reality allows for freedom.[13] Only creatures living a human life may experience the contrast between necessity and freedom. Again, it is from the phenomenological viewpoint of experience that the opposition of necessity and freedom becomes meaningful.

There might be another reason why Arendt replaces the traditional opposition of necessity and contingency with the one of necessity and freedom. There is a tendency in Arendt's work to dismiss necessity, as an ontological and epistemological category, in favor of contingency. That is, while substituting contingency as the primary ontological and epistemological category, Arendt reinterprets necessity and freedom as existential and experiential categories. Arendt's work implies not only that necessity and freedom are on the same level—the existential, specifically human level of life—but, moreover, that the experience of both is enabled by contingency, that is, by time and change.[14] Again, it is Arendt's distinction between the natural and the human that best elucidates the import of this reinterpretation. Both natural and human life are contingent; that is, both are marked by change, but in very distinct ways. According to Arendt, the time sequence of natural life is cyclical or, in other words, repetitive. All organisms are bound to the same repetitive sequences of birth, procreation, and death, and within life, the same repetitive sequences of physical survival. Now, in contrast to the repetitive and cyclical temporality of natural life, the temporality of (specifically) human life is linear but not continuous, as is mostly assumed in the classical accounts of time by, for instance, Aristotle and Kant. The temporality of human life, Arendt maintains, is linear and *dis*continuous because the linear sequence of human life is interrupted by new beginnings and new events. While the repetitive time sequences of natural life are experienced as necessity, the interruptions of the linear time sequence of human life *may* be experienced as freedom. For it is not a matter of course that they will be experienced as freedom. Throughout her work, Arendt argues that the experience of freedom has fallen in disrepute and is consequently forgotten due to the influential metaphysical fallacy that has elevated necessity to the highest form of being, degrading contingency to meaningless change and blind chance. The overall effect has been one of occluding completely the phenomenon of the new and the related experience of freedom. From the viewpoint of necessity, which is taken as norm and truth, contingency is the privation of truth: an illusion, a haphazard, a meaningless play of changes that fools our senses and isn't quite real. Due to this Platonic worldview—which is surprisingly tenacious, for it lives on in the modern sciences' proclivity for determinism—contingency is neglected, and the phenomenon contingency gives rise to, newness, is hardly acknowledged as something real.

New Beginnings

When Arendt proposes that the linear sequence of human life is interrupted by new beginnings and new events, what does she mean by new beginnings? Once again, the history of Western philosophy provides the key frame of reference. Throughout the history of Western philosophy, reflections on the temporality of human existence have, almost without exception, focused on mortality and finiteness. The acknowledgment that one first has to be born before dying becomes an option; the acknowledgment, in other words, of natality is a blind spot, and obviously a very gendered blind spot, of Western philosophy and culture.[15] Inspired by Saint Augustine, Arendt, in *The Human Condition,* emphasizes natality, which she interprets as a new beginning. Upon birth, human beings enter the world not only as new creatures, but also as beginners. Throughout our life we retain the capacity for new beginnings, which is the capacity of action, as Arendt explains:

> With word and deed we insert ourselves into the human world, and this insertion is like a second birth, in which we confirm and take upon ourselves the naked fact of our original physical appearance. This insertion is not forced upon us by necessity . . . its impulse springs from the beginning which came into the world when we were born and to which we respond by beginning something new on our own initiative. To act, in its most general sense, means to take initiative, to begin. . . . [And] it is in the nature of beginnings that something new is started which cannot be expected from whatever may have happened before.[16]

The temporal existential condition of natality refers not only to physical birth but also to the second birth of political speech and action. In Arendt's phenomenology of the political this very important second birth refers to the capacity and possibility to engage in public, pluralist, noninstrumental, and nonstrategic interaction in word and deed. For Arendt, physical birth is a new beginning only when people assume and respond to the condition of natality by inserting themselves into the public world of "human affairs," as she often calls it, that is, the public arena of noninstrumental and nonstrategic interaction: the political in Arendt's sense. This type of interaction introduces a double newness in the world. First, the second birth of public interaction reveals what every first, physical birth potentially is, namely a new and unique addition to human plurality. In Arendt's view human plurality, far from being simply a given, can realize and manifest itself only in and through speech and action. We are not born as unique individuals; we individuate through interaction with others. Hence the newness introduced by the second birth of speech and action is the newness of a new, unique individual who, together with other unique individuals, past, present, and future, constitutes human plurality—the great mosaic of equal yet distinct individuals. Political interaction introduces a second newness as well, the newness of unexpected and therefore unpredictable events and states of affairs. Words and deeds evoke responses and reactions, leading, because of the plurality of agents, to an open-ended and unpredictable web of consequences. The events, states of affairs, and facts resulting from political interaction are therefore not simply contingent, but rather unpredictable and sometimes spectacularly or horrifyingly new. This does not mean, of course, that they are always as spectacularly unexpected as, for instance, the fall of the Berlin Wall in November 1989, or as horrifyingly unprecedented as, for instance, the extermination camps of World War II. But these examples demonstrate what is true of every new event or state of affairs: because they exceed established frameworks of understanding, we have to come up with new interpretive narratives in order to give the new events a place in the worldly space of human affairs.

Summing up, contingency is a necessary but not sufficient condition of newness. In order for new events to happen and new states of affairs to come about, human interaction is required. Pluralist interaction, according to Arendt, may be the beginning of something new exactly because the events and states of affairs that result from this type of action are unintended and unpredictable. Whereas the implementation of plans and intentions in instrumental and strategic action, and of policies in politics as it is commonly understood, leads to more or less predictable results, the open-endedness of pluralist interaction cannot but lead to unpredictable consequences and, if successful, new events or states of affairs. For political interaction will always have unpredictable results, but not always new results. Political interaction may fail in this respect, and probably most often will fail if we take twentieth-century history as our model. Too many examples in recent history to enumerate here teach us that to be clamped down by force or to be recuperated by established bureaucratic institutions are two frequently occurring ways in which genuine political interaction fails to be the beginning of something new.

Freedom

Arendt's conception of political interaction relates freedom to contingency and newness. Public, pluralist interaction qualifies as political only if it is undertaken not out of (moral) obligation, nor because it is compelled by norms or laws—whether laws of reason, nature, or otherwise—but as one's own initiative, in other words, if it is undertaken freely. This aspect of initiative is crucial, for it underlies the distinction between mere change or mere contingency on the one hand, and a new beginning on the other. A new beginning is more than simply a change. Temporality and contingency imply continuous changes, but by far the most of those changes are not new beginnings. They are causally explainable and (sometimes) predictable changes, which means that the changes are reducible to preexisting causes and, therefore, not really a new beginning, in the sense of a discontinuity in the linear sequence of time, nor the start of something new. Most natural phenomena are of this kind, but also a lot of human behavior is explainable and predictable in terms of the habits, rules, and institutional practices on which it is based. Only those courses of interaction that are started spontaneously, from our own initiative, qualify as new beginnings, and may lead to new events and states of affairs. This looks like a very hard condition because most action, as Arendt herself emphasizes, is habitual or institutionally embedded, and, as such, semi-automatic. It is not compelled or forced, but neither is it free in Arendt's sense, for it constitutes not a discontinuity, but rather a continuation and confirmation of the status quo. One shouldn't forget, however, that pluralist interaction consists for a large part in speech-acts. And speech-acts are much more easily conceivable as spontaneous initiative. Unless we censor ourselves or are censored by external forces, we are able to and often do speak our minds freely.

Though spontaneity and initiative can be equated with free volition, it would be completely wrong to interpret Arendt's conception of freedom in terms of what traditionally is called the free will. Freedom, in Arendt, is a worldly reality realized through pluralistic interaction in word and deed. The free will is a mental phenomenon that, if understood correctly, is an indispensable ingredient of freedom, but not more than that: an ingredient. In the second volume of *The Life of the Mind,* dedicated to the topic of willing, Arendt vigorously opposes the traditional reduction of freedom to free will. With the sole exception of Duns Scotus, who understood the "I will" as an "I can," thereby relating freedom to action, the Christian tradition since Saint Paul reduced freedom to the paradoxical mental phenomenon of a divided and impotent will where the "I will" is followed by an "I cannot."[17] This was not the only way in which Western tradition emasculated the phenomenon of the will, thereby obscuring the possibility of action and the reality of freedom. The distortion of the free will to sovereignty, autarky, and utter autonomy on the one hand, or its subjugation under the dictates of reason on the other hand, have also been major factors in the Western tradition's forgetting of (the experience of) pluralistic interaction as the realization of freedom. The former substituted the solipsistic model of hierarchical rule; the second abolished the freedom of the will. While easily adaptable to a framework of instrumental and strategic action, both are deeply incompatible with the pluralistic open-endedness of political action and freedom in Arendt's sense. Like Duns Scotus—the only philosopher, according to Arendt, who understood the will—Arendt understands the will as the initiative to act. In contrast to a long tradition of obscuring and distorting the phenomenon of the will, this understanding is the only one that relates the will to action and freedom.

Arendt's conceptualization of newness and freedom as a discontinuity in the linear sequence of time raises another problem that is maybe more difficult to dispose of. The notion of discontinuity is embedded in the opposition Arendt construes between causality, on the one hand, and freedom and newness, or new beginning, on the other hand. The following passage from the essay "Understanding and Politics" is a clear example of this opposition:

> Newness is the realm of the historian, who—unlike the natural scientist, who is concerned with ever-recurring happenings—deals with events which always occur only once. This newness can be manipulated if the historian insists on causality and pretends to be able to explain events by a chain of causes which eventually led up to them. . . . Causality, however, is an altogether alien and falsifying category in the historical sciences. Not only does the actual meaning of every event always transcend any number of past "causes" which we may assign to it, . . . but this past itself comes into being only with the event itself. Only when something irrevocable has happened can we even try to trace its history backward. The event illuminates its own past; it can never be deduced from it.[18]

In this passage and elsewhere Arendt insists that in the historical sciences—or the humanities as we would probably say nowadays—we should not use causal explanations because they are reductive. They reduce what Arendt considers to be the quintessence of the historical, newness. The title of the essay—"Understanding and Politics"—and the context of the passage suggest that we need the herme-neutic approach of understanding (*verstehen*) in order to be able to appreciate the singularity and newness of events. Arendt's opposition of causal explanation and hermeneutic understanding raises the question whether her conception of the new is inscribed in a dualism of nature and history. Though it makes sense to distinguish between (the experience and knowledge of) nature and history in the way I discussed in the first section, dualism of nature and history implies a lot more than a distinction in this sense. Dualism of nature and history implies the existence of two distinct and exclusive ontological realms with distinct and exclusive characteristics. It implies a conception of nature as the ontological realm of changing but repetitive phenomena, excluding newness, and of history as the ontological realm of singular, new events, excluding repetition. It is obvious, how-ever, that this is false. Despite the many reductively deterministic interpretations of it, evolution almost per definition entails newness, namely the emergence of new species. And history does not consist only of singular, new events, but also of a lot of repetitive phenomena, for instance when we focus on the emergence and consolidation of institutions and their bureaucracies. Insofar as Arendt does sometimes show a tendency to relapse into an ontological dualism of nature versus history and a methodological dualism of causal explanation versus hermeneutic understanding, I would argue in favor of a deconstruction of the ontological dualism and a transformation of methodological dualism into methodological pluralism in both the humanities and the natural sciences.

Conclusion: Time and Freedom

Throughout her work Arendt criticizes the Western tradition's penchant to valorize necessity and disparage contingency. What starts with the ontological elevation of unchanging, necessary being in Greek philosophy, and continues with the epis-temological elevation of the necessary truths of reason, logic, and mathematics in modern philosophy and science, culminates in the determinist philosophies of history, of which Hegel provides the exemplary example. By reducing every change and every new event to a phase in the unfolding with dialectical necessity of reason, society, and nature, this type of philosophy all but eliminates contingency and newness. Arendt is of course not the only one to take issue with this way of thinking. Nietzsche, Kierkegaard, and Lyotard are among the philosophers who, from various perspectives and motivated by different issues, have criticized this type of, in Lyotard's words, "master narrative." Nor is Arendt the only philosopher to recognize that the metaphysical hierarchy of necessity versus contingency is symptomatic for a conception of time that valorizes the unchanging eternity of

the timeless over and above the contingency of time. Though there are no references or clear indications of this, it may arguably be assumed that Arendt's work
is influenced in this respect by that of her teacher Heidegger who, at the time
when Arendt was his student, was deeply immersed in a deconstructive analysis
of the metaphysical conception of time. Another explicitly acknowledged source
of inspiration is the work of Henri Bergson, who, like Arendt, criticized the Western tradition of philosophy's pervasive lack of understanding of radical novelty
and unpredictability.[19] The specific achievement of Arendt's work, however, is to
provide an extensive phenomenological elucidation of the political consequences
of the metaphysical hierarchy and its underlying conception, or, rather, denial
of contingency and newness. When philosophers and scientists systematically
reduce the freedom practice of pluralist speech and action to causally explainable
and predictable behavior, or to manifestations of necessary historical processes or
laws of nature, it is no wonder that the experience of freedom is forgotten. In this
forgetfulness originates the vicious circle that, according to Arendt, is characteristic of the modern Western tradition. The privileging of necessity undermines
the experience of freedom that, in its turn, leads to the misconceived notion of
politics as rule, administration, organization, policy—in short, politics as the result
of instrumental and/or strategic action. These misconceptions of politics, in their
turn, enable and validate causalist and determinist approaches of human reality.

Among the few philosophers who have understood the crucial connection
between freedom and time, Arendt is the only one to analyze and explicate the
phenomenological-existential interdependence of the practice of freedom and
the recognition of the possibility of unexpected newness. Against the backdrop
of a global civilization that in religion, philosophy, science, and politics tends to
replace the risk of freedom with the (mostly illusionary) certainty of calculation
and control, digitalization and predictability, and the belief in historical, social,
and natural inevitabilities, Arendt foregrounds freedom as human beings' capacity
to avoid inevitable disasters and to make the miracle of the improbable happen.

Notes

1. Wollstonecraft, *A Vindication of the Rights of Woman*.

2. Okin, *Justice, Gender, and the Family*.

3. If you take a large enough time span you will, however, find a few titles, including
Allen, "Hannah Arendt"; Barber, "Phenomenology and the Ethical Bases of Pluralism";
Betz-Hull, "A Progression of Thought and the Primacy of Interaction"; Steven Galt Crowell,
"Who Is the Political Actor?"; Hinchman and Hinchman, "In Heidegger's Shadow"; Ta-
miniaux, "Bios Politikos and Bios Theoretikos in the Phenomenology of Hannah Arendt";
Vollrath, "Hannah Arendt and the Method of Political Thinking."

4. In a 1964 interview with Guenther Gauss, Arendt says that she doesn't belong to the circle of philosophers, and that she is not accepted as such by the philosophers (Arendt, *Essays in Understanding 1930–1954*, 1).

5. Arendt, *The Human Condition*.

6. Ibid., 176.

7. Dilthey, *Einleitung in die Geisteswissenschaften*.

8. In (implicitly) identifying meaningfulness as the most important feature of worldliness, Arendt is clearly influenced by Heidegger, though her analysis of the worldly condition of human existence in *The Human Condition* is in most other respects very different from Heidegger's analysis of the worldliness of human *Dasein* in *Being and Time*. For Heidegger's analysis of worldliness in terms of involvement (*Bewandtnis*) and significance (*Bedeutsamkeit*), see Heidegger, *Being and Time*, §18.

9. *The Life of the Mind* was published posthumously because Arendt died after finishing the volume on willing. After her death, lecture notes on judging were published instead of the missing third volume of the trilogy (Hannah Arendt, *Lectures on Kant's Political Philosophy*).

10. Arendt, *The Life of the Mind*, 60.

11. Ibid., 60.

12. Strictly speaking, necessity is the denial of contingency. Against the overwhelming sensory experience of change, necessity refers to what does not change, what is not other than it is.

13. Though this is a very Kantian view, Arendt does not subscribe to the Kantian dualism that separates animal (natural, bodily) life from a specifically human life, in the sense of a life based on reason, the organ or faculty that is supposed to enable freedom and morality. Arendt's work allows only for a gradual distinction between the human and the natural. Humans and animals are, for instance, both worldly beings: "Living beings, men and animals, are not just in the world, they are *of the world*, and this precisely because they are subjects and objects—perceiving and being perceived—at the same time" (Arendt, *The Life of the Mind*, 20).

14. Here are two indications of the rejection of necessity as an epistemological and ontological category. A few lines below the quotation I cited, Arendt explicitly rejects the main instance of epistemological necessity, i.e., necessary truth, here in the form of the truths of mathematics and logic: "there are no truths beyond and above factual truths: all scientific truths are factual truths, those engendered by sheer brain power and expressed in a specially designed sign language not excluded" (Arendt, *The Life of the Mind*, 60). Another example is provided by Arendt's insistence that "Being and Appearing coincide" (Arendt, *The Life of the Mind*, 19). As appearance and disappearance go together—something Arendt learned from Heidegger—the interpretation of being in terms of appearing entails that change and, therefore, contingency are coextensive with being.

15. See on this topic the excellent article of Christina Schües, "The Birth of Difference."

16. Arendt, *The Human Condition*, 176–78.

17. It is no accident that Duns Scotus is according to Arendt "the only thinker for

whom the word 'contingent' has no derogatory association" (Arendt, *The Life of the Mind*, 2:134). As one of the very few philosophers who acknowledged the free will and its relation to action, he understood that contingency is "the price to be paid for freedom" (ibid.).

18. Arendt, *Essays in Understanding 1930–1954*, 318–19.

19. References to Bergson occur throughout *The Life of the Mind*. Of specific interest, in this context, is a long quotation on page 32 of vol. 2 (*Willing*) of *The Life of the Mind*.

Bibliography

Allen, Wayne. "Hannah Arendt: Existential Phenomenology and Political Freedom." *Philosophy and Social Criticism* 9 (1982): 171–90.

Arendt, Hannah. *Essays in Understanding 1930–1954: Uncollected and Unpublished Work.* Ed. Jerome Kohn. New York: Harcourt Brace, 1994.

———. *The Human Condition*. Chicago: University of Chicago Press, 1958.

———. *Lectures on Kant's Political Philosophy*. Ed. and with interpretive essay by Ronald Beiner. Chicago: University of Chicago Press, 1982.

———. *The Life of the Mind*, vols. 1 and 2. New York: Harcourt Brace, 1978.

Barber, Benjamin. "Phenomenology and the Ethical Bases of Pluralism: Arendt and Beauvoir on Race in the United States." In *The Existential Phenomenology of Simone de Beauvoir*, ed. W. O'Brien and Lester Embree, 149–74. Dordrecht: Kluwer, 2001.

Betz-Hull, Margareth. "A Progression of Thought and the Primacy of Interaction." *Journal of the British Society for Phenomenology* 30, no. 2 (1999): 207–28.

Crowell, Steven Galt. "Who Is the Political Actor? An Existential Phenomenological Approach." In *Phenomenology of the Political*, ed. K. Thompson and L. Embree, 11–28. Dordrecht: Kluwer, 2000.

Dilthey, Wilhelm. *Einleitung in die Geisteswissenschaften*. [1883] Stuttgart: Teubner, 1922.

Heidegger, Martin. *Being and Time*. Trans. John Macquarrie and Edward Robinson. Oxford: Blackwell, 1962.

Hinchman, Lewis, and Sandra Hinchman. "In Heidegger's Shadow: Hannah Arendt's Phenomenological Humanism." *Review of Politics* 46, no. 2 (1984): 183–210.

Okin, Susan Moller. *Justice, Gender, and the Family*. New York: Basic Books, 1989.

Schües, Christina. "The Birth of Difference." *Human Studies* 20, no. 2 (1997): 243–52.

Taminiaux, Jacques. "Bios Politikos and Bios Theoretikos in the Phenomenology of Hannah Arendt." *International Journal of Philosophical Studies* 4, no. 2 (1996): 215–32.

Vollrath, Ernst. "Hannah Arendt and the Method of Political Thinking." *Social Research* 44, no. 1 (1977): 160–82.

Wollstonecraft, Mary. *A Vindication of the Rights of Woman*. [1792] Ed. with intro. by Miriam Brody. London: Penguin Books, 1985.

9.

QUESTIONING "HOMELAND" THROUGH YAEL BARTANA'S *WILD SEEDS*

Helen A. Fielding

Adriana Cavarero claims that the uniqueness of the voice is that which grounds the political. Drawing upon the work of Hannah Arendt, she argues that the *polis* is not a place as such, but is rather the "in-between," that which "relates and separates [humans] at the same time, revealing their plural condition."[1] This in-between, she argues, is lacking in the contemporary articulation of democracy, which, on the one hand, is supposed to extend and guarantee equal rights to all humans, yet on the other hand, relies upon national identity, which is inherently exclusive. This spatially formulated understanding of identity is based on the fusion of individual voices, requiring a version of history that does not sufficiently allow for dissension, suturing over the violence required for such cohesion. Moreover, as an identity, national citizenship can be extended to people who do not actually inhabit a state and be denied to others who do. This cohesion then is attained through the denial of relations among multiple embodied and particular individuals, the *polis,* in favor of the unitary body of the state, that is, the nation. Although the in-between suggests the spatial, it is, however, essentially temporal since, as relational, it is necessarily intermittent.

In this paper I argue that Yael Bartana's video artworks, in particular *Wild Seeds* (2005), draw upon the particularity of embodied voices to reveal the fissures in national identity.[2] Video provides a potent medium for investigating identity since it cannot avoid questions of time. In general, a painting can be observed in the glance of the eye, cursory as this glance might be; sculptures usually require that one walk around them, but this movement unfolds at the viewer's own pace. Video art is otherwise. Temporality is woven into its structure in terms of the work's length, whether or not the viewer is required to watch it in its entirety, whether the video is repetitive with no definitive start or finish, and even in terms of the length of each shot. These might be merely technical aspects of video art, yet in any artwork the technical aspects, the very materiality of the piece, are intrinsic to the working of the work. In the case of Bartana's videos, the temporal aspect of video allows her to open up a time-space, or rather a spacing as a relation rather than a place.[3] It is a spacing that takes place only when the artwork sets to work in its engagement with viewers, that is, when the video is playing in a public space.[4] As Veronica Vasterling points out, it is the temporal aspect of freedom, the contingent, that allows for the new over and above necessity and that can alter the course of history.

In her choice of subject matter, Bartana generally takes up temporally circumscribed events that are deeply embedded in the past, yet show up either disjuncture or parallels between national identity and individual embodied narratives. While national identity might rely upon fusion, Bartana's videos upset that identity by opening up a spacing where identity can be questioned. Filming events such as a demonstration or an initiation into military weapons training, as well as play, her videos draw upon ritualized events that, in their repetition, are often meant to work performatively at a corporeal level to create a national and cultural unity. She draws upon two aspects of repetition: first, she tries to show up the unintended results of these repetitions, the appearance of fissures in national and cultural unity; second, meaning is shown to be contingent and can be modified in the repeated replaying of the actual video work—meanings shift in terms of who is viewing as well as with each viewing. Thus, Bartana's videos affectively and phenomenally draw the viewer into the corporeal experience of these rituals, yet only to show up the ruptures; indeed, they seem to suggest that it is at the level of the corporeal that this cohesion can be both effected and also undone, perhaps precisely because the corporeal is through and through temporal.

Her stated methodology, to make "the everyday strange," is to reveal the strangeness, the uncanniness, at the heart of the quotidian.[5] In German, the "uncanny" is the *Unheimliche,* the unhomely, the alien at the heart of the familiar; in revealing the *Unheimliche* as such, her videos open up a space for reflecting upon that which is usually taken for granted: home, embodiment, the everyday.[6] Indeed, this approach relies upon the phenomenological insight that the everyday we corporeally inhabit, which too rarely is exposed to scrutiny or interrogation, can actually be transformed through such questioning. Bartana's videos suggest, moreover, that embodied being itself can lend itself to this fusion or unity that national rituals seem to support, but also, and more importantly, to a being-with that can take place only where fusion is foregone. There is an inherent risk of violence in being with others that belongs to the political that cannot be equated with the violence done to others, the violence of force. Thus, to be with others means making oneself vulnerable to the risks of violence that that being-with implies.

If we take Arendt's concern that the *polis,* or public, where we appear before others through our action and speech, is collapsed in modernity with the private, resulting in what she refers to as the "social," which is neither private nor public—that is, it is a space where we can neither be with others nor withdraw from the world—then any notion of homeland must be rigorously interrogated for its complicity in this collapse. If nation configured as home requires fusion rather than being-with, then there is no potential for critical dialogue that allows for the objective acknowledgment of others' embodied realities. Moreover, in losing the possibilities of appearing before others, we simultaneously forfeit the space for withdrawal and reflection. She notes that in the aftermath of two world wars, the "rightless" lost first their homes, and with them the "entire social texture into which they were born and in which they established for themselves a distinct place in the world."[7] Thus having a home is about more than simply having one's own space; it also situates someone within a relational and contextual structure, that is, the world, where "opinions [are] significant and actions effective," where one can engage in the intermittent political relations of action and speech.[8]

What Bartana's videos accomplish, then, is to establish the temporal aspect of space, that is, a spacing where the taken-for-granted corporeal complicity with national identity can be brought to the fore in the questioning of homeland; for not only is the political deeply embodied, as the videos reveal, but this political aspect of embodiment, this being-with, is in danger of being lost. Thus, rather than focusing on national identity, which is exclusive and hence primarily spatial, corporeal being-with emphasizes the temporal—the *polis* is figured as embodied intermittent relations or spacings rather than as an actual territory or space. At the same time, such relations need to take place; they need to be bounded and supported by spatial structures, for example, by a home, in order to prevent them from dissipating into nothing.

For speaking and acting require some kind of shared reality, beyond mere identification, that is affirmed by others. Film theorist Laura Marks notes that identity politics "depends strategically on the recognition of ethnic, national, gender, and other affiliations"; thus it is those "people who slip between the cracks" of these categories who "stir up political ferment." And these are the people who "are just beginning to find their voices."[9] For Cavarero, the voice is significant not only because it is unique, but also because it is always addressed *to* someone. For Arendt, while the in-between of the *polis* relates and separates humans, "the *inter-est,* which lies between people . . . can relate and bind them together."[10] In speaking and acting, not only do we share and confirm "some worldly objective reality," but agents are disclosed by acting for spectators and speaking to one another. Acting and speaking are not tangible in that they do not leave behind "end products." But, she reminds us, the in-between of the relation among agents has its own reality in the "'web' of human relationships."[11] This inter-est, perhaps even desire, is that which binds humans together.

Perhaps this is one of the reasons *Wild Seeds* is so compelling. The film, which makes reference to a few lines in Genesis, to the giving of these lands to the seeds of Abraham, records a game invented and played by a group of Israeli youths, refuseniks who oppose Israeli occupation of the West Bank.[12] Named "Evacuation of Gilad's Colony," the game was the adolescents' response to "the forced withdrawal of Jewish settlers from the Occupied Territories" and the resultant "violent confrontation between soldiers and settlers at Gilad's Farms in 2002."[13] The game, which can be played anywhere at any time, is simple: two youths play the part of soldiers who attempt to win by pulling apart the remaining youths, who take the role of protesting resisting settlers. Though the game is ostensibly the acting out of the resistance of settlers to soldiers, it also mirrors the exile that Palestinians have been forced to endure. The youths are seventeen, some just sixteen, years of age, and in the artist's view, they would not, even a year later, have participated in the game.[14] As such, Bartana captures them at the threshold between youth and adulthood, an intense stage of becoming, at the brink of an adult self-consciousness, and of articulating identity, of sensing out one's desires, one's place in the world.

Playing games is a way for children to become aware of their spatial world. Games allow children to discover and invent new movements, ways of touching, of working out their emotional worlds. For Louis Hammer, this play is about the spatial: "it was play that brought to life the growing structures of home."[15] But play is also inherently temporal in that it involves repetition, and it is inherent to corporeal becoming. Perhaps, like all children's games, this one was an attempt to understand and work through complex feelings attached to events over which they have little control. Likely many the grandchildren or great-grandchildren of Holocaust survivors, they are what Griselda Pollock in her discussion of Bracha Lichtenberg Ettinger terms "witnesses without an event."[16] In reversing Dori Laub's claim that the rounding up, shipping off, and extermination of large populations in Nazi Germany meant that everyone was implicated in this "rational, bureaucratic and administrative transformation of death into a dying worse than death," thereby leaving no outside witnesses who could attest to the event, Pollock is interested in the ways that trauma continues to resonate and reverberate in surviving generations, often gaining in force and momentum.[17] While Laub seeks to therapeutically support survivors in becoming witnesses to their own suffering and the suffering of others, Pollock reflects upon the unanticipated effects of the continued resonances between and among subsequent generations. Thus an event that cannot be "fully captured in *thought, memory* and *speech*" can be psychically transmitted in a border-linking transgenerational transmission.[18] In other words, traumatic events of a historic and political scale are taken up differently at the level of the discourses of national identity and those of corporeal intersubjectivity. Such events can have psychic and corporeal effects that cannot be accounted for in discourses of national identity and that in fact contribute to the failure of representation and identity.

In the case of the youths filmed in *Wild Seeds,* it is a question of having incorporated events for which they have neither memory nor experience, and yet, because our corporeal being is always already an intercorporeality, there is an affective response, an intertwining with the embodied being of family members, friends, and community, including Arab and Palestinian neighbors. As Cathy Caruth claims, "we can also read the address of the voice . . . not as the story of the individual in relation to the events of his own past, but as the story of the way in which one's own trauma is tied up with the trauma of another, the way in which trauma may lead therefore, to the encounter with another, through the very possibility and surprise of listening to another's wound."[19] *Wild Seeds,* I would thus suggest, explores the embodied reverberations of the multiple experiences of shared traumas in the ways that they exceed the unifying gestures of national identity; the youths respond through their game, not only to the pressures to conform to a national identity they also resist, but also to their desire to find their own voices, and to respond to those of others, to change the course of history. As Vasterling points out, freedom is not something we think, it is something we enact, and it is the contingency of action that allows for something new.

Though rules can offer a framework of protection, as Arendt observes, "human institutions and laws" cannot completely guarantee what will happen within a "body politic," just as the "boundaries of the territory" do not provide absolute protection "against action from without."[20] Though, according to Bartana, the game can be played anywhere at any time, where the game is played does make a difference.[21] And this "anywhere anytime" is at first supported by the camera's lens capturing rolling expansive green-yellow hills that at first appear endlessly open. Yet, ultimately the space is bounded; the game is played and filmed in a very particular place—the beautiful hills of Prat's settlement, situated in the occupied territories. From time to time the expansive rolling hills that appear in the camera's lens are punctuated with the hint of small settlements on the horizon. Despite a feeling of openness that the space provides, Bartana chose to film in a place surrounded by closed military areas and security zones, perhaps revealing that though boundaries and rules might limit what we can do, action itself is ulti-

Wild Seeds. Courtesy of the Annet Gelink Gallery, Amsterdam, and the artist

mately boundless, which is what allows it to establish new relations.[22] In this way action is like play. Play is playful in part because it has the potential to allow for the unexpected within the boundaries of play. And the unexpected is temporal.

The video begins as the adolescents walk down a slope toward the site—they touch, then grasp each others' hands and limbs, creating one mass of intertwined bodies that clasp, hug, and laugh. The timing of the video has been slowed down, which has the effect of intensifying the experience, of allowing the viewer to phenomenally sense the tension, the suspension or slowdown of time that can precede the start of sport or competition. Indeed, the viewer too becomes corporeally engaged, echoing and reverberating with the adolescent passions. This video is compelling because the youths not only perform resistance, they are physically, emotionally, corporeally engaged in it as they hold, pull, grab, scream, and laugh, revealing how resistance is an embodied relation. We see and almost feel precisely how hands, legs, and mouths resist. And we feel simultaneously how the line between play and aggression is not firmly drawn.

We see moreover the overlapping of bodies, the ways that bodies move into and around and over each other, literally revealing a web of relations. There are human bundles of intertwining bodies—we see the fleshiness of these negotiations. One hand strokes another. The colors are fluorescent. The reds and greens punctuate

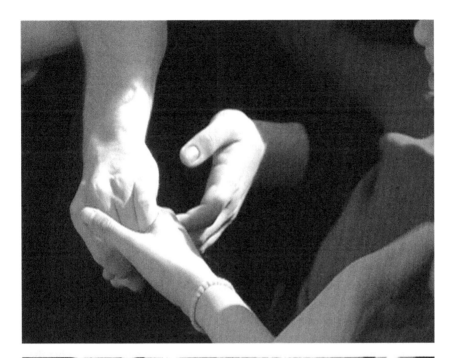

Wild Seeds. Courtesy of the Annet Gelink Gallery, Amsterdam, and the artist

the screen. The camera's gaze sweeps the grass from close up, mimicking what one might see as a participant in the game, thus implicating the camera, which cannot maintain a status of the objective viewer. Another body is pulled along the ground. A shirt rips at the seam, exposing the vulnerable flesh of armpit and the inside of the arm. A mass of bodies tumble around each other as they roll down a hill. One youth rocks his body to gain momentum and force to aid him in pulling the other bodies apart. We can see how hard it actually is to force bodies that resist without actually hurting them. Thus not only does playing this game allow the youths to feel corporeally the texture of resistance, but the viewer's body also takes up this embodied experience as her body overlaps with those on the screen.

Laura Marks suggests in her interrogation of intercultural film that haptic perception privileges the materiality of the image rather than representation. This concept, coming out of psychology, refers to a "combination of tactile, kinesthetic, and proprioceptive functions," the experience of touch both inside and out.[23] But Marks, drawing upon the use of the term by nineteenth-century art historian Aloïs Riegl, is interested in the way that optical visuality, which focuses on distinct forms viewed at sufficient distance so that they can be taken in at a glance, differs from haptic visuality, which is more likely to "move over the surface of its object . . . not to distinguish form so much as to discern texture."[24] She argues that haptic visuality is accordingly more objective since it is engaged with what is there rather than merely with the projection of the subject's organizational structures onto what is seen. Moreover, whereas the optical image provides sufficient information for the viewer to understand the narrative, the haptic image is less easily decoded and requires the viewer to draw more substantially upon her own bodily memories and affectivity as she engages with the image. Of course, Marks recognizes that there is no distinct division between haptic and optic visuality; nevertheless, haptic images more readily tend to invite the viewer into a relation with what is seen because they draw upon other forms of sense experience and make a claim on the body as a whole, foregrounding relations between bodies; whereas optic visuality leans toward the representational, securing the viewer's own boundaries.[25]

Video, like film, relies upon vision and sound—only two of the five senses. Yet, since our senses, which cannot be collapsed into one another, nevertheless intertwine, overlap, and come together in the synergic system of being in the world, one can see the hardness of ice, and hear the brittleness of glass as it breaks. This makes sense, as Merleau-Ponty explains, if we understand the senses as opening existentially upon the world.[26] Thus video might not literally be able to provide the experiences of smell, taste, or touch, yet these senses are evoked in *Wild Seeds* in the ways that they overlap with our sensuous bodies that have, over time, sedimented a carnal knowledge of certain smells, tastes, and ways of touching and being touched. To watch this video is to corporeally engage with it, that is to say, to bring into relation the temporal existence of three different kinds of bodies, that of the embodied viewer, that of the filmmaker, and that of the technical film that unfolds over time.[27]

Marks argues that haptic vision is thus inherently erotic not because it relies upon voyeurism, since that would require the distancing of optical vision, but rather because the viewer is implicated in the viewing. The eye that is invited to caress or engage closely with haptic images can explore the "resistant alterity" at the heart of the erotic, an alterity that, in evading sameness, participates in the movement of life that opens toward a future even as it is grounded in embodied relations in the present, without, for all that, appropriating the other.

In seeing, as Merleau-Ponty describes in his lectures on nature, the body is "mediator of an isomorphism," that is, of a correspondence between "the structure of the distributions of light" that comprise the "'image' of the film" and the scanning of these structures "by the perceiving body."[28] This is the esthesiological and also libidinal body that is "an opening to things and to others" and that moves into things and beings and takes them up.[29] When Merleau-Ponty looks in the mirror, he sees something of himself in the things that he contemplates. This is not a tactile mirror, he writes; whereas "touching immediately touches itself," vision must operate differently since it operates at a distance beyond the limits of his body, and it does so in the way that the mirror operates, through a visual contemplation whereby he sees himself in the things. Schilder does not only sense the pipe in his hand, but he can feel it in his mirror reflection, just as the "body can assume segments derived from the body of another."[30] This is the circuit of being where outside and inside interpenetrate.[31] Thus, vision is privileged over touch for Merleau-Ponty, because he finds in his visible body all his other attributes, but the tactile does not similarly confer the visual.[32] For this reason, film can incorporate the tactile into its visual structure. As I view *Wild Seeds,* the tactile relations amongst the youths find echoes with the tactile visual structures that my phenomenal body has already incorporated.

This intertwining of my body with the world, with other bodies and with "other bodies between them," is the promiscuous encroachment (*empiétement*) of corporeal schemas connected by perception, imagination, and thought, which holds the promise of both violence and potential. It is an action that is a passion: for, as Merleau-Ponty further explains, to make the other "pass into my body is also to make a body pass into me which, like mine, bites. Retaliation."[33] As Emmanuel de Saint Aubert points out, this promiscuous relation of the *Ineinander* is both wounding and creative because, in that our corporeal being is never achieved once and for all and our desire is inexhaustible, we are vulnerable to "the pain of frustration and the opacity of misunderstanding"; and yet, at the same time, we are also driven by the "insurgence of desire," the "upheaval of our personal being. . . and of our interpersonal communion (our shared engendering [co-naissance]."[34] For the viewing subject, this tension inherent to our intercorporeal relations also belongs to haptic vision since the gaze that is invited to participate can be disrupted in an abrupt shift to the distance and mastery of optical vision. This tension thus holds a potential violence to which the viewer who engages with the film remains vulnerable.[35] It is in fact precisely because the viewer has opened herself to the vulnerability of a desiring perceptual relation with the image that she is also open to the risk of violence. The viewer experiences this tangible tension in *Wild Seeds* as that between the eroticism of feeling affectively drawn into this tight knot of moving and grasping bodies and the apprehensible possibility of violence, to those bodies and to the viewer's invested gaze. And indeed, at one level, the violence of the game is fulfilled over and over, in that the game ends only when all bodies have been pulled apart, dispersed from their cohesion.

Thus, in the *Phenomenology of Perception*, Merleau-Ponty argues that we cannot simply compartmentalize our sexuality, which draws upon the emotional and affective aspects of our embodied being.[36] In his nature lectures he takes this insight further in his formulation of corporeal being as inherently libidinal: "The sexual is coextensive with the human not as a unique cause, but as a dimension outside of which nothing remains."[37] And certainly *Wild Seeds* is an intensely erotic work; the images dispel any notion of one central or omniscient eye. Bartana had two handheld cameras at work, and they shot the game being played six times, weaving around and among the bodies.[38] The viewer is drawn into the midst of these bodies—the lenses focus on hands, on faces, grimaces, thighs, a foot levering against another body. The viewer's implication in this work also reveals the erotic's political potential as a source of power.[39] The critique of mastery that is inherent to haptic visuality is effective because it engages desire as well as pleasure; in other words, the implication of the viewer does not correspond to a self-conscious Brechtian distancing. Instead, ideally, there is a relationship of "mutuality" between the viewer and the haptic image; "the viewer is more likely to lose herself in the image," for when "vision is like touch, the object's touch back may be like a caress."[40] This is vision that acknowledges that activity and passivity are at work in both the seer and what is seen for, as Irigaray reminds us, "seeing corresponds to being touched by something or someone—first of all by light waves."[41] The erotic element of haptic visuality, understood by Marks as a respect for difference as well as a "loss of self in the presence the other," is accordingly at work in *Wild Seeds* in the ways the viewer is corporeally drawn into the video in a refutation of distance and detachment.[42]

It is precisely because our senses open existentially upon a world that video art can explore the implications of this phenomenal aspect of the body for disjuncture, for that which does not appear within the logic of a system. Merleau-Ponty explains that "when I say that I see a sound, I mean that I echo the vibration of the sound with my whole sensory being."[43] Thus, in his example, when a film is dubbed, it is not merely that the word and image do not seem to fit, but the film does not have an "auditory existence"; the film world breaks down. Bartana draws on this effect by playing with sound. In moving beyond a representational account she does not simply record the sounds that accompanied what was filmed. Instead, she works with sound in order to create an experience of depth, the depth of our relationality, the depth that animates us, transforming "the work from a two-dimensional screening into an experiential three-dimensional installation" that establishes its own spatial boundaries or limits.[44] The film space makes room to include the viewer in the space of the play, to make room for and include the outsider into the relational space of the polis. When the video is exhibited, the sound is played on four speakers, which augments the experience of being in the center of the fray. The experience would likely be somewhat different for those who understand Hebrew; still, for non–Hebrew speakers, even though the words themselves carry no representational significance as such, words take up gestures and gestures words, "and they inter-communicate through the medium" of the body.[45] All viewers are surrounded by screams, laughs, breathing, voices that sound fearful, in pain crossing over to pleasure, shrieking; being surrounded by sound creates the sensation of inclusion in the space of this game, as though the viewer has almost been thrust among these moving bodies. Daniel Meir's soundtrack includes evocative music—voices chanting indistinct words. The youths' voices, moreover, from time to time fade in and out, mirroring and directing phenomenal attention that tends to be taken up by something, before slipping off to some dream world or some other perceptual stimuli, an aspect of experience that is inherent to corporeality, and yet rarely comes to the fore. The video reveals how attunement to sound, which the video encourages, contributes to a corporeal encounter in the present. Listening to *Wild Seeds* reveals not meaning or signification as such, but rather the experience of being corporeally open to the rhythms of sensual encounters, to relation. This suspension but not negation of meaning and of preconceived structures allows aural boundaries to open up, minimizing the force of colonized perception and the disembodied reliance upon cognitive signification. It allows for ways of seeing, hearing, and touching beyond the structures that belong to the dominant logic of perception.[46]

Haptic hearing, which Marks only briefly gestures toward, both draws upon but also turns upside down Merleau-Ponty's understanding that we echo the vibration of sound with our whole sensory being; haptic hearing can both permeate our senses synesthetically and break open synesthetic couplings. It is a way of hearing sound "as an undifferentiated whole" before it coagulates into signification, before we existentially find ourselves in a situation.[47] Phenomenally we tend to listen for meaning, and meaning is shaped by past sedimentations; to hear haptically is to be open to an ambient texture that does not precede preconceived structures of meaning. It requires attending to the passive receptivity of our corporeal capacity to hear. In fact, just as in order to see, our eyes are literally hit by light waves, sound too vibrates our bodies. Thus, to really listen is to listen with one's whole body, and attending to *Wild Seeds* seems to demand this of viewers. In this sense, then, *Wild Seeds* also provides an opportunity to corporeally question the ways in which our bodies fit into and take up previously or socially sedimented ways of understanding the world. Bartana accomplishes this first with the tightness of her frames, which provide little context or distance for the viewer, and second with her use of sound.

I want to argue that the experience of haptic sound intermingled with haptic vision is key to this work because the viewer becomes intersubjectively engaged rather than dominating the scene in a comprehensive and masterful glance, revealing how subjectivity is always already relational. This suspension of domination allows for a spacing where new meanings can emerge—but in holding this questioning gap open, the work does not in itself provide the answers. Haptic vision is erotic because it is intensely intersubjective, sensually implicating the viewer and requiring that she suspend her controlling gaze and ability to master what is seen in a glance; it requires that she become involved with the texture of the visual, textures requiring touch that takes time. Haptic hearing similarly requires an engagement that precedes cognition, or at least suspends it, immersing the hearer in a textural acoustic landscape that overlaps and interweaves with other senses. This overlapping is not precisely the same as that described by Merleau-Ponty in the phenomenal apprehension of an event or scene that relies upon the logic of existence, the perceptual logic that allows me to see the wind as it whips a flag around the pole. Instead, haptic hearing is phenomenal in that it requires an attunement to that which has not yet been laid out as a system, allowing for something new to emerge—something that is not yet meaning since its appearance precedes cognition.

Yet, the video does not lack a formal system of signification; the work is a two-screen projection played on adjacent walls. The images and soundtrack are projected on the primary screen, but on the other, Bartana has provided text, a selective translation of the adolescents' conversation, which is an intermingling of political slogans, exclamations, and sexual banter, along with descriptions of nonsemantic bodily sounds. In fact, the text shows the ways in which the corporeal, the banal, the sexual, political, and relational all interweave. The textual screen begins:

> we have a plan to conquer this land/ give me your hand/ you are in the middle, you are safe/ ow ow ouch/ my muscles hurt/ shift up a bit (girl grunts)/ I can't, I'm stuck/ let's get tighter/ like chewing gum/ whose foot is this? the thorns are right up my ass/ (background voices)/ ahhhh/ (boy screams)/ . . . / soldier I love you/ you're squeezing my balls/ go away/ (girl screams)/ stop!/ . . . / if you rip my shirt, I'll kill you/ you ripped my shirt/ (girl screams)/.[48]

In providing the split screen with a gap between them, Bartana further emphasizes a temporal interval between the affective and signification. It is possible to do this with video art because the viewer can choose to sit, stand, or walk around the space—stay for a few minutes or linger for a longer time; thus, the experience of viewing includes movement and relation in a way that watching a film, sitting statically in a movie theater, does not.[49] In fact, it is impossible to watch both screens at the same time, and the viewer must make a choice. I found in particular that my eyes would turn to the text at the times when the voices would suddenly cut out and the work's hold on me, my immersion among the bodies, was momentarily relaxed, allowing the cognitive to come to the fore. For example, at one such moment when one hears music but no voices, on the adjacent screen the banter continues, but this time as script: "criminals/ join the refusniks/ you fascist."[50] Moreover, splitting off the affective relation from the political slogans also brings into relief the non-relational, order-directed nature of the slogans, which are even further set off by their interspersion with translations of the cries and sexual banter. The effect is to cut off the relational space of the *polis* from the political clichés, which accordingly lose their potency.

Indeed, the gap between the affective emotional experience of resistance and our intellectual understanding of what is at stake in resisting provides a spacing that allows for thought, and it is this questioning that is at the heart of the *Unheimliche*,[51] that allows us to make the everyday strange. As incarnate beings, humans can see the world, but it is as humans that they have the particular ability to see with their "own eyes," as viewing subjects, since it requires a "reflexive and reflective consciousness."[52]

The problem with the nation-state, as Cavarero points out, is that it relies upon a logic that assumes reconciliation between universality and territoriality. The modern state, which claims to be territorial, in fact sustains a common national identity through the idea of a homeland that unites those who belong to it. According to this "contradictory logic, which is however quite intrinsic to modernity, the warm bond of the mystique of the nation corrects the cold juridical, procedural, rational bond of the state."[53] This logic becomes particularly apparent for Cavarero in the national anthem. The words of the anthem are generally "dedicated to exalting the historical roots of the homeland and to emphasizing continuity, homogeneity, and shared values." It is not, however, so much the words that are significant as the way the anthem works toward a "fusion of individuals in the song that symbolizes their union."[54]

Wild Seeds is, in a way, a unique kind of anthem that reveals the fissures in national identity itself—an identity that, in the case of Israel, is articulated for Bartana in terms of an "occupation regime."[55] The adolescents grasp each other, creating a mass of bodies—they seem to hang on at any cost until each is literally dragged away from the others. In providing the split screen between the sounds of their voices, their grunts and cries, laughter and moans, juxtaposed against a text that is distanced from the action, a separation of the affective-relational and the order-signification is brought to the fore. This separation is one that grounds the concept of the modern nation-state since democracy guarantees the rights of a general universal subject, signified in constitutions and bills of rights, whereas the affective sounds of their voices remind of us of the corporeal particularity of each individual, who may or may not be guaranteed state rights, as demonstrated for Bartana by the Israeli demolition of Palestinian houses in the occupied territories.[56] Bartana's work, rather than maintaining a separation, ultimately sets the two in relation. It breaks open the system of affective-relational and order-signification by literally presenting them on adjacent screens that require the viewer to corporeally shift from one to another in a process that takes time within the space-time that the video itself establishes. This process calls attention to the fact that the viewer cannot take in both screens at one time; one screen must always be sacrificed. This back-and-forth movement in turn sets into motion a resonance, opening up a temporal interval that calls upon the viewer to reflect upon how the affective-relational and order-signification are brought into relation. Not only does this interval provoke a critical evaluation of the clichés, which, dislodged from their place in Israeli national identity, stand out as the clichés that they are, but it also reminds the viewer that identity itself is relational rather than given.

Indeed, what the particular voice provides, that universal signification does not, is resonance. Resonance, in the vibration of voice, is, as Cavarero reminds us, first of all, always a relation; it is addressed to an other. Even the first cries of a newborn, which do not register according to a code of signification, can speak directly to the mother who responds with her own voice which might just consist of comforting coos. In the resonance of "reciprocal communication," in the relation, lies the power to destabilize the "rigidity of codes that organize the system of language." At the same time speech is more than just the pleasure of the relation but also engages in signification. I suggest that Bartana's video shows up both this contrast between the two, as well as their necessary interdependence. For even without the textual screen, without knowledge of Hebrew, the voices gesture and signify in their vocality.[57]

In another video work, *Siren's Song*,[58] Bartana provides another "national anthem." An adolescent brass band from Holon's Conservatory of Music plays Israeli marching songs while standing beside a highway that wends along the Tel Aviv beach. What is compelling about this video is the way the musicians, even as they play the designated music, reverberate with the sounds about them.[59] With the musicians we feel and attend to what is happening around us: in their notes we hear the swish of passing cars caught in dense traffic. The sounds of the band indeed seem to merge with the stop-and-go traffic, beginning the song only to fall into a cacophony of sounds before returning to the tune.

The camera's lens does not position the viewer to be the band's audience. We observe the musicians only fleetingly. Instead there are images of sneakered feet stepping up to a stone pedestal, of shadows lined up on the road, distorting as cars drive by, as well as of horns gently swaying in a line. We see a musician's back, and faces reflected in a car's window. Thus, rather than standing over and against the musicians, the viewer is encouraged to resonate alongside them even as they, in turn, reverberate with the traffic and the people around them, showing up the dissonance, the breaks in unity and flow, the fissures in a national identity that are apparent if one listens carefully. The film begins with a view of the sirens positioned on the beach prepared to warn people of impending danger. Bartana's musicians sound another kind of siren, revealing another kind of danger present among them. In both films, Bartana focuses on adolescents, young people on the threshold of adulthood, at the time when they are finding their voices, their speech in the world.

For it is precisely in speaking and acting in the presence of others that we reveal ourselves as unique beings. The *polis* is not a space as such; it is not a physical location but rather an "organization of the people as it arises out of acting and speaking together," even as this togetherness needs to be bounded by a place that supports its flourishing.[60] This relation of speaking to someone and acting before spectators can take place only "where people are with others and neither for nor against them," privileging, for Cavarero, the "relational and contextual" aspects of language over the "normative, rational and universal" ones.[61] Moreover, the political is thus temporal in that the potency or power that is generated through interaction takes place only when it is actualized and lasts only as long as there is an active relation. Since power cannot then be stored up in reserve for future use, "the realm" or space of politics is marked by intermittence, and "power is actualized only where word and deed have not parted company."[62] Though it is potentiality that can be actualized, it can, nonetheless, never be fully materialized, and it comes into being only where people live together.[63] When people isolate themselves from others and resist being together, they surrender power; they become "impotent, no matter how great [their] strength and how valid [their] reasons." Accordingly, violence and tyranny, which rely on force and not power, for Arendt, "can destroy power."[64]

Cavarero concludes that the difference between ontology and politics is that the *polis,* or the political, is constituted only when there are active relations—otherwise the uniqueness of each individual remains a given but is not political.[65] Similarly, the work of art sets to work, is potent, only when it is encountered by someone who interacts with the work. If what is political is the saying and not merely the said, then the text provided by Bartana is political not so much in terms of the slogans blurted out by the youths, which in fact become mere clichés, but rather in the saying of these phrases in this particular context, in this particular playing of the video at this moment addressed to my ear and to my spectatorship, to my being both with the work and with other viewers. For in order for an artwork to set to work we must work with it rather than against it; we must for a time attend to the work, without closing off our perceptual attunement. Thus, while I am hearing these words as affective gestures sutured across the gap with the screen text, they still reverberate against my eardrums in a new context. Their voices, while incomprehensible to my ears, still reveal a "destination to speech."[66] So that the written words—"give up, you fascist/ burn you bastard/ desert the army, traitors/ (girl screams)/ a jew does not deport another jew/ where is your conscience? / you left it at home?/ go back where you came from/ no! this is our land/ ow ow ow/ (screaming and laughing)/"[67]—take on a particular political meaning demanding that I, the viewer, reflect upon these phrases in their capacity as slogans—in terms of what they are supposed to effect.

What is particular to a game is that, as in belonging to a nation-state, one must play along with the rules in order to participate as a team member. As a viewer I experience the potential of the political, of the relation; the cries and slogans are relationally addressed to my ear. In the concept of the political that understands a nation-state to be grounded in the universal subject, the economy of the One or the Same, there is ultimately no relation because there is only one subject and "no common space to share."[68] In making room for the viewer as participant, Bartana's film is political in that it enacts a gap or space as a spacing, a temporal in-between that allows for an individual questioning, or a broader reflection on the experience of exile and forced evacuation, that is, for thought.

A third video, made one year earlier than the other two, *Low Relief II*,[69] seems, in contrast to *Wild Seeds,* to reveal the hopelessness and anonymity of demonstrations precisely in its erasure of voice. In this video Bartana wants to capture the experience of participating in demonstrations that oppose Israeli state policies, Jews alongside Arabs, as the feeling of participating in something that belies majority attitudes, yet, for all that, still provokes feelings of powerlessness.[70] To demonstrate is to act and speak in public before spectators; thus, feelings of lack of potency in the face of the Israeli regime are captured in the erasure of individual voices that the video provides. *Low Relief II* captures this contradiction: the feeling that the demonstrators' actions seem futile while at the same time affirming Bartana's belief that it is still important to take part in them, to declare oneself before others as a political act.[71]

Reliefs are generally celebrations of heroes, but in this video there are no heroes, just anonymous figures whose features are all but wiped out. Daniel Meir's soundtrack consists of nothing more than the desolate sounds of blowing wind. There are no voices, and no cries. Just as one feels intimately engaged with *Wild Seeds, Low Relief II* provokes a detached feeling of repetition and monotony. Using a filter and special software, Bartana creates a contradictory effect: stone in movement. Rather than picking out particular details, shapes emerge in fluid patterns of light, appearing then flowing away. The colors are monotone. In *Wild Seeds* there is an implicit tension that emerges from the possibility of violence that hovers at the edges of bodies participating in a ritual that crosses the limits where touch becomes force. By contrast, in *Low Relief II,* the banal is interspersed with the violent in an air of indifference—it all seems the same. We watch someone drink water. A police officer smiles while eating an apple. Demonstrators yell and scream though their voices remain mute; one demonstrator is carried away, each limb held by one of four police officers.

Politics, then, seems to privilege the temporal, and video art thus lends itself to this enactment; the in-between, while a space and not a territory, is more a spacing, a taking place between people that arises wherever people act and speak together, that is, where they appear to one another. If reality is accordingly "guaranteed by the presence of others," by their acknowledgment of a shared existence, then for those whose speech and actions are not recognized, their appearing comes and goes like a dream but lacks reality.[72] Spectators are also witnesses, and their acknowledgment is required. Thus the artwork achieves the political if, even for a moment, it engages the viewer to reflect, and perhaps also to discuss her reflections with others. It is after all shown in a public space.

In understanding the *polis* as tied not to territory as such but rather to an interactive yet bounded space where individuals can appear through what they say and do, the film engages the viewer to reflect upon what is meant by home and nation, by exile and partition. For to be at home in a nation means to suspend critical reflection in the immersion in the everyday, and is thus politically suspect. I do not mean to dispel the importance of home as our ties to particular places, for places with their accompanying laws and customs do provide boundaries that allow for action, for things and relations to presence, for the appearance of a shared reality. Thus the spatial of course supports the political, but I am arguing for an inherent temporal dimension to the political; it is action that is, in fact, inter-action, the speaking and acting before others, that imbues potency in the act of saying. The possibilities of the polis are, hence, revealed as embodied intermittent relations or spacings rather than as actual territories or spaces.

Notes

1. Cavarero, *For More than One Voice,* 192; Arendt, *The Human Condition,* 52.

2. Bartana, *Wild Seeds.*

3. See Irigaray, "To Paint the Invisible," 396–97, and Olkowski, "The End of Phenomenology."

4. See Heidegger, "The Origin of the Work of Art," 42–44.

5. Reckitt, "Yael Bartana: Ritual." Indeed, Bartana understands herself as an amateur anthropologist (Eilat, "A Conversation with Yael Bartana," 42).

6. See Freud, "The 'Uncanny' (1919)."

7. Arendt, *The Origins of Totalitarianism,* 293.

8. Ibid., 296.

9. Marks, *The Skin of the Film,* 55.

10. Arendt, *The Human Condition,* 52, 182.

11. Ibid., 183.

12. These biblical lines, which are provided alongside the exhibition of Yael Bartana's short film *Wild Seeds* (2005), exhibited at "Yael Bartana: Ritual," *The Power Plant,* Toronto, 2007, read: "Sojourn in this land and I will be with you and will bless you. For to you, and to all your seed, I will give all these lands and I will establish the oath which I swore to Abraham your father. I will multiply your seed as the stars of the sky, and will give to your seed all these lands. In your seed will all the nations of the earth be blessed" (Genesis 26:3–4).

13. Reckitt, "Yael Bartana: Ritual." Bartana describes the game as being "created by a group of young Israeli activists, some of them just before their IDF recruitment, others future objectors. I met the group through my niece, who is now 19. She was among the few young people who refused to be recruited by the Israeli army. The video was taken in the Occupied Territories, in the beautiful landscape of the Prat settlement, but the game may be played any place and at any time the group chooses" (Eilat, "A Conversation with Yael Bartana," 37).

14. Bartana, Walking Tour of Exhibition.

15. Hammer, "Architecture and the Poetry of Space," 381.

16. Pollock, "Aesthetic Practice as Introduction to Bracha Ettinger and the Concepts of Matrix and Metramorphosis," 23.

17. Laub, "An Event without a Witness," 10.

18. Ibid., 78; Pollock, "Aesthetic Practice as Introduction to Bracha Ettinger and the Concepts of Matrix and Metramorphosis," 14.

19. Caruth, *Unclaimed Experience,* 8.

20. Arendt, *The Human Condition,* 191.

21. Indeed, the game was staged publicly in New York on July 12, 2009, with participants from the Whitney Museum Independent Study Program at Union Square (http://www.artisrael.org/event2009-07/yael-bartana-wild-seeds-in-america-performance-in-union-square-park-new-york). Though I was not present at this event, I would suggest that the place and circumstances would shift the meaning, perhaps considerably.

22. Arendt, *The Human Condition,* 191.

23. Marks, *The Skin of the Film,* 162.

24. Ibid.

25. Ibid., 162–63.

26. Merleau-Ponty, "The Film and the New Psychology," 50.

27. Vivian Sobchack points out that the body of film as technological is different from that of the human body (*The Address of the Eye,* 243).

28. Merleau-Ponty, *Nature,* 278.

29. Ibid., 281.

30. Merleau-Ponty, "Eye and Mind," 168.

31. Moreover, the discovery of mirror neurons by G. Rizzolatti and V. Gallese supports this phenomenological argument. As Dieter Lohmar explains, they "found in experiments with primates that a set of neurons in the premotor cortex represents the visually registered movements of another animal. The activity of these mirror neurons presents exactly the same pattern of activity as appears in the movement of one's own body" (Lohmar, "Mirror Neurons and the Phenomenology of Intersubjectivity," 5).

32. Merleau-Ponty, *Nature,* 278.

33. Ibid., 280.

34. Saint Aubert, "De la négation de l'éthique à une éthique de la négativité," 382. This is my translation.

35. Marks, *The Skin of the Film,* 184–85; Irigaray, "The Fecundity of the Caress," 187.

36. Merleau-Ponty, *Phenomenology of Perception,* 178–201. Giovanna Colombetti, drawing upon research in contemporary cognitive psychology, argues in favor of a phenomenological approach to emotions that understands the appraisal of a situation as corporeal; that is, the affective is not mediated by a "separate non-corporeal appraising experience. The emotionally aroused body is rather that through which the subject evaluates her world" (Colombetti, "Enactive Appraisal," 544).

37. Merleau-Ponty, *Nature,* 282.

38. Bartana, Walking Tour of Exhibition.

39. See Lorde, "Uses of the Erotic."

40. Marks, *The Skin of the Film*, 184.

41. Irigaray, "To Paint the Invisible," 397.

42. Marks, *The Skin of the Film*, 192–93.

43. Merleau-Ponty, *Phenomenology of Perception*, 272.

44. Eilat, "A Conversation with Yael Bartana," 41.

45. Merleau-Ponty, *Phenomenology of Perception*, 273.

46. Bartana writes of the sound she employs in *Wild Seeds*: "The link between the video and exhibition space is made by sound, which transforms the work from a two-dimensional screening into an experiential three-dimensional installation. The works strive to convey an authentic feeling through sound, rather than to play the sound that existed in situ during the shooting. Sound is total and can convey numerous physical dimensions that an image is incapable of conveying. The sound guides and directs the viewer. Once it encounters the image, it can lead to a sense of pause" (Eilat, "A Conversation with Yael Bartana," 41).

47. Marks, *The Skin of the Film*, 183.

48. Yael Bartana, *Wild Seeds*. Note that the slash indicates text on a new screen.

49. For a discussion of this phenomenon in video art, see Olkowski, "Bodies in the Light," 166–67.

50. Bartana, *Wild Seeds*.

51. Heidegger defends a translation of the ancient Greek *deinon* in the choral ode of Sophocles' *Antigone* as the *Unheimliche*, the "uncanny," arguing for this interpretation of the human as the most unhomely since humans are the ones capable of questioning being, of being in relation to being (Heidegger, *Hölderlin's Hymn "The Ister,"* 61, 115). Further, at the end of "Building Dwelling Thinking," an essay written in the aftermath of the war, when homelessness was of crisis proportions, Heidegger stressed that the real problem of homelessness (*Heimatlosigkeit*) was that humans "*must ever learn to dwell*," that to be human is to always question their relation to being (Heidegger, "Building Dwelling Thinking," 161; Heidegger, *Vorträge und Aufsätze*, 156). In Arendt's and Cavarero's refiguring of this claim, what must ever be rethought is our relation to others.

52. Sobchack, *The Address of the Eye*, 51.

53. Cavarero, *For More than One Voice*, 201–202.

54. Ibid., 202.

55. Bartana, "Summer Work Camp."

56. Ibid.

57. Cavarero, *For More than One Voice*, 200.

58. Bartana, *Siren's Song*.

59. Apparently they play a "popular Israeli song 'Tomorrow,' but the dream of a tomorrow 'when the Israeli army can throw off their uniforms . . .' is drowned out by the horns of passing cars" (http://catalogue.montevideo.nl/art.php?id=11592).

60. Arendt, *The Human Condition*, 198.

61. Ibid., 180; Cavarero, *For More than One Voice*, 192.

62. Cavarero, *For More than One Voice*, 196; Arendt, *The Human Condition*, 200. See

also Heidegger's discussion of "standing reserve" [*Bestand*] (Heidegger, "The Question Concerning Technology," 17; Heidegger, *Vorträge und Aufsätze*, 21).

63. Arendt, *The Human Condition*, 199–200.

64. Ibid., 203.

65. Cavarero, *For More than One Voice*, 196.

66. Ibid., 212.

67. Bartana, *Wild Seeds*.

68. Cavarero, *For More than One Voice*, 191, 212.

69. Bartana, *Low Relief II*.

70. Bartana, Walking Tour of Exhibition.

71. Ibid.

72. Arendt, *The Human Condition*, 198–99.

Bibliography

Arendt, Hannah. *The Human Condition*. Chicago: University of Chicago Press, 1958.

———. *The Origins of Totalitarianism*. New York: Harcourt, Brace, Jovanovich, 1968.

Bartana, Yael. *Low Relief II*. 4:00. DV&DVD. Soundtrack Daniel Meir. Production: Israel, the Netherlands, 2004.

———. *Siren's Song*. 4:00. DV&DVD. Soundtrack Daniel Meir with a brass band from the Holon's Conservatory of Music. Production: Israel, 2005.

———. "Summer Work Camp." In *Liminal Spaces*. 2007. http://liminalspaces.org/?page_id=27.

———. Walking Tour of Exhibition. In "Yael Bartana: Ritual." The Power Plant, Toronto, Ontario, April 22, 2007.

———. *Wild Seeds*. 6:40. DV& DVD. Soundtrack Daniel Meir. Production: Israel, the Netherlands, 2005.

Caruth, Cathy. *Unclaimed Experience: Trauma, Narrative and History*. Baltimore, Md.: Johns Hopkins University Press, 1996.

Cavarero, Adriana. *For More Than One Voice: Toward a Philosophy of Vocal Expression*. Trans. Paul A. Kottman. Stanford, Calif.: Stanford University Press, 2005.

Colombetti, Giovanna. "Enactive Appraisal." *Phenomenology and Cognitive Science* 6 (2007): 527–46.

Eilat, Galit. "A Conversation with Yael Bartana." In *Yael Bartana: Videos and Photographs*, ed. Charles Esche and Esra Sarigedik Öktem. Eindhoven, Netherlands: Van Abeemuseum, 2006.

Freud, Sigmund. "The 'Uncanny' (1919)." In *Art and Literature*, trans. James Strachey, 339–76. Harmondsworth, Middlesex: Penguin Books, 1985.

Hammer, Louis. "Architecture and the Poetry of Space." *Journal of Aesthetics and Art Criticism* 39, no. 4 (1981): 381–88.

Heidegger, Martin. "Building Dwelling Thinking." In *Poetry, Language, Thought*, trans. Albert Hofstadter, 143–61. New York: Harper and Row, 1971.

———. *Hölderlin's Hymn "The Ister."* Trans. William McNeill and Julia Davis. Bloomington: Indiana University Press, 1996.

———. "The Origin of the Work of Art." In *Off the Beaten Track,* trans. Julian Young and Kenneth Haynes, 1–56. Cambridge: Cambridge University Press, 2002.

———. "The Question Concerning Technology." In *The Question Concerning Technology and Other Essays,* trans. William Lovitt, 3–35. New York: Harper and Row, 1977.

———. *Vorträge und Aufsätze.* Pfullingen: Neske, 1954.

Irigaray, Luce. "The Fecundity of the Caress." In *An Ethics of Sexual Difference,* trans. Carolyn Burke and Gillian C. Gill, 185–217. Ithaca, N.Y.: Cornell University Press, 1993.

———. "To Paint the Invisible." Trans. Helen Fielding. *Continental Philosophy Review* 37 (2004): 389–405.

Laub, Dori. "An Event without a Witness: Truth, Testimony and Survival." In *Testimony: Crises of Witnessing in Literature, Psychoanalysis and History,* ed. Dori Laub and Shoshana Felman, 75–92. London: Routledge, 1991.

Lohmar, Dieter. "Mirror Neurons and the Phenomenology of Intersubjectivity." *Phenomenology and the Cognitive Sciences* 5 (2006): 5–16.

Lorde, Audre. "Uses of the Erotic: The Erotic as Power." In *Sister Outsider: Essays and Speeches.* Trumansberg, N.Y.: Crossing Press, 1984.

Marks, Laura U. *The Skin of the Film: Intercultural Cinema, Embodiment, and the Senses.* Durham, N.C.: Duke University Press, 2000.

Merleau-Ponty, Maurice. "Eye and Mind." In *The Primacy of Perception,* trans. Carleton Dallery, 159–90. Evanston, Ill.: Northwestern University Press, 1964.

———. "The Film and the New Psychology." In *Sense and Non-sense,* trans. Hubert Dreyfus and Patricia Allen Dreyfus, 48–59. Evanston, Ill.: Northwestern University Press, 1964.

———. *Nature: Course Notes from the Collège de France.* Trans. Robert Vallier. Evanston, Ill.: Northwestern University Press, 2003.

———. *Phenomenology of Perception.* Trans. Colin Smith. London: Routledge, 2003.

Olkowski, Dorothea. "Bodies in the Light: Relaxing the Imaginary in Video." In *Thinking Bodies,* ed. Juliett McCannell, Juliet Flower, and Laura Zakarin, 165–80. Stanford, Calif.: Stanford University Press, 1994.

———. "The End of Phenomenology: Bergson's Interval in Irigaray." *Hypatia* 15, no. 3 (2000): 73–91.

Pollock, Griselda. "Aesthetic Practice as Introduction to Bracha Ettinger and the Concepts of Matrix and Metramorphosis." *Theory, Culture and Society* 21, no. 1 (2004): 5–65.

Reckitt, Helena. "Yael Bartana: Ritual." In *The Power Plant.* 2006–2007. http://www.thepowerplant.org/exhibitions/winter_06_07/YaelBartana/info.htm.

Sobchack, Vivian. *The Address of the Eye.* Princeton, N.J.: Princeton University Press, 1992.

Saint Aubert, Emmanuel de. "De la négation de l'éthique à une éthique de la négativité." *Alter* 13 (2005): 373–87.

10.

SHARING TIME ACROSS UNSHARED HORIZONS

Gail Weiss

The focus of this essay arises out of a political issue with which I have been concerned for some time, namely, the very real social barriers that divide individuals and groups of people with very different histories and experiences from one another when there are no corresponding temporal or spatial barriers preventing their communication. Both phenomenology and hermeneutics, I would argue, provide us with extremely useful ways of grappling with this problem. In phenomenological terms, we might understand it as a question of how it is possible to "share time" across unshared horizons, that is, how it is possible for people to, in Alfred Schutz's language, "grow old together" with all the intimacy that this implies, even when they lack a shared "stock of knowledge" that constitutes the typical parameters of daily life. From a hermeneutical perspective, this lack of shared understanding is clearly tied to significant interpretive differences that can stem from conflicting or even incompatible horizons of significance. The challenge of communicating with others with whom we share space and time across varying cultural horizons clearly has direct implications, both positive and negative, both for how one is identified by others as well as how one comes to identify oneself. In particular, I would like to explore how "sharing time across unshared horizons" can promote new understandings of personal as well as group identity that are grounded in a recognition of and respect for difference.

Using the Bergsonian distinction between time and temporality, or between "outer time" and "inner time," the problem I am interested in examining is how people can share what Schutz calls "civic" or "standard time," that is, quantitative time, and attribute completely different (sometimes even incompatible) meanings to their experiences. Of course, from a Bergsonian perspective, no two people will "live" time in the same way; there will always be differences between the durée of one person and that of another even when they are engaged in the same activity. Each individual's distinctive corporeal relationship with the world of her concern is sufficient to guarantee the idiosyncratic nature of her respective temporal experience, and thus, the unique significance of specific events in her life.[1] Nonetheless, Schutz claims that "because it is common to each of us, standard time makes an intersubjective coordination of the different individual plan systems possible."[2] He appeals to the universality of what he calls the "world of working," or the concrete, ongoing engagement of our bodies in specific motor tasks, as a ground for a common intersubjective experience. In a passage that echoes Husserl's famous description of the natural attitude in *Ideas I,* Schutz asserts:

> The wide-awake man within the natural attitude is primarily interested in that sector of the world of his everyday life which is within his scope and which is centered in space and time around himself. The place which my body occupies in the world, my actual Here, is the starting point from which I take my bearing in space. It is, so to speak, the center 0 of my system of coordinates. Relatively to my body I group the elements of my surroundings under the categories of right and left, before and behind, above and below, near and far, and so on. And in a similar way my actual Now is the origin of all the time perspectives under which I organize the events within the world such as the categories of fore and aft, past and future, simultaneity and succession, etc.[3]

Although Schutz doesn't say this explicitly, his implication is that because human bodies share basic physiological similarities despite their manifest differences of age, sex, skin, hair, eye color, height, weight, and so on, there will be corresponding structural similarities in our temporal experiences. However, recent work by disability theorists has challenged even this rudimentary assumption. For someone who is incapable of assuming the vertical posture typical for children and adult human beings, for instance a quadriplegic, the body *might* still serve as the "center 0 of her system of coordinates" and her "actual Now" may still serve as "the origin of all the time perspectives under which" she "organizes the events within the world," but this world itself will not have the same spatiality, nor I would argue, the same temporality as it would for someone who is able-bodied. Moreover, the inhospitability of our built environment for quadriplegics, paraplegics, and other people with serious motor disabilities virtually guarantees that they cannot be full participants in the "world of working" that, according to Schutz, forms the basis of the natural attitude. This does not mean that the disabled, too, don't have their own "world of working," just that the presuppositions that govern the world of working for the able-bodied individual (presuppositions regarding their basic manner and mode of engaging the world) are often inoperative or just simply inapplicable in the former's world. Not being able to draw upon the same basic motor capacities as "normates" (a term used by leading disability theorist Rosemarie Garland Thomson) and being socially stigmatized for this "failure" certainly lead to different ways of experiencing the world for disabled and non-disabled individuals. Because our bodies comprise an ongoing horizon of significance in all aspects of our lives, it is inevitable that disabled individuals and able-bodied individuals face significant challenges in bridging the physical barriers that spatially, temporally, socially, and politically divide them.

While it is perhaps easier to see how someone who is physically impaired, who continually experiences what Thomson calls a "mis-fit" between her body and her environment, may bring different horizons to bear upon her experience than an able-bodied person, disabled people are certainly not the only ones who may experience themselves as "misfits" in relation to the "world of working" that, as previously mentioned, comprises the basis for a shared, intersubjective existence for Schutz. People who are socially and politically disenfranchised, physically and/or psychically oppressed, because they are deemed to be the "wrong" race, the "wrong" ethnicity, or the "wrong" gender, or to possess the "wrong" sexuality also, I would argue, may find that the horizons of significance that structure the meaning of daily life for their oppressors are not salient for them. This experience of "unshared horizons," in turn, is often concretely manifested through what Ruth Frankenberg calls "racial social geographies," the powerful, yet often invisible, barriers that physically, socially, and psychically segregate groups of people who are perceived (and/or perceive themselves) to be essentially different from one another, even when they inhabit a single, shared space and time such as daily lunch period in a high school cafeteria.[4]

Linda Alcoff's discussion of both the positive and the negative ways in which identities are visibly marked, in *Visible Identities: Race, Gender, and the Self,* has a direct bearing on the question of incommensurable durées, for she is concerned with how identities that have been sedimented through oppressive experiences can nonetheless serve as positive "interpretive horizons" for those who live them. More specifically, Alcoff defends many people's strong sense of pride in their distinct racialized, ethnic, and gendered identities, even when these latter have resulted from long histories of oppression. Her rich and provocative descriptions of how race and gender actually function as social identities in the United States today accords well with Husserl's emphasis on providing as comprehensive a description as possible of the phenomenon one is investigating, and she well recognizes that to achieve this latter goal philosophy needs to move beyond rigid methodological and disciplinary boundaries. Philosophy, in other words, to echo Judith Butler's concerns articulated in the final chapter of her book, *Undoing Gender,* needs to confront its own othering practices, and needs to let that which has been designated other speak, in its own words, on its own terms, and I might add, in a manner that expresses the other's own sense of time.[5]

In its Cartesian zeal for "clear and distinct knowledge," the legacy of the modern philosophical tradition (and the Socratic and Aristotelian traditions as well) has been an intolerance for ambiguity, and, as Alcoff persuasively shows throughout her work, this poses huge problems for understanding the evolving meanings of racialized and gendered identities since these latter are paradigmatic sites of ambiguity, confusion, and discomfort. Turning now to Alcoff's work, I hope to open up a more general discussion of how we can best continue the dialogue to which she has so richly contributed, a dialogue concerned with identifying the concrete strategies that can best serve to alleviate the deleterious effects of oppressive identities as they unfold over time without devaluing the personal, political, theoretical, and practical significance of identity and the durées that constitute them.

At the very outset of *Visible Identities,* Alcoff makes it clear that she is offering "a sustained defense of identity as an epistemically salient and ontologically real entity."[6] "The reality of identities," she tells us, "often comes from the fact that they are visibly marked on the body itself, guiding if not determining the way we perceive and judge others and are perceived and judged by them."[7] Although she explicitly links the "realness" of identities to their "visibility," Alcoff also repeatedly acknowledges that visibility is woefully inadequate as a criterion for assessing a given individual's identity. Indeed, in her discussion of mixed-race individuals, including her own experience, Alcoff stresses that it is frequently the case that one's skin color, hair texture, and other physiognomic features may reflect only one identity rather than two or more, leading others to falsely identify the individual exclusively with one race alone. As Alcoff affirms, the rule of hypodescent described by Gloria Marshall and many other critical race theorists is alive and well, revealing the strong historico-political motivation for identifying a mixed-race individual, even with racially ambiguous features, with the racial group that is most oppressed.[8]

Hybrid identities, especially identities that are usually thought to be oppositional to one another, can produce confusion and anxiety not only for those who embody them but also for those who recognize their coexistence in another person's life. Not only do they reveal the limits of the clear-cut categorical distinctions that philosophers hold dear, but they also pose challenges to our most basic ontological, epistemological, and temporal presuppositions.[9] In *The Republic,* Plato attempts to justify the purity of identity categories through the "Myth of the Metals," famously proclaiming that each person is formed out of one metal alone, gold, silver, or bronze.[10] The metal we are made of, he argues, determines our aptitudes in life and, in his view, should therefore dictate the individual's goals and aspirations. Although the concept of racial identity did not exist as such in Plato's time, the legacy of this seemingly harmless myth that defines an individual in terms of his possession of a specific "natural" aptitude and holds him accountable for how well or poorly he develops it is readily found in racist ideologies that either implicitly or explicitly argue that a given individual's race can or should determine the type of person they are, the occupations for which they are most suited, the accomplishments of which they are capable, and the social class with which they should be associated.

Despite the dangers of viewing an individual's identity as if it were a simple, singular, or "pure" entity, Alcoff nonetheless affirms that identities help to make sense of and unify our lived experience. "Identities," she tells us, "must resonate with and unify lived experience, and they must provide a meaning that has some purchase, however partial, on the subject's own daily reality."[11] On the surface, it might seem that the best way to accomplish this would be if our identities themselves were unified. Indeed, our proper names serve symbolically as unifiers of our identity, and, as Louis Althusser and Judith Butler respectively maintain, they facilitate our interpellation as singular individuals.[12] Both Althusser and Butler emphasize, however, that while it is through interpellation that we become subjects in our own right, at the same time, it is also through being interpellated by others that we are subjected to those others. While neither Althusser nor Butler specifically focuses on the temporality of the interpellative process, it is evident that a great deal of the power of the act of interpellation arises out of its repetition over time; the sedimentation of both individual and group identities that results is thus an intersubjective temporal phenomenon. Moreover, the process of subjectivation that occurs through the act of interpellation is depicted by Butler in particular as both enabling and disabling: enabling insofar as it grants us social recognition, disabling because we ultimately lack control over the forms that recognition will take since it issues from others and not from ourselves.[13]

To the extent that our identities are constituted out of multiple facets of our own experience, including multiple encounters with (the experiences of) others, it is inevitable that our identities themselves will express that very multiplicity, even when they appear to be unified and coherent. Indeed, the different temporal and spatial contexts within which these identities are performed contribute to this sense of multiplicity even as these identities themselves become consolidated in and through their repetition in varying situations. Appealing to Teresa de Lauretis's work, Alcoff reinforces these points when she claims that "the fluid historical context in which we negotiate our identities is a context in which we are both subjects of and subjected to social construction."[14] If we view our identities as involving a constant negotiation between our own view of ourselves and the perspectives others have of us, or between what Alcoff refers to as our subjective lived experience on the one hand and our social identities on the other, it is evident that even the most rigidly defined identity is never fixed in stone but can always be transformed.[15]

There are countless historical examples of such transformations in both individual and group identities. For instance, as Michel Foucault emphasizes in *Discipline and Punish,* a single illicit action may forever after brand an individual with the identity of criminal, an all-encompassing identity that has the power to fundamentally alter how that individual views himself and how he is viewed by others. And, as Lewis Gordon, Frantz Fanon, and many other critical race theorists have argued, the very appearance of a black man in an antiblack world is capable of generating a phobic response that becomes part and parcel of his identity in a racist state, placing "ontological limits" on his own subjectivation.[16] Accordingly, Alcoff argues, "identities are constituted by social contextual conditions of interaction in specific cultures at particular historical periods, and thus their nature, effects, and the problems that need to be addressed in regard to them will be largely local."[17]

Since it is clear that there may be contexts in which I ascribe a particular identity to myself that others do not ascribe to me (or vice versa), we must reckon in any discussion of identity with a traditional philosophical concern, namely, with how to resolve the self/other binary according to which there is a fundamental separation between my view of myself and the view the other has of me.[18] Within this dualistic framework, identity is seen as encompassing both a "subjective" perspective that reflects and expresses my own view of myself and, at the same time, the perspective of the other (or others), which is distinct from my own. Working within such a binary model, the central issue then becomes, how are these dual (and often competing) perspectives reconcilable into a coherent identity that is lived by and associated with a concrete individual?

As Alcoff discusses, Merleau-Ponty raises this type of concern in relation to Sartre's ontological distinction between the experience of being-for-itself (*être pour-soi*) and the experience of being-for-others (*être pour-les-autres*). Merleau-Ponty attempts to move beyond this oppositional framework by positing a chiasmatic relationship between the perspective we have of ourselves and the perspective the other has of us. To call the relationship between my own perspective and the perspective of the other chiasmatic means that it is a reversible relationship that allows us to experience the perspective of the other toward ourselves (even without having full access to it) even as the other can do the same for us, all the while preserving the differences between the two perspectives. In the essay *Eye and Mind,* he suggests that we chiasmatically encounter inanimate as well as animate others. On his account, we are reckoning with the perspective of others all the time, even if we can never *know* them with Cartesian clarity and distinctness. Insofar as we can enter into chiasmatic relationships with nonconscious entities, it should be evident that a chiasmatic relationship does not, for Merleau-Ponty, presuppose that one or both of us must be aware of that relationship in order for it to exist. In his most famous example of a mundane chiasmatic encounter, namely, one hand touching the other, one doesn't have to be *aware* that one hand is touching the other in order to have the experience. Awareness does, undeniably, affect and transform the experience (of touching and being touched) and therefore alters its meaning, but it does not create the experience in the first place *nor* is it required to make the special temporal reflexivity that is operative within the experience significant in our lives.

Merleau-Ponty opposes the self/other binary because he maintains that even *before* the recognition of the unique perspective of the other occurs, we are always already acting within an intersubjective context and so are already affected by the perspective of the other, whether or not we are aware that this is occurring. This is why he proclaims that

> what is given . . . is the taking up of each subjectivity by itself, and of subjectivities by each other *in the generality of a single nature, the cohesion of an intersubjective life and a world.* . . . True reflection presents me to myself not as idle and inaccessible subjectivity, but as identical with my presence in the world and to others, as I am now realizing it: I am all that I see, I am an intersubjective field, not despite my body and historical situation, but, on the contrary, by being this body and this situation, and through them, all the rest.[19]

Irigaray, though accusing Merleau-Ponty of ultimately privileging subjectivity (and male subjectivity at that) over intersubjectivity, agrees with his claim that subjectivity is grounded within a fundamentally intersubjective experience. The experience of the look, as Sartre describes it in *Being and Nothingness,* or of the master's need and demand for recognition by the slave, as depicted by Hegel, both of which Alcoff discusses at some length, highlights the moments we are forced to *acknowledge* the radical alterity of the other; but they fail, Irigaray argues, to acknowledge properly the significance of more primordial contacts with the other, most particularly, the encounters that begin even before we are born, as our bodies grow over time within the bodies of our mothers.[20]

Through a compelling historical analysis of the rationalist philosophical tradition, Alcoff reinforces Irigaray's critique, demonstrating that the inherently intersubjective features of identity have most often been seen as a threat to our status as autonomous moral agents. Within this tradition, with relatively few exceptions, the roles played by others, society, history, politics, and even, I would argue, temporality itself in the formation of our identities have often been downplayed.

To the extent that these influences are acknowledged, they have frequently been seen as collectively determining the "accidental" features of our identities, not the essential ones. And, Alcoff contends, within these accounts the most essential aspect of identity turns out to be general and universal (and, I might add, it is also depicted as atemporal), namely the capacity for rationality itself.

A major problem with such an ahistorical approach to identity is that there are countless individuals (all of whom possess their own distinctive identities) whose disabilities, sex, and/or race have precluded them from being seen as having the capacity for rationality in the first place.[21] Not surprisingly, with regard to the self/other binary that frames these discussions, the emphasis is overwhelmingly placed on the autonomous self's ability to express its own identity through its willed choices. And, as feminists, critical race theorists, and disability theorists have all emphasized, those individuals who are viewed as unable to do this often have their very humanity placed in question.

On this Cartesian view, then, the perspective of the other is not granted the same legitimacy as one's own perspective, and, as Heidegger illustrates in his condemnation of the perspective of the "they" in *Being and Time,* the choice to give weight to the view of the other regarding oneself can even be regarded as potentially inauthentic.[22] Existentialists, then, as well as rationalists have placed the primary weight upon the self in determining its own identity even while recognizing that to be human means, to use Sartre's language, to be not only a being-for-itself but also a being-for-others.[23]

In his essay "Identity: Cultural, Transcultural, and Multicultural," Peter Caws reinforces this position, maintaining that "there is a sense—the existentialists were good at dramatizing it, but I think they were also right—in which I am alone in the world and have to forge my identity in isolation."[24] From this perspective, identity is an individual project, and Caws distinguishes it from an identification, which can be imposed on one by others. This occurs, for instance, when one is identified as a citizen of a particular country (e.g., a Spaniard or a Turk). Caws observes that children are born into a "first" or "native" culture that is "imposed from without." It is a culture, he claims, that they belong to but that they have not "made their own."[25] For Caws and other existentialist thinkers, identity is something we fashion ourselves, working from the "raw" (and not-so-raw) materials provided by the world around us, including all the people, places, and things we come in contact with on a daily basis. In Caws's words, "Identity, psychologically as well as logically, is a *reflexive* relation, a relation of myself to myself, but it can be a mediated relation: I relate to myself through my interaction with others *and with the world.*"[26] Ultimately, for him as well as for Sartre, identity is something we individually *choose;* however, it also must be distinguished from the mundane choices we make from moment to moment throughout our lives. For Sartre, the choice of an identity should be understood as an *existential* choice that unifies my less momentous choices such as which outfit to wear in the morning, what to eat for lunch, and with whom to spend time.[27]

In contrast to the strong individualist emphasis in the existentialist tradition, Marxists maintain that others play the crucial role in determining an individual's identity (including how it is temporally constructed and experienced), and they understand this identity to be primarily a function of one's social class. Even when one emerges from the "false consciousness" of believing one's class status to be natural and inevitable, one does so not by affirming one's individuality but by recognizing that one is a member of a socially constructed, subjugated (or dominating) economic group. In short, one attains *class consciousness.*

While the recognition that others play a central role in the formation of one's identity is a compelling feature of a Marxist position, on the other hand, this view also runs the danger of making it seem as if the individual has virtually no agency in determining her identity. Moreover, it is not only Marxists who are subject to this critique. In her book *Volatile Bodies,* Elizabeth Grosz calls positions that emphasize the role of society in determining the identity of the individual "outside in" perspectives, and she argues that Friedrich Nietzsche, Michel Foucault, Gilles Deleuze, and Félix Guattari all ascribe to this model, in which the individual's identity is primarily constructed not by herself but by the society in which she lives.[28] Pierre Bourdieu's discussions of the power of the habitus to shape an individual's desires, hopes, fears, and beliefs in accordance with the standards of taste operative for their social class are a perfect example of this view. It should not be surprising that, just as the Cartesian emphasis on the autonomous self has been critiqued for its "subjectivism," so too have serious objections been made concerning Bourdieu's reduction of an individual's aesthetic predilections to the taste that has been indexed for that individual's social class.

Rather than embracing one side of the self/other binary or the other, Alcoff attributes equally primary roles both to the self and to the other in the constitution of identity. Like Merleau-Ponty, she views subjectivity and intersubjectivity as inseparable from one another; both philosophers maintain that we always emerge as subjects in and through our interactions with others. Insofar as these interactions are multiple, it follows that our identities themselves are multiple. This helps us to understand why even if an individual has a dominant identity, the meaning of that identity is never fixed in her life but changes over time and in different situations in accordance with her own experiences as well as with the way society as a whole and other individuals respond to (or fail to respond to) her. While society may promulgate specific standards for particular identities, it is clear that even the person most devoted to these standards will inevitably end up embodying them in her own way. This is why Alcoff declares that "social identities are relational, contextual, *and* fundamental to the self."[29]

Up to now, I have focused more generally on the complexity of the issues that must be addressed when one seeks to make claims about the meaning of particular identities. As we have seen, there are a variety of conflicting perspectives regarding how much weight to give to the self and how much weight to attribute to the other (including society at large) in the construction of an individual's identity. Since I cannot do justice to all of the possible issues that can be raised with regard to the changing meanings of an individual's multiple identities over time, I would like to turn instead to a particular set of concerns, namely, how multiple identities seem to be very inclusive insofar as they can provide access to different horizons simultaneously, and yet, how the often competing demands placed upon one by dual identities are frequently so all-encompassing that it is virtually impossible to live these identities in a unified, coherent manner throughout one's life. Rather than abandoning the notion of multiple identities or even a hybrid identity as an impossible project, I would argue, both with and against Alcoff, that we need to recognize the limits of privileging a unified identity as a goal we should be striving for to live meaningful lives. Moreover, I would also argue that we need to stop privileging *visible* identities over invisible identities, since the latter can be just as salient for a given individual and her community even if there are no visual markers present to indicate that that identity is present and operative in her life.

In an all-too-brief section of *Visible Identities*, Alcoff argues for what she calls a "pluritopic hermeneutics," though, unfortunately, she doesn't develop what this involves in much depth. She explains this notion by observing that "one's very own horizon, constitutive of one's identity, is itself pluritopic and multicultural, constituted by sometimes contradictory background meanings or value assumptions."[30] She goes on to claim that "we cannot assume that any hermeneutic horizon or background of understanding is in fact coherent or closed to other horizons."[31] This leads her to conclude: "Thus, it is not simply that the other makes up the self, but that multiple others are constitutive aspects of our interpretive horizon, offering alternative and in some cases competing background assumptions and perceptual practices, fracturing the meanings of visible appearance and complicating embodied knowledge."[32]

If we accept, as I think we should, Alcoff's view of identity as an interpretive horizon, and acknowledge that this latter is intersubjectively constituted out of "competing background assumptions and perceptual practices" that fracture "the meanings of visible appearance" and complicate "embodied knowledge," then why privilege visible appearance at all? Although I agree with much of what Alcoff says about identity, the places I find myself least persuaded with her account are precisely those places where she is at pains to distinguish racialized and gendered identities from other types of identity, such as religious or ethnic identity, on the basis of the visibility of the former as compared to the latter. Even though Alcoff acknowledges that other types of identity can certainly be visible, she nonetheless doesn't acknowledge sufficiently that many individuals' ethnic or religious identities may be even more visible (to themselves as well as to others) than their racial identity, if not their gender identity, and that, as Robert Murphy and other disability scholars have argued, the visibility of a wheelchair can render *invisible* its user's race or gender altogether.[33] Alcoff does *not* argue that race and gender are more important or more meaningful aspects of our identity because they are allegedly the most visible aspects of one's identity, but her emphasis on the salience of visibility for identity opens up her account to this type of misreading. Moreover, as she herself acknowledges in the case of mixed-race individuals, racial identity is not always visible, and as transsexuals' experiences frequently attest, neither is gender identity. So, the questions I am posing for Alcoff are: (1) Why do we need to distinguish between visible and non-visible identities, especially if this isn't a salient distinction in an individual's own life? (2) Are race and gender really more visible than other kinds of identities? I realize that one of the reasons why Alcoff emphasizes visibility so much is because it so readily reveals the materiality of identity to the "eye of the beholder," and yet the materiality and even temporality of our non-visible identities can be revealed through other sensory avenues as well.

By calling identities interpretive horizons, Alcoff is suggesting that our identities serve as indispensable frameworks that structure the meaning we give to our everyday experiences. At the same time, our identities, as we have seen, are not fixed but fluid, continually being reshaped over time and across space by the events and relationships through which they are constructed in the first place. In his chapter "On Multiple Realities" in *The Problem of Social Reality,* Schutz argues, following William James, not only that different people can construct different "realities" but also that each of us inhabits more than one reality. These latter include not only the "world of working" that undergirds the natural attitude but also the "world of phantasms," the world of memories, the world of anticipations, and so on. Rather than seeing the distinctiveness of these multiple realities as separating one person from another, Schutz also reminds us that "the world of daily life into which we are born is from the outset an intersubjective world. This implies on the one hand that this world is not my private one but common to all of us; on the other hand that within this world there are fellow-men with whom I am connected by manifold social relationships."[34]

When the other communicates with me, when I listen to the other and try to figure out what he is saying, Schutz maintains, I am engaged in interpretive activity. Through this intersubjective engagement, he argues, "a new dimension of time" is established.[35] In his words: "He and I, *we* share, while the process lasts, a common vivid present, *our* vivid present, which enables him and me to say: '*We* experienced this occurrence together.' By the We-relation, thus established, we both—he, addressing himself to me, and I, listening to him—are living in our mutual vivid present, directed toward the thought to be realized in and by the communicating process. *We grow older together.*"[36] Unlike Alcoff, however, Schutz does not focus intently on the personal, social, and political obstacles that often keep individuals from entering into "we-relationships" with one another, that is, on the self-imposed and socially imposed "limits" of interpretation.

If we view identities as interpretive horizons, as Alcoff suggests, this can, I would argue, help us to understand how and why temporal experiences can be so radically different even when the individuals in question are "spending time together." If an individual refuses the possibility of establishing a "we-relationship" with another person because the horizons that constitute the basis for the latter's own interpretive activity are seen to be too different from her own, this means, on Schutz's account, not only that she is foreclosing the possibility of expanding her own interpretive horizons but also that she is depriving herself of the potential to establish new ways of experiencing time. Schutz's emphasis on the temporal implications of forming or even refusing to form "we-relationships" thus has the potential to deepen Alcoff's account of how identities are formed by attuning us to one of the most important yet less visible aspects of identity construction, namely, that identities are themselves products of time and can in turn transform how time is embodied and expressed.

While Bergson, Schutz, Merleau-Ponty, Alcoff, and I would all agree that the uniqueness of our respective durées is a source of experiential richness that contributes inexhaustible depth and meaning to our collective being-in-the-world, nonetheless, it is also crucial to acknowledge, as Alcoff does, the very real individual and cultural prejudices, as well as the political and physical barriers, that form part of the fabric of the "natural attitude" and that must be denaturalized in order to be overcome. Anticipating Levinas, Schutz stresses the importance of the face-to-face relationship in this process. The face-to-face relation, he tells us, is "a basic structure of the world of daily life."[37] The importance of this direct encounter with the other cannot be underestimated, because, Schutz argues, "all the other manifold social relationships are derived from the originary experiencing of the totality of the other's self in the community of time and space."[38] As Schutz himself would acknowledge, however, "the community of time and space" is not homogeneous, nor can it be taken for granted insofar as it is possible for "multiple realities" to be experienced in and through this primary intersubjective encounter. Or, as Bergson might argue, several different durées can and do unfold within what Schutz is calling a community of time and space. While Levinas would disagree that we ever do experience the "totality of the other's self" in the face-to-face relation, both he and Schutz emphasize the transformative potential this relationship has precisely because it is an encounter with the alterity of the other, an encounter that enables us to transcend the limits of our own "stock of knowledge."

To take seriously Alcoff's view of identity as an interpretive horizon enables us to explore the possibilities available to us to transform our own identities, our own horizons, and thereby the very meaning of our experiences, through our interactions with others. Taken together with Schutz's analysis of the temporal possibilities opened up by the we-relationship, we can see the cost not only to the marginalized other but also to the dominant individual who refuses to engage in this process. For, as the numerous anti-immigrant protests that ushered in the new millennium in France, the United States, and elsewhere in the world poignantly reveal, the refusal to enter into we-relationships with those who are deemed to be too different from oneself inevitably not only harms these others (both visibly and invisibly) by attacking, diminishing, and literally delegitimizing key features of their identity, but also impoverishes one's own lived possibilities insofar as one closes oneself off from alternative ways of living space and time.

Does this mean that oppressed individuals should feel compelled to enter into we-relationships with their oppressors?[39] Aren't some ways of living space and time more desirable and enriching to experience than others? These are important questions raised by my analysis, and though they deserve more attention than I can give to them here, let me conclude by observing that since a we-relationship requires a willingness of both parties to "share a common present," this relationship is impossible to enact when the horizons of significance that each party brings to bear on the situation are viewed (by either or both parties) to be incommensurable. Thus, while no two individuals can or should share the same horizons (indeed if they did, they would have nothing of interest to *share* with one another), there must nonetheless be a ground of *mutual* respect for the differences between our identities and experiences in order for we-relationships to be established and maintained. We-relationships, then, presuppose not sameness of experiences, but a genuine openness to and appreciation for difference. This means that respect for the alterity of the other must always be present in order for time to be shared across unshared horizons. The mutuality of this respect is impossible when one party dominates another. Nor is it something that can be achieved once and for all, since it is an ongoing, intersubjective project that both unfolds within and also makes possible a shared experience of time.

Notes

1. Bergson, *An Introduction to Metaphysics.*

2. Schutz, *The Problem of Social Reality,* 222.

3. Ibid., 222–23.

4. Frankenberg, *White Women, Race Matters.*

5. Butler, *Undoing Gender.*

6. Alcoff, *Visible Identities,* 5.

7. Ibid.

8. Marshall, "Racial Classifications."

9. One temporal presupposition disrupted by mixed-race individuals includes the common belief that an individual can have only one identity at a time rather than two identities (or some sort of amalgamation of two identities) at the same time.

10. It is important to note, however, that the myth didn't even apply to all people, just to recognized citizens or potential citizens of the Republic. This eliminated slaves from consideration altogether, and, given Plato's own ambivalent views about women's capacity for rationality, it renders the applicability of the account to freeborn women very problematic as well.

11. Alcoff, *Visible Identities,* 42.

12. See Althusser, "Ideology and Ideological State Apparatuses" and Butler's chapter "Arguing with the Real" in *Bodies That Matter,* as well as her subsequent book, *Excitable Speech: A Politics of the Performative,* for in-depth accounts of the power of interpellation.

13. Althusser emphasizes the role of the state even more than the role of other individuals in this process. Subjectivation, he argues, is ideological through and through. In his words, *"the category of the subject is only constitutive of all ideology insofar as all ideology has the function (which defines it) of 'constituting' concrete individuals as subjects"* (Althusser, "Ideology and Ideological State Apparatus," 116). For Althusser (following Marx), the state ideology that "constitutes concrete individuals as subjects" is always the dominant ideology of the ruling class. In *Bodies That Matter,* Butler further develops Althusser's insight that the disabling aspects of subjectivation produce enabling effects by granting the subject recognition as a subject, albeit a subordinated subject. In her words, "This 'subjection,' or *assujettissement,* is not only a subordination but a securing and maintaining, a putting into place of a subject, a subjectivation" (Butler, *Bodies That Matter,* 34). Butler traces this enabling/disabling view of subjectivation back to Hegel's famous discussion in the lordship and bondsman chapter in *Phenomenology of Mind* of the subordination of the master to the slave insofar as the master requires the slave's recognition of his status as master (and therefore a confirmation by the slave of the slave's own subordinated status) in order to secure his own subjectivation as master.

14. Alcoff, *Visible Identities,* 146.

15. This goes against William James's strong claim in the "Habits" chapter of *The Principles of Psychology* that a person's character is "fixed like plaster by the time we are thirty" and is more in keeping with the existentialist emphasis upon the ongoing re-creation of the self espoused by both Jean-Paul Sartre and Simone de Beauvoir.

16. I am using Lewis Gordon's expression "antiblack world" to capture the all-pervasive presence of antiblack racism in social life, that is, the ways in which antiblack racism operates as an "ontological limitation of human reality" for blacks (as well as for non-blacks) (Gordon, *Bad Faith and Antiblack Racism,* 1).

17. Alcoff, *Visible Identities,* 266, 9.

18. Alcoff provides an excellent historical survey of both political and philosophical approaches to identity in chapters 2 and 3 of *Visible Identities.*

19. Merleau-Ponty, *Phenomenology of Perception,* 452.

20. Irigaray, *Speculum of the Other Woman.*

21. Eva Kittay offers one of the most moving accounts of just such a person in chapter 6 of *Love's Labor,* namely her oldest child, Sesha, who has had no trouble expressing her identity with caretakers, family, and friends, despite severe mental and physical disabilities that render her incapable of using language or of getting about in the world independently.

22. The same point holds for Sartre as well, and it is illustrated in depth both in the "Bad Faith" section of *Being and Nothingness* and in his play *No Exit.*

23. Kierkegaard's, Heidegger's, and Sartre's respective understandings of the authentic individual as someone who is at least conceptually able to separate herself from others have been integral to both the phenomenological and the existential traditions. It is a major reason for the ongoing critique of these traditions as being too "subjectivist." Alcoff provides an excellent explanation of this critique and a response to it in chapter 4 of *Visible Identities.* Sara Heinämaa also tackles this critique head-on in chapter 1 of *Toward a Phenomenology of Sexual Difference,* with reference to both Kierkegaard and Beauvoir, arguing that it is possible to affirm the "Kierkegaardian notion of the separation of the self" without this affirmation leading to "solipsism or subjectivism" (Heinämaa, *Toward a Phenomenology of Sexual Difference,* 10).

24. Caws, "Identity: Cultural, Transcultural, and Multicultural," 379.

25. Ibid., 371.

26. Ibid., 379. It is striking that Caws claims that identity, as reflexive, "can" be mediated rather than that it is mediated. This suggests that it might be possible for the self to relate to itself without mediation by others and/or by the world of her concern. In fact, Caws supports this interpretation when he maintains that one can and should transcend one's culture of origin, though he is quick to clarify that this "does not mean turning one's back on it" (385). To make one's identity one's own, as we have just seen, involves stepping away from identifications that have been imposed on one by one's society. In his words, "the mature person is likely to leave his or her culture of origin behind as limiting to the development of personal identity" (372). While he acknowledges the positive role that an ethnic identification can play in an individual's life, he views it as exceedingly problematic

for the individual to merely accept this identification as her identity. Instead, appealing to Sartre, Caws maintains that she needs to actively commit to this particular identity as a self-conscious choice in order to avoid the charge of bad faith. In what follows, I will argue that though this may seem like a very appealing view of identity, especially to individuals who were oppressed growing up within their native cultures, it presupposes that we can, indeed, transcend the influence of our culture of origin through our rational choices. Moreover, it is exceedingly problematic to imply, as Caws does, that the "mature" person leaves her native culture behind. This makes it seem as if one's native culture resembles the immature Freudian id that must be repudiated. However, even Freud recognized that the desires of the id can never be transcended or vanquished altogether. Instead we must reckon with them on an ongoing basis, just as, I would argue, we continue to reckon with the influence of our native culture, which we have a tendency to regard as immature when we are most in tension with it!

27. See the "Existential Psychoanalysis" chapter of *Being and Nothingness* for a good description of what it means to make an existential choice.

28. See part 3 of *Volatile Bodies* for an in-depth description of these types of theories. Grosz herself seems more sympathetic to "outside in" perspectives, despite her recognition of their shortcomings, than to the "inside out" perspectives she associates with the phenomenological and psychoanalytic traditions.

29. Alcoff, *Visible Identities*, 90.

30. Ibid., 125.

31. Ibid.

32. Ibid.

33. Murphy, *The Body Silent*.

34. Schutz, *The Problem of Social Reality*, 218.

35. Ibid., 219.

36. Ibid., 219–20.

37. Ibid., 221.

38. Ibid.

39. I am indebted to an anonymous reviewer for drawing my attention to the danger of ignoring the power differentials that make it not only unfeasible but also undesirable for oppressed individuals to seek to engage in "we-relationships" with their oppressors.

Bibliography

Alcoff, Linda. *Visible Identities: Race, Gender, and the Self.* Oxford: Oxford University Press, 2006.

Althusser, Louis. "Ideology and Ideological State Apparatus (Notes towards an Investigation)." In *Lenin and Philosophy and Other Essays*, trans. Ben Brewster, 85–126. New York: Monthly Review Press, 2001.

Bergson, Henri. *An Introduction to Metaphysics.* Trans. Thomas E. Hulme. New York: Macmillan, 1955.

Bourdieu, Pierre. *The Logic of Practice.* Trans. Richard Nice. Stanford, Calif.: Stanford University Press, 1990.

Butler, Judith. *Bodies That Matter: On the Discursive Limits of "Sex."* New York: Routledge, 1993.

———. *Excitable Speech: A Politics of the Performative.* New York: Routledge, 1997.

———. *Undoing Gender.* New York: Routledge Press, 2004.

Caws, Peter. "Identity: Cultural, Transcultural, and Multicultural." In *Multiculturalism: A Critical Reader,* ed. David Theo Goldberg, 371–87. Oxford: Blackwell, 1994.

Fanon, Frantz. *Black Skin White Masks.* Trans. Charles Lam Markmann. New York: Grove Press, 1967.

Foucault, Michel. *Discipline and Punish: The Birth of the Prison.* Trans. Alan Sheridan. New York: Vintage Books, 1977.

Frankenberg, Ruth. *White Women, Race Matters: The Social Construction of Whiteness.* Minneapolis: University of Minnesota Press, 1993.

Gordon, Lewis R. *Bad Faith and Antiblack Racism.* Atlantic Highlands, N.J.: Humanities Press, 1995.

———. *Existentia Africana: Understanding Africana Existential Thought.* New York: Routledge, 2000.

Grosz, Elizabeth. *Volatile Bodies: Toward a Corporeal Feminism.* Bloomington: Indiana University Press, 1994.

Hegel, Georg W. F. *The Phenomenology of Mind.* Intro. George Lichtheim. Trans. James B. Baillie. New York: Harper and Row, 1967.

Heidegger, Martin. *Being and Time.* Trans. Joan Stambaugh. Albany: SUNY Press, 1996.

Heinämaa, Sara. *Toward a Phenomenology of Sexual Difference: Husserl, Merleau-Ponty, and Beauvoir.* Lanham, Md.: Rowman and Littlefield, 2003.

Husserl, Edmund. *Ideas Pertaining to a Pure Phenomenology and to a Phenomenological Philosophy.* First Book. Trans. Fred Kersten. Dordrecht: Kluwer Academic Publishers, 1982.

Irigaray, Luce. *An Ethics of Sexual Difference.* Trans. Carolyn Burke and Gillian C. Gill. Ithaca, N.Y.: Cornell University Press, 1993.

———. *Speculum of the Other Woman.* Trans. Gillian C. Gill. Ithaca, N.Y.: Cornell University Press, 1985.

James, William. *The Principles of Psychology.* Vol. 1. New York: Dover Publications, 1950.

Kierkegaard, Søren. *Fear and Trembling/Repetition.* Ed. and trans. Howard Hong and Edna Hong. Princeton, N.J.: Princeton University Press, 1983.

Kittay, Eva. *Love's Labor: Essays on Women, Equality, and Dependency.* New York: Routledge, 1999.

Marshall, Gloria. "Racial Classifications: Popular and Scientific." In *The Racial Economy of Science: Toward a Democratic Future,* ed. Sandra Harding, 116–27. Bloomington: Indiana University Press, 1993.

Merleau-Ponty, Maurice. "Eye and Mind." In *The Merleau-Ponty Aesthetics Reader,* ed. Galen A. Johnson. Translation ed. Michael Smith. Evanston, Ill.: Northwestern University Press, 1993.

————. *Phenomenology of Perception*. Trans. Colin Smith. London: Routledge and Kegan Paul, 1962.

Murphy, Robert F. *The Body Silent*. New York: W. W. Norton, 1990.

Plato. *The Republic*. Trans. Francis MacDonald Cornford. Oxford: Oxford University Press, 1978.

Sartre, Jean-Paul. *Being and Nothingness*. Trans. Hazel E. Barnes. New York: Washington Square Press, 1956.

————. "No Exit." In *No Exit and Three Other Plays*. Trans. S. Gilbert, 1–47. New York: Vintage Books, 1976.

Schutz, Alfred. *The Phenomenology of the Social World*. Trans. George Walsh and Frederick Lehnert. Evanston, Ill.: Northwestern University Press, 1967.

————. *The Problem of Social Reality: Collected Papers I*. Ed. Maurice Natanson. The Hague: Martinus Nijhoff, 1982.

Thomson, Rosemarie Garland. *Extraordinary Bodies: Figuring Physical Disability in American Culture and Literature*. New York: Columbia University Press, 1997.

CONTRIBUTORS

Helen A. Fielding is Associate Professor of Philosophy and Women's Studies and Feminist Research at the University of Western Ontario, Canada. She has coedited *The Other: Feminist Reflections in Ethics* with Gabrielle Hiltmann, Dorothea Olkowski, and Anne Reichold, and vol. 7 of *Chiasmi International* with Mauro Carbone. She has published articles on Irigaray, Heidegger, Nancy, and Merleau-Ponty in journals such as *Continental Philosophy Review* and the *Journal of the British Society for Phenomenology,* as well as articles in various collections such as *Feminist Interpretations of Merleau-Ponty,* ed. Dorothea Olkowski and Gail Weiss. She is currently working on a book manuscript titled *The Cultivation of Perception.*

Linda Fisher is Associate Professor in the Department of Gender Studies at Central European University, Budapest. Her research areas include contemporary Continental philosophy, phenomenology, hermeneutics, feminist philosophy and gender studies, philosophy and literature, and aesthetics. Her current work in feminist phenomenology explores the intersections of temporality, intersubjectivity, difference, and embodiment, with the aim of developing a phenomenology of gendered experience. She is particularly interested in the thematics of voice and vocality as a locus of identity and intersubjectivity. She is author of *Good Reasoning Matters!* (with Leo A. Groarke and Christopher W. Tindale), and editor of *Feminist Phenomenology* (with Lester Embree), and *Feministische Phänomenologie und Hermeneutik* (with Silvia Stoller and Veronica Vasterling), and has written on topics such as difference and gender difference, Beauvoir, identity and alterity, Husserl, multiculturalism, Gadamer, Merleau-Ponty, opera, Shakespeare, and David Mamet. She is currently working on a monograph entitled *In Her Own Voice: A Feminist Philosophy of Voice and Vocality.*

Annemie Halsema is Assistant Professor at the Department of Philosophy of VU-University Amsterdam. Her recent research focuses on the relationship between hermeneutics and feminist philosophy. She is especially interested in the notion of the self in the work of Ricoeur, Irigaray, and Butler. She has published in the field of feminist philosophy, especially on Irigaray and Butler. English publications include: "The Gift of Recognition: Self and Other in the Multicultural Situation," in *The Other: Feminist Reflections in Ethics,* ed. Helen Fielding, Gabrielle Hiltmann, Dorothea Olkowski, and Anne Reichold; and "Horizontal Transcendence: Irigaray's Religion after Ontotheology," in *Religion: Beyond a Concept,* ed. Hent de Vries.

Sara Heinämaa is docent and senior lecturer of theoretical philosophy at the University of Helsinki, and is currently an Academy fellow at the Helsinki Collegium for Advanced Studies. Her expertise is in phenomenology of embodiment, personhood, and intersubjectivity. Her best-known work is *Toward a Phenomenology of Sexual Difference: Husserl, Merleau-Ponty, Beauvoir,* and her latest publications include articles on desire, generativity, and the phenomenological ethics of renewal.

Dorothea E. Olkowski is Professor and former Chair of Philosophy and former Director of Women's Studies at the University of Colorado at Colorado Springs. She has recently completed three books: *The Universal (In the Realm of the Sensible), Feminist Interpretations of Maurice Merleau-Ponty* (edited with Gail Weiss), and *The Other: Feminist Reflections in Ethics,* ed. Helen Fielding, Gabrielle Hiltman, Dorothea Olkowski, and Anne Reichold. She is also author of *Gilles Deleuze and The Ruin of Representation* and editor of *Resistance, Flight, Creation, Feminist Enactments of French Philosophy;* she has edited *Re-Reading Merleau-Ponty, Essays beyond the Continental-Analytic Divide* (with Lawrence Hass); *Merleau-Ponty, Interiority and Exteriority, Psychic Life and the World* (with James Morley); and *Gilles Deleuze and the Theater of Philosophy* (with Constantin V. Boundas). She is currently working on a book entitled *Nature, Ethics, Love.*

Christina Schües is Associate Professor at the Institute of Social Sciences and Philosophy, University Vechta. Her research areas are the history of philosophy, phenomenology, feminist theory, anthropological philosophy, time, ethics, and the philosophy of education. Her book publications include: *Philosophie des Geborenseins; Die andere Hälfte der Globalisierung. Menschenrechte, Ökonomie und Medialität aus feministischer Sicht,* coedited with Birgit Hartmann, Steffi Hobuß, Nina Zimnik, and Julia Pätrut; *Der Traum vom "besseren" Menschen. Zum Verhältnis von praktischer Philosophie und Biotechnologie,* edited with Rudolf Rehn and Frank Weinreich; *Changes of Perception: Five Systematic Approaches in Husserlian Phenomenology; Bildungsphilosophie. Grundlagen—Methoden—Perspektiven,* edited with Rudolf Rehn. She has recently published articles on natality, generativity, ethics, and medical ethics. She is currently working on the interrelation between ethics and time and on the theme of the *conditio humana*.

Silvia Stoller is University Docent in the Department of Philosophy at the University of Vienna, Austria, and editor of *Journal Phänomenologie*. Her research areas are phenomenology, feminist philosophy, gender studies, and philosophical anthropology. Selected publications include: *Existenz—Differenz—Konstruktion: Phänomenologien der Geschlechtlichkeit bei Beauvoir, Irigaray und Butler; Feministische Phänomenologie und Hermeneutik,* ed. Silvia Stoller, Veronica Vasterling, and Linda Fisher; "Asymmetrical Genders: Phenomenological Reflections on Sexual Difference," in "Contemporary Feminist Philosophy in German," ed. Gertrude Postl, special issue, *Hypatia: A Journal of Feminist Philosophy* 20, no. 2 (Spring 2005). She is currently editing a volume on Simone de Beauvoir's essay "La Vieillesse."

Veronica Vasterling is Associate Professor in the Department of Philosophy and the Institute for Gender Studies of Radboud University Nijmegen in the Netherlands. She is member of the board of the International Association of Women Philosophers (www.iaph-philo.org), and coordinator of a European project on interdisciplinarity in gender studies. Her research is in gender and feminist theory, political philosophy, philosophical anthropology, hermeneutic phenomenology, and psychoanalysis. Recent publications include: "Cognitive Theory and Phenomenology in Arendt's and Nussbaum's Work on Narrative," *Human Studies* 30, no. 2 (2007); "Plural Perspectives and Independence: Political and Moral Judgement in Hannah Arendt," in *The Other: Feminist Reflections in Ethics,* ed. Helen Fielding, Gabrielle Hiltmann, Dorothea Olkowski, and Anne Reichold; *Practising Interdisciplinarity in Gender Studies* (editor); *Feministische Phänomenologie und Hermeneutik,* edited with Silvia Stoller and Linda Fisher.

Gail Weiss is Chair of the Department of Philosophy and Professor of Philosophy and Human Sciences at the George Washington University. Her areas of specialization include phenomenology and existentialism, feminist theory, and philosophy of literature. She is author of *Refiguring the Ordinary* (IUP, 2008); *Body Images: Embodiment as Intercorporeality;* editor of *Intertwinings: Interdisciplinary Encounters with Merleau-Ponty;* and co-editor of *Feminist Interpretations of Maurice Merleau-Ponty* (with Dorothea Olkowski), *Thinking the Limits of the Body* (with Jeffrey J. Cohen), and *Perspectives on Embodiment: The Intersections of Nature and Culture* (with Honi Fern Haber). She is currently completing a monograph on Beauvoir and Merleau-Ponty and has published numerous journal articles and book chapters on philosophical and feminist issues related to human embodiment.

INDEX

Page numbers in italics indicate illustrations.

Printed and bound by CPI Group (UK) Ltd, Croydon, CR0 4YY

13/04/2025

14656551-0002